The Ageless Warrior

The Life of Boxing Legend Archie Moore

by
Mike Fitzgerald

Foreword by Jake "Raging Bull" LaMotta

Preface by Bert Randolph Sugar

Afterword by Pete Ehrmann

Sports Publishing L.L.C.
www.sportspublishingllc.com

Director of production: Susan M. Moyer
Project manager: Jim Henehan
Dust jacket design: K. Jeffrey Higgerson
Developmental editor: Doug Hoepker
Copy editor: Cynthia L. McNew
Photo editor: Erin Linden-Levy

Hardcover ISBN: 1-58261-255-2
Leather Edition ISBN: 1-58261-846-1

Printed in the United States of America

Sports Publishing L.L.C.
www.sportspublishingllc.com

To my friend and mentor, boxing historian Pete Ehrmann, whose assistance and contributions throughout this project did not go overlooked.

Special thank you also to Sports Publishing's marketing man, Nick Obradovich, whose foresight and belief in Archie Moore's life story brought this project to fruition.

Contents

Foreword

Even as a kid I never believed in Santa Claus. But I am 100 percent behind a legend just as timeless and dazzling as the fat man in the read suit. This one carried a bag full of tricks, and his name was Archie Moore. Like jolly old St. Nick, the Ol' Mongoose seemed to be around forever. In boxing, a career that lasts over 25 years qualifies as forever, and in the span of his career Archie fought Rocky Marciano and Muhammad Ali and just about everyone in between who would get in the ring with him.

When I was growing up in the Bronx, I remember my Dad threatening to shoot Santa to get out of buying us Christmas presents. I know for a fact that there were a whole lot of very good fighters in the '40s and '50s—including some world champions—who would have preferred shooting Archie to fighting him. But even with a gun, a lot of them would've been underdogs to one of the cagiest boxers in the history of the ring.

Although I was a bull and Archie was a matador, he and I had a lot in common. We both learned to box while doing a stretch in reform school. Back in our day, you needed to be connected right or you were last in line to get a shot at real glory and the big money. Archie and I spent a lot of time at the back of the line. I was an uncrowned champion for five years, and Archie was for a lot longer than that. We both had to fight tough, top-ranked contenders, like middleweight Nate Bolden and light heavyweight Lloyd Marshall, just to turn a decent buck in boxing.

Bolden handed me an early pro defeat, but Archie beat him in his New York debut in 1944. But instead of the title shot Archie had already earned, he had to get back in line and wait another nine years for a crack at the title. They didn't even want him back in Gotham for a long time.

Archie and I both had to fight Marshall on his turf in Cleveland. That was like going up against a frog in an ugly contest and giving him odds. We just didn't have the right "in." I didn't really have a manager, and Archie had the wrong one for a hell of a long time.

When we were fighting, there was just one champion in each weight division, and there were only eight weight divisions. Today there are twice as many weight classes and at least eight guys in each one claiming to be world champion. It's a whole different game. If he were around today, Archie would be collecting titles easier than Paris Hilton collects boyfriends.

Today's boxers qualify for a world title with fewer than 20 fights! It took Archie Moore 17 years and over 100 fights to get his chance. And like me, on his way there he had to fight all the guys nobody else wanted to fight. There are some so-called experts today who say that Roy Jones Jr. would have no trouble in the ring against Archie. They ought to go lie down for a long time, and then become experts in some other field.

I have a ton of respect for Archie Moore and what he accomplished. We both trained at Stillman's Gym in New York, but we never fought. It almost happened, but things didn't work out. I'm not saying who would have won, but without question it would have been a great fight. Archie started out as a middleweight, but eventually moved up to light heavyweight and even heavyweight. I starved myself to stay around 160 pounds, because that's where Sugar Ray Robinson and the money fights were for me. Archie eventually had problems staying at the 175-pound light heavyweight limit even with the famous secret diet he picked up while fighting in Australia a few years before we met. I never met any Aborigines in the Bronx, and so I did my dieting the old-fashioned way.

When he finally got his shot, Archie won the light heavyweight title on the first try and then defended it for a decade against some of the greatest names in the history of that division. He almost pulled it off when he went for the grand prize against Rocky Marciano, but that one got away. Archie was boxing's all-time knockout king. He was a credit to our sport and to humanity.

Over the years, Archie and I became good friends. We attended many of the same boxing functions and were both inducted into the International Boxing Hall of Fame in Canastota, N.Y. around the same time. At all the events we attended, fans formed long lines to shake the hand of this great champion and man. If I hadn't already known Archie, that's a line I would gladly have joined myself.

His life story is one of overcoming tremendous hardships to realize his dreams. It's a great story that will inspire everybody who reads it. Mike Fitzgerald has done a fantastic job of writing it. He had a fight or two himself, and obviously made the right decision when he traded his boxing gloves for whatever the hell these guys write with nowadays.

—*Jake LaMotta,*
former Middleweight Champion of the World

Preface

Old age has been toasted, coffee'd, egg'd and griddle-caked in literature (*The Old Man and the Sea*), nursery rhyme (*Old King Cole*) and song ("Ol' Man River" or "Mose"), but none of those regaled in words and music ever came close to that Ol' gray head with the Ol' gray fist named Archie Moore.

Archie Moore was boxing's version of Methuselah, a credential courier of old age who, like old wine, aged well—well enough to topple lads half his age who would never grew old, at least not in the way Archie had.

The boxer known as Archie Moore was born Archibald Lee Wright in Benoit, Mississippi, in either 1913 or 1916, depending upon who was keeping score, Moore or his mother. Archie, with no unconditional surrender to undeniable facts, tried to explain away the discrepancy by saying, tongue firmly implanted in cheek: "I have given this a lot of thought and have decided that I must have been three when I was born." Like the vaudeville entertainer of old, Archie took his boxing act on the road, traveling more highways and byways than Mssrs. Rand & McNally ever mapped in search of fights. Over 29 years, he fought an estimated 215 times, winning 183, 145 by KO.

"Estimated," we say, because most of his early fights were fought in tanktowns and in "bootleg" fights on the so-called "Chittlin'" (short for chitterlings, or pig's intestines) Circuit in the only fights open to "colored" fighters, far away from the gaze of mainstream media and unreported.

Reading and re-reading Moore's voluminous record in *The Ring Record Book* conjured up mental pictures in our wayback machine of the black and white TV image of an old fighter in trunks that looked as if they had been made by Omar the Tentmakar with arms crossed in front of his face in what he called his "armadillo" defense disassembling into smaller pieces the likes of Harold Johnson, Tony Anthony and Yvon Durelle.

But these were, in the main, major televised fights, seen by millions and reported on the sports pages. What of Moore's earlier fights when he fought in almost total anonymity? As the-then editor of *The Ring Record Book* and unofficial keeper of boxing's historic flame, we were equally concerned about those fights as part of the overall record of one of boxing's all-time greats. And surely missing from his record.

And so it was that on one fine morning back in the late '70s the man they called "The Old Mongoose" appeared at my desk in *The Ring* offices, attempting to sell us on a story on his ABC ("Any Boy Can") Foundation. Drawing a picture as well as a dictionary will allow, the man in front of me sported (if that's the right word) a red black-and-green Black Solidarity cap that covered his graying looks and an open-necked shirt that showed wisps of graying hair on his manly chest. He launched into a monologue about his foundation with as gifted a cauliflower tongue ever heard this side of William Jennings Bryan.

Without interrupting his spiel, of which there was next to no chance, an idea occurred to Yours Truly: Why not have him check his own record in *The Record Book* for missing fights?

Politely he took *The Record Book* to a desk in the corner and for the next hour pored over his pages like a scientist analyzing a new strain of molecular matter. Finally he arose and offered his findings: there were five missing fights he could identify—not all of them winning fights, mind you, but five missing from his record, the first one of which was in 1935 against the formidable-sounding Piano Mover Jones. His pay for that night was the small coin collected in a hat passed amongst his fellow CCC camp members. And the result was, as expected, a knockout, the first of what we were to calculate as a boxing—and Guinness—record 145.

That morning was to become, in the closing words of Humphrey Bogart in the movie *Casablanca*, "the beginning of a beautiful friendship" between the Old Mongoose and Yours Truly. One that would continue, and blossom, throughout the years, from dinners—where he spat his meat into table napkins saying something or other about an "Aborigine" diet he followed that allowed him to chew the juice out of the meat, but not swallow the meat itself—through pre-fight encounters where he would regale his audience of one with sage observations, peppered with words like "breathology" and "escapeology," to all-night dissertations at the Boxing Hall of Fame, where, drawing on his fine command of both memory and the English language, he would regale his audience with stories about his career, getting up to about 1950 by the hour of four. And those trying to interrupt him had about as much effect on his stream-of-talkativeness as a deck chair blowing off the QEII.

One story in particular sticks in my mind: the story of his classic fight with Yvon Durelle, where, after being knocked down for the fourth time by Durelle, he went back to his corner and, unable to focus correctly, was told by his manager, Doc Kearns, to wave at his wife over in the other corner, behind Durelle, to show her that he was all right. His wife, however, was seated behind him, not in the other corner. And the wave, supposedly in the direction of his wife, was instead in the direction of Durelle, who thought Moore, despite all the punishment he had taken over five rounds, was waving scornfully at him and lost heart and the fight.

To have known Archie Moore—either through his record or personally—was to have known greatness, in and out of the ring. He was proof positive that boxing not only builds character, but characters as well, none being bigger or greater than Archie. If he hadn't existed, boxing would have been forced to invent him.

—*Bert Randolph Sugar, "Boxing's Foremost Historian"*

Sugar is the author of *Bert Sugar On Boxing* (or *The Best of Bert Sugar, The Worst of Bert Sugar: What the Hell's the Difference?*)

Acknowledgments

All the people interviewed for this book were giving with their time in sharing with me how Archie Moore had touched their lives.

For biographical details on Moore's life, all three previous books were used: *The Archie Moore Story* by Archie Moore and Bob Condon, *Any Boy Can* by Leonard Pearl and Archie Moore, and *The Ol' Mongoose: The Authorized Biography of Archie Moore, Undefeated Light Heavyweight Champion of the World* by Dr. Marilyn Douroux.

Special thanks go to my wife Deb, who did much of the word processing for the manuscript and encouraged me throughout this lengthy mission. Thanks also go to my good friend, Marshall Terrill, for contacting Archie Moore's agent, Jerry Haack, and recommending me for the project. Jerry and Judy Haack deserve thanks for their assistance throughout this project.

Thanks also go to Rena Moore, who set up my week in San Diego to interview her father and assisted throughout the project. Thank you to other members of Archie Moore's family who contributed to this book, including Billy Moore, J'Marie Moore, the late Mrs. Joan Moore, Arnold Wright and John Stump.

This book could not have been finished without the support of freelance boxing journalist Pete Ehrmann. Pete edited the manuscript, offered suggestions, and confirmed the boxing facts relating to this book.

I would also like to thank others who contributed to this book including: Jake LaMotta, for his foreword to this book; Bert Randolph Sugar for his preface; George Rugg of the University of Notre Dame sports research department; Ed and Jeff Brophy from the International Boxing Hall of Fame in Canastota, New York; boxing historian Henry Otty; friend Katy Milewski; former San Diego Sports Hall of Fame curator Todd Tobias; my three friends and boxing associates, Mr. Bill Martin, Bob Lynch and Gary Pliner.

Finally, thanks go to my parents, Mike Sr. and Claudiadair, who are much happier now that I am writing about the sport of boxing, as opposed to the concern they felt when I was an active participant.

CHAPTER 1

Theft on a St. Louis Trolley

"Moore is down! He's hurt! Durelle goes to a neutral corner as Moore struggles to get up...Moore is up now, and Durelle charges, throwing bombs from every angle, and Moore seems unable to defend himself. Moore goes down again for the third time! This fight could be over in the very first round. Moore is badly hurt! Well...Father Time has finally caught up with 'The Old Mongoose.'"
—Announcer Jack Drees
Montreal, December 10, 1958

Archie Moore, boxing's ageless wonder, lay on the canvas looking older by the second as the referee stood over him counting them off. The light heavyweight champion of the world had been down before in his long career, but it appeared he would not beat the count this time. Moore strived to gain his footing as the referee continued to count, six...seven...eight. But apparently listening to his heart and not his head, Moore's legs somehow righted him just before the count of 10.

Referee Jack Sharkey, the former world heavyweight champion, signaled for the action to resume. Moore tried to come back swinging, but once again he was sent to the canvas by an overhand right from brawling Yvon Durelle. In Archie's seventh defense of his 175-pound title, it appeared that Father Time had not only caught up with Moore, but then used his scythe to chop him down at the knees. Many fighters in Moore's position—horizontal—would've stayed that way. But it took Moore 17 years to get his shot at the world championship, and he had vowed that they would have to carry him out of the ring unconscious before he would ever surrender what he had worked so hard to achieve.

On this cold, rainy night at The Forum in Montreal, Canada, Moore was within a week of being either 45 or 42 years old, depending on whether one believed Archie, who claimed the former, or his mother, who swore he was three years younger. Whoever was right, Moore was still an antique by boxing standards.

As a boy growing up in St. Louis, Missouri, he ran the streets and ended up in the state reformatory. As a fighter he had long been denied the opportunity to advance to the front rank of his chosen profession because of the color of his skin. Twice along the way he almost died. So a few booming right-hands from local hero Durelle—including the one that sent Moore down a third time in the opening round and had Jack Drees and most of the national TV audience writing Archie's boxing obituary—weren't enough to separate Archie from his consciousness and his title.

When the bell sounded to end the opening round, Moore wobbled back to his corner for the 60-second intermission. Waiting for him there was his manager, Jack "Doc" Kearns, a figure as legendary in boxing as Moore himself. Almost 40 years before, Kearns had guided Jack Dempsey from the hobo jungles to the heavyweight championship. Kearns was an unabashed hustler who once said, "Maybe I'm fast with a buck, the booze, and the broads, but I was always pretty quick with ideas, too." He once likened himself to a strip-teaser, claiming that "you couldn't get anywhere without a little exposure."

But the most important item in Kearns's bag of tricks now was the ice water he poured down Archie's trunks to get Moore ready for the second round. Archie was still groggy when the bell rang, but he fought out of the ether in the ensuing three rounds and even seemed to be turning the tide, scoring with a big body punch in the fourth. However, in the fifth round Durelle landed another solid right that dumped Moore to the canvas for the fourth time. Once again, boxing's eldest statesman courageously regained his feet and, on unsteady legs, traded bombs with the brawling fisherman until the bell rang. Now it was time for sheer genius, not ice water.

Moore's wife was seated behind Durelle's corner, and Kearns's brainstorm was to have Archie stand up in his corner and wave to her. He did as instructed, and the stunned Durelle, thinking the champion was gaily waving at him, wondered what he had to do to let the air out of the old man once and for all. He'd punched Moore down four times and seemingly had him on the verge of a knockout, and here was Archie waving at him as if they were playing a game of tag. The fact was that Moore himself was too dazed to know what he was doing, but Kearns's ploy worked to perfection. Durelle was disheartened, and Moore went out and took charge. In the eleventh round, he put Durelle down for the count, achieving one of the most astonishing and memorable come-from-behind victories in boxing history.

The Durelle fight was the centerpiece of a career that lasted until 1963, almost 30 years, and saw Moore become boxing's all-time knockout king. Boxing took him around the world and made Archie an international idol. He held the light heavyweight title for nearly a decade and was a shining counterpoint to the stereotype of a boxer as all brawn and no brains. Moore's career highlights included knocking down champion Rocky Marciano in a bid for the heavyweight title, training a young Muhammad Ali, advising George Foreman in his miraculous comeback, and, most important to Archie, coaching and motivating troubled youngsters.

* * *

Archie Moore was born Archibald Lee Wright on either December 13, 1916, or December 13, 1913. Moore always kept his true age a secret, claiming the less you told people about yourself, the more interested in you they would become. Throughout his life, his birth date remained in constant question, which suited Archie just fine. When he ran for Congress in California in 1960, he even registered as a candidate using both birth dates. Whenever pressed for a definitive answer to the riddle and reminded that his own mother differed with him on the subject, Moore would muddy the waters even further by claiming that he must have been three years old at birth.

This much is known fact: Archie was born in Benoit, Mississippi, the second of two children of Lorena and Thomas Wright. The first was a daughter, Rachel, born two years before Archie. Moore's mother—who was correct on her son's true age—was only 17 when he was born. His parents were only children themselves and had difficulty facing the responsibility of raising their own family. Not long afterwards, Lorena and Thomas separated, and Archie and Rachel were sent to St. Louis to live with their aunt and uncle, Willie Pearl and Cleveland Moore. To prevent any embarrassing questions in that stricter, more moralistic time, Archie's last name was changed from Wright to Moore.

Cleveland Moore came from the Deep South. Like most African-Americans living below the Mason-Dixon line, he was a sharecropper. It was grueling work for small pay, and when Cleveland heard about construction jobs available in St. Louis, he and Willie Pearl headed north in 1917. Construction work did provide a better living, but with the addition of Archie and Rachel to the family, Cleveland worked six days a week to put food on the table.

To Archie, his aunt Willie Pearl was "one of the finest women a man could know, and she was everything a mother could be." His aunt was a wise woman of high moral character who never had children of her own, and she raised Archie and Rachel as if they had been born to her. Willie Pearl had a favorite poem she recited often to Archie, and throughout his life he applied it to every challenge that confronted him. It went:

> *When a task is once begun,*
> *Never leave it until it's done,*
> *If the labor is great or small,*
> *Do it well or not at all*

In the Moore household, cleanliness was not only a virtue but also a commandment. "My family was too poor to paint and too proud to whitewash, so we kept everything spotless," Archie said. "We grew up with bare wood floors, and on Saturdays scrubbed them with lye soap. The house was so clean it was like a hospital. My auntie taught us that we might not have the best furniture or wear the best clothing, but we could sure keep them clean."

Uncle Cleveland was a large, muscular man who ran a strict household. Moore grew up with a lot of respect for him. "My Uncle Cleveland never hit me for misbehaving," he said. "I knew better than to go against his ways. He always meant what he said, and I knew that it would never be in my best interest to cross him!"

In the summer, after school let out, the Moores would visit relatives in Mississippi. These vacations were much anticipated as there were plenty of relatives to visit with lots of young cousins to enjoy being around. Their relatives lived in a shack, but it was considered one of the nicer shacks in the area. Archie's grandfather farmed his own land and thus was a step above a mere sharecropper. His shack had four rooms, and guests slept on straw mats on the floor. The property stretched over several acres, and the Moores never lacked for good food when vacationing in the South. An abundance of fruit grew near the shack, and there was always plenty of chickens and hogs on the property. This is where Archie developed the famous appetite that often caused him grief years later when it came time to keep his weight at the 175-pound light heavyweight limit.

"I always looked forward to visiting my cousins in Mississippi," Archie recalled. "There was a big swimming hole that provided a break from the summer weather. We used to play there all day. Then later in the evening we'd pull a big melon up from the water well. After soaking all day, it was cool and delicious by nightfall. We'd chase each other around and spit the melon pits at each other. I have great memories from those days."

In St. Louis, the Moores lived in an all-black area on the city's south side, and the school Archie attended had only black students. The ugly face of racism was unknown to him until he was eight, at which time racism introduced itself on his last summer vacation in Mississippi. It was a hot summer day, and Archie was riding bareback on one of his grandfather's horses. His sister Rachel was leading the horse into town down a country road. From out of nowhere a young white boy jumped in front of them and lashed out at the horse with a stick. The panicked animal reared up, kicking its front feet up high, and Archie went tumbling off. He picked himself up and then grabbed and violently shook the white boy until the latter started to cry. Meanwhile, Rachel raced back to the shack and informed everyone there about the incident. After Moore led the frightened horse back home he was greeted by a furious Aunt Willie Pearl. She warned Archie about racial tension in the South and the inherent danger of mixing it up with Caucasians even if the one in question had deserved what he got. The very next day, the Moores headed back to St. Louis. It was their last vacation in the Old South.

Not long afterwards, Archie got his first taste of boxing fever. "When I was eight years old and living in St. Louis," he recalled, "I was coming home with a wagon full of chips from the ice house and heard noise coming from behind a fence. Behind the fence people were screaming and yelling. I peeked through a hole in the fence noticing people shouting with excitement and I saw two men were slugging it out. The people screamed, the men punched, and I was thrilled. I almost fainted with ecstasy. I decided that I gotta be the champ someday."

* * *

Archie's birth mother, Lorena Wright, met and married World War I veteran Mordell Brown. Through that union, Archie and his sister acquired a stepbrother, Samuel, who went by the name of Jackie. When Mordell Brown took ill and passed away soon after the marriage, Jackie moved in with the Moores.

Archie's mother married once more and gave birth to another son, named Louis. Recalled Moore of his half-brother: "Louis liked to get into trouble. He was a hustler as a teenager. Shooting dice or placing bets. I would only see him on and off through the years. I used to visit my mother on weekends, and Louis and I would run around. We were only separated by a few years."

Archie had only slight memories of his father, Thomas Wright, who had fallen out of touch. Wright went into the grocery store business with his brother in St. Louis and fathered eight children after Archie. One of them, Arnold Wright, recalled that his father, "was like a rolling stone. Wherever he laid his hat he called home." Archie would not see his father again for over 30 years. Rena Moore, Archie's daughter, said in a 1998 interview, "Daddy never really mentioned his father to us kids. I don't think they were ever close."

Archie attended Dumas Grade School in St. Louis. It was located next to the Loose Wiles Biscuit Company, where, Moore often recalled with a smile, for a nickel you could get a large bag of broken cookies. Archie was an excellent student, doing especially well in history and music.

Not all the lessons he learned at Dumas came out of textbooks, however. One in particular that always stood out in his mind occurred when Archie's fifth grade teacher, tired of his laughing and carrying on in class, slapped him in front of the other children. Recalled Moore, "I was embarrassed and contemplated leaving school. Later, I asked the teacher why she had done that to me. The teacher made me realize that if I was going to turn into something special someday that I shouldn't carry on like that. I should hold myself with more dignity. The teacher cared about me as a person and about my future. It just took me a while to figure that out at that young age."

That same year, Moore had his first real fistfight after his best friend, Mose Howell, laughingly sicced his dog on Archie and the animal tore a hole in the seat of Moore's pants. "I laid for Mose and gave him a shiner," Moore later recollected. "Hit him with a right. Mose got his brother Rube after me. Rube was two years older. He followed me and Rachel after school and kept goading me. Finally, Rachel slapped his face. Then Rube hit Rachel. I never knew I had so much fire in me. I tore into him and we scrambled for five minutes until somebody broke it up. Neither of us wanted to continue. I was satisfied with a draw. I had saved our pride, and Rachel and I walked home arm in arm with our heads up."

There were street gangs in the 1920s, but not the kind that we hear about today. "Back when I was a kid in St. Louis, a gang fight meant only fists, and it was usually an ethnic thing," Moore recalled. "The Irish against the Italians or the blacks took on the Latinos. It was the type of fight that an adult could break up with a few stern words. No killings, that's for sure, maybe a black eye or fat lip. I could hold my own, so I never had any worries."

Except if Aunt Willie Pearl found out it. "Auntie was opposed to street fighting," Moore said. "If she saw I had a black eye or heard I'd been fighting, I'd have to face her punishment, too." Archie was small for his age—just barely over 100 pounds—too short for basketball and too light for football. However, Moore lived near a professional fighter named Kid Roberts, who gave him his earliest boxing lessons. Two school buddies, Robert Stamps and "Pretty" Eddie Williams, also had an interest in boxing, and the three of them became regulars at Roberts's place.

Roberts showed Archie how to properly hold his hands in a boxer's stance and throw a left jab. Archie was a quick study, and soon he was the best fighter in his neighborhood. Then he branched out into the Italian and Jewish neighborhoods. It was good-natured competition, and after the bouts the kids would pool their money and buy fruit and soda.

Archie's passion for boxing grew until he spent most of his free time practicing. He worked hard to build his muscles for the fight game, employing some unconventional methods. He spent a great deal of time walking on his hands, climbing up and down stairs on them and even going around the block that way. Moore also attacked the chin-up bar, one time chinning himself 250 consecutive times. He'd also stand in front of a mirror for hours with five-pound flatirons in each hand, throwing punches.

On the home front, Moore spent a lot of time with his sister, until Rachel discovered men. After she fell in love with a man named Elihu Williams, she and Archie would only see each other on the way to school. Eventually, Rachel and Williams were married. Around that same time, Archie's interest in school began to diminish. He had always received decent grades, but in his junior year he decided to drop out of high school after another slapping incident in front of his classmates. This time Moore's crime was yelling "Ouch!" after a student stuck a splinter in his leg.

Difficult times were ahead for the Moore household. Rachel became pregnant with twins and died shortly after delivery. Her son died soon after birth, leaving the girl, June, to be raised by Aunt Willie Pearl. Another major blow was the death of Uncle Cleveland in a work-related accident. On his deathbed, Uncle Cleveland called for Archie. "Put your hand in mine," he told his nephew. "Promise me one thing, Archie—take care of your auntie for me, will you please?" Moore agreed. It was a promise he never broke.

The family received some insurance money, but Willie Pearl typically lent it out to relatives, and the Moores were soon on welfare along with the rest of the neighborhood. Even worse, Archie started to run with a gang of friends who involved themselves in minor criminal activities. Petty theft was at the top of the list. They began stripping empty houses, removing the lead pipes and selling them as well as trimming the wiring for the copper it contained. One of Moore's pals, Arthur "Knox" James, was in on it, too. His mother treated Archie like a son, offering pie or cookies whenever Archie visited. But it was illicit goodies that tempted Moore and

James the most. Together they were caught three times attempting various illegal schemes. Their last one landed Moore in jail.

The plan was to rip off a cable car. Arthur got aboard first and pulled down the pole that carried the current from overhead to stall the car. When the conductor went back to investigate the problem, Archie jumped on board and stole the unattended change box. Unfortunately for him, Moore's getaway route took him right past an on-duty police officer. Sizing up the situation, the cop fired a couple warning shots into the air, halting Archie in his tracks.

Archie was sent to Juvenile Hall to await trial. He passed the time by looking out the window, knowing that his aunt was suffering even more than him. Archie remembered, "I found myself gazing out the window, reminiscing about the good times I had, and then my mind wandered to going before a judge. I then felt guilty for putting my wonderful aunt through the ordeal."

Willie Pearl and Archie's mother were alongside him when the judge pronounced sentence. "I glanced at my aunt and my heart was about to break because I knew that this was a beautiful woman," Moore would recall. "Then, I looked at my mother, and my mother held my hand, and I said, 'Mother, don't cry.' And when I said that, two big tears welled up in my eyes and, try as I could, I couldn't fight them back. They rolled down my cheek like big drops of rain."

The sentence was a three-year term at the state reformatory for young men in Booneville, Missouri. Moore left the courtroom in chains. Aunt Willie Pearl sobbed uncontrollably. She had always been there for him, and hurting her like that made Archie realize his mistake more than any punishment. He vowed right then to be a better person and to make something of himself. He couldn't have known it then, but his reform school stint would help him keep that vow.

New reformatory inmates were assigned to the brickyard detail, back-breaking work designed to instill discipline. But Moore's brickyard duty was short-lived. He injured his hand in a scuffle and was transferred to the laundry room. There the work was less physically demanding, but the scalding steam on top of the hot summer weather made the duty unbearable. Eventually Archie switched to working in the dining room.

When he wasn't working, Moore recalled, "I had many hours to sit down and work at many of the mind-accelerating programs available to inmates. I read everything I could, especially history. I enjoyed reading about heroes of the past, especially western heroes. I didn't go to school at the reformatory, but I spent a lot of time in the library."

The 15-year-old Moore was one of the smallest inmates. That made him a natural target for reform school bullies, but that ended when Archie whipped one of the largest inmates after an incident during mealtime. Absolute silence was the rule during meals, so the boys used sign language to communicate. But some signs had double meanings. An upraised little finger meant pass the sugar, but it also was used as a homosexual signal. When the big inmate raised his little finger at Archie, Moore had no doubt what he had in mind and then disabused him of the notion by smacking the kid with a solid right hand that sent him crumbling to the ground. The rest of the inmates watched in disbelief as the smallest kid in the reformatory whipped one of the biggest. It was the last time Archie had any trouble in reform school.

The reformatory in Booneville had a boxing program open to all inmates, and Archie joined up. Moore fought 16 matches in reform school, knocking out all but one of his opponents. The discipline and his own determination to make his aunt proud of him again made him a model inmate, and his good behavior eventually led to an early discharge. He was at Booneville for 22 months.

Aunt Willie Pearl arranged through a parole officer for Moore to get a job with an ice and coal dealer. Archie's job was to carry buckets filled with ice up several flights of stairs. It was hard work for which he was supposed to be paid a dollar a day. But at the end of his first full day on the job, when Archie attempted to collect his daily wage, he was told it had not been a profitable day and so he would only get 50 cents for his 12 hours of hard labor. His employer knew that as a parolee Moore was required to work full-time and figured he had Archie over a barrel. There were two ice picks sticking in the wall, and Archie somehow managed to resist the urge to grab one and stab his boss. But he did quit on the spot.

Moore had to find another job quickly to satisfy his parole officer. Afraid of being exploited again, he confided his fears to the mother of his old friend Arthur James. She worked in a factory full-time but also rented out rooms in her home for extra income. Mrs. James came up with the idea of having Archie work for her twice a week, cleaning, doing maintenance work and any odd jobs that needed to be done around the house. It was a perfect arrangement for Moore, giving him plenty of free time to practice his boxing, which was gaining importance in his life.

Moore's hero was Kid Chocolate, the featherweight titlist, an exceptional boxer with gleaming charisma. Whenever one of the Kid's bouts was aired on the radio, Moore would rush over to the James residence for the broadcast. He vividly recalled listening to his hero battle Tony Canzoneri for the latter's lightweight title on November 20, 1931. Chocolate lost the decision, but that didn't stop Archie from wanting to be just like him, although Aunt Willie Pearl preferred that he become a gospel-preaching minister.

Looking for a way to improve both as a boxer and a man, Moore found the answer in the Civilian Conservation Corps. The CCC had been established in 1933 by President Franklin Roosevelt to provide work for unemployed men at the height of the Great Depression. Over three million of them enrolled in the program. It was run military-style, and all the enrollees were relocated to camps in national parks, where they built roads, trails, bridges and campgrounds. Everyone was given food, shelter, clothing, and $30 per month, of which they were required to send $25 home to their families. The remaining $5 was for spending money.

Moore's parole officer was Thomas Brooks, a decent man who always had Archie's best interest at heart. Once Brooks caught Moore violating his parole by staying out past curfew and instructed him to go home immediately. The cocky Moore didn't feel like being ordered around and let Brooks know it. Instead of writing him up, Brooks answered by smacking his parolee in the mouth and ordering him home. Archie went. Later, when approached by Moore for permission to join the CCC, Brooks arranged everything, figuring Archie would profit from the experience.

CHAPTER 2

Bootleg Boxing in Arkansas

In late summer of 1935, Archie was assigned to a new Civilian Conservation Corps camp in Poplar Bluff, Missouri. The facility included a main building, four 50-man barracks, a mess hall, recreation building, library and separate quarters for army and technical personnel.

Plenty of options were available to CCC recruits. They could choose to learn such skills as photography, auto mechanics, forestry and cooking. Moore elected to be in the forestry division. After being locked up in the reformatory, he wanted to be outdoors as much as possible and do physical work that would develop his strength and muscles for boxing. In addition to their jobs, recruits were required to help around the camp or work in the kitchen. In the evenings they were free, and Archie helped start a boxing team to compete in area amateur tournaments.

Moore was the most experienced boxer in camp and worked hard to improve his skills. He would spend hours shadowboxing in front of a mirror, observing and critiquing his moves. Even on the job he found ways to practice for the ring. He would stand in the back of the truck taking the forestry crew back to camp from the work site and duck as it passed under low-hanging tree branches, claiming it was good bobbing and weaving practice.

Moore resumed his amateur boxing career as a CCCer, and at the same time he engaged in several paid matches on the sly, using his own name or patriotically campaigning as the "Fourth of July Kid."

According to the *Ring Record Book and Boxing Encyclopedia*— "The Bible of Boxing"—Moore's first professional bout was in 1935 in Hot Springs, Arkansas, against an opponent called Piano Man Jones. In fact, Archie insisted, the other boxer's name was Piano Mover Jones, and he worked in a furniture store moving pianos. According to Archie, the musical purist, calling him "Piano Man" was not only incorrect but also an injustice to the music industry.

Moore said to the *Los Angeles Times*, "A promoter from Hot Springs, Arkansas, wanted me to turn pro there. He offered me nine dollars, plus room and board, if I would go down to Hot Springs and fight Jones, so I did. Piano Mover was a local heavyweight who had beaten up everyone in the area. He weighed 195 pounds; I weighed 150 pounds. We fought in a school gym, and I remember there wasn't a black face in the crowd. I could hear white farmers at ringside, betting bushels of corn on the outcome. Early in the first round, I feinted at Jones, and he lunged. I knew I had him. I knocked him out in the second round. I played a tune on the Piano Mover. After the fight they passed a hat. That small collection resulted in my first fight purse."

An early professional bout not listed in the *Boxing Register*, a more recent record book published under the imprimatur of the International Boxing Hall of Fame, is Moore's victory over Billy Simms on September 3, 1935 in Poplar Bluff, Missouri. The main event featured talented Allan Matthews of St. Louis. Moore attended the bout with 75 fellow CCCers to cheer on Matthews. Simms, a Poplar Bluff knockout artist, stopped Sammy Fulson in the first round on the undercard and then pumped his fists in the air and brazenly challenged anyone in the crowd to go a few rounds right then and there. The CCC boys shoved Archie forward. Simms accepted the challenge and was knocked out by Moore in the third round. An article about the fight in the *Poplar Bluff Times* touted Moore as a good prospect for some smart manager, since Simms was no slouch as a fighter himself.

While engaging in an occasional surreptitious fight for pay, Archie was also in training for the Southeast Missouri-North Arkansas Golden Gloves competition, slated for February 7, 1936. A few weeks before that, a Poplar Bluff promoter contacted Moore at the CCC camp about fighting a man named Four-H Posey in a professional bout. Posey was a popular local white fighter with almost a 20-pound weight advantage over Archie. He knocked Moore down early in the bout, but Moore recovered and proceeded to knock Posey down several times. It became clear that the deck was stacked against Archie when each time Posey hit the canvas, the bell was rung to signal the end of the round and to give the local hero time to regroup. The fight dragged on that way, and eventually it was obvious that Posey was in trouble no matter how short the rounds became. So after another knockdown, the referee just dispensed with any pretense of fairness and declared Posey the winner. This naturally upset the large contingent of CCC members rooting for Archie, and a small riot broke out. It was 15 miles back to the CCC camp, and the truck carrying Moore and his compatriots back home was pursued the whole way by some hot-eyed Posey backers intent on continuing the battle royale.

Unluckily for them, the CCCers radioed ahead to request that the front gate be opened for them and then manned by armed guards. When the Posey posse arrived, the guards pointed out the penalty for trespassing on government property. That ended matters, although the retreating faction warned that hostilities would resume whenever Moore and the other CCCers were spotted in Poplar Bluff.

In Hot Springs, Arkansas, on January 31, 1936, Moore was billed as the "Fourth of July Kid" in a scheduled eight-round match against Pocahontas Kid, a lumber camp worker from nearby Glenwood. Pocahontas had built a decent reputation in the

Razorback State, but he went out in the third round against
Archie. The pay for these early professional fights was only a few
dollars, but it nearly equaled his $5 monthly CCC allowance, and
Moore dutifully sent his winnings to Aunt Willie Pearl.

It was back to the simon-pure ranks the following week. The
finals at the Southeast Missouri-North Arkansas Golden Gloves
tournament were held before a full house at the VFW Arena in
Poplar Bluff, where, their bold talk notwithstanding, no Posey
backers interfered. Moore decisioned Kneibert Davidson to
advance to the championship round and then knocked out local
boxer Dale Richardson for the open division middleweight title.
Archie controlled the bout from the start, flooring Richardson
right after the opening bell. Richardson went to the deck twice in
the second round and was finished by a hard right to the chin.

His regional Golden Gloves title qualified Moore for the St.
Louis Golden Gloves championships. The four-day Tournament
of Champions, involving Golden Gloves titlists from 11 regions,
began February 17 at the Municipal Auditorium. In the opening
bout, Moore defeated Ray Halford, a St. Louis boxer, by a unanimous three-round decision. Two days later, Moore advanced to the
finals by winning unanimously over Bill Harper. His final opponent was Courtland Schultz. In a bout between two counter-
punchers, Schultz came on in the third and final round to take the
decision over Moore. While disappointed, Moore's strong showing
enhanced his reputation, and he headed back to CCC quarters
pleased with himself.

Not long afterwards, Archie and some buddies returned to St.
Louis to see some friends and check out the boxing opportunities
at some local professional gyms. To save money, Moore and his
pals decided to hop a moving freight. It was a risky move that
almost cost Archie his life. He and his friends first climbed aboard
a cramped tank car carrying molasses. In search of more spacious
accommodations, they then hopped aboard a different train up the
line. Moore was last in line, and as he ran alongside the freight he
heard footsteps trailing behind. He turned to see who was following just as a club swung by the pursuing security guard was com-

ing at his head. Archie ducked, and the club missed him and smashed on the steel side of the car, shattering into pieces. Had the club hit its intended target, it might have been Moore's head in pieces on the ground. Archie grabbed onto the train, hauled himself aboard, and then leaped from rooftop to rooftop in search of his companions. In the process, Moore dropped his knapsack containing all his boxing gear. Fortunately, everyone made it safely to St. Louis. There the fellows went their separate ways, planning to meet back in Poplar Bluff in a few days.

Upon his return to the camp, Moore was amazed to find that the boxing gear he'd lost on the train was there. It had been found and mailed back to him by a Good Samaritan.

A model CCCer, Archie was honorably discharged in the spring of 1936. His sights set on a ring career, he returned to St. Louis.

CHAPTER 3

Turning Pro... Officially

Back home, Moore soon found employment with the Works Project Administration (WPA), another New Deal enterprise, and started boxing nights at the Pine Street YMCA in downtown St. Louis. There, Moore reacquainted himself with two men who would have a significant impact on his career.

Bantamweight George Porter and heavyweight Monroe Harrison were acquaintances from Moore's Golden Gloves days. It was Harrison who convinced Moore that he could become a great fighter. Harrison was coach and captain of the Pine Street YMCA boxing team, which was sponsored by the black weekly newspaper, the *St. Louis Argus*. He had a younger brother, Matthew, who started boxing at the same time as Moore. Matthew worked hard but was no match for Moore in their daily sparring sessions. Monroe was so impressed that he turned his attention to Archie and began to work with him in the gym.

Harrison was one of the city's top amateur boxers. Two years earlier, he had competed in the national Amateur Athletic Union boxing championships hosted by St. Louis. It was the first time in over 50 years that the tournament was held outside Boston or New York. A local rule against interracial boxing in St. Louis had to be rescinded first. In addition to Harrison, among the 161 boxers from all over the United States in the tournament was an unheralded, quiet man from Detroit identified in the papers as "Joe Lewis." The media would get it right when Joe Louis began his ascent to the world heavyweight title after knocking out Ario Soldail of Chicago for the 175-pound AAU title and being named the most outstanding boxer of the tournament.

Harrison won his first bout in the light heavyweight competition, but then was eliminated on a disputed decision in his next match. He and Louis never met in the ring, but Harrison would provide quality sparring whenever Louis passed through St. Louis during his professional career. "Oh, he could fight!" Moore said of Harrison. "He played a great part in Joe Louis's life. Talk about Mike Tyson! Tyson can fight. Louis, though, was much more revered and feared than Tyson. Louis had to get 20 sparring partners in order to get three or four good rounds of work. He knocked guys out every day. Monroe was the only guy who gave Louis problems. He gave Louis plenty of problems."

Moore called Harrison the greatest teacher he ever had in boxing. It was Harrison who taught him the unique "cross-arm" stance and the tremendous defensive techniques that would become Moore trademarks. "Monroe rarely took a solid punch, or any punch," recalled Archie. "He didn't have a scar on him."

Later, Harrison also played a major role in the early career of Charles "Sonny" Liston, who would become one of the most feared heavyweight champions. He continued to coach amateur and professional fighters in the Gateway City until his death in 1979.

George Porter and Moore had attended school together. "George Porter knew something about everything," Archie said. "He was a worldly guy who had his smarts on at all times. George helped teach me the basics of boxing. He taught me the importance of the jab and also how to properly punch the heavy bag. We used to hang out together all the time." Moore and Porter had both fought in the 1936 St. Louis Golden Gloves tournament. Fighting for the Pine Street YMCA, Porter defeated Mickie Collins, a teammate of Moore's at the Poplar Bluff CCC camp. It was Porter who encouraged Moore to box at the Pine Street YMCA upon his CCC discharge.

For the eight St. Louis amateur boxers, including Archie Moore and Monroe Harrison, who traveled to Cleveland, Ohio, for the 1936 national AAU boxing tournament, there was added incentive to do well. The boxers who made it to the semifinals would be eligible to compete in May trials for the 1936 U.S. Olympic team. Thus, the tournament was a double disappointment for Moore and Harrison. Archie lost to Frank Nelson, of Davenport, Iowa, and Harrison was defeated by Daniel Merritte of Cleveland, by decision.

Moore's defeat was acutely embarrassing on account of an article in the next day's *St. Louis Post Dispatch*, which hurt him more than Nelson's punches. Sportswriter W.J. McGoogan stated that Moore had fought nonchalantly and never seemed particularly interested, and even suggested Archie had mostly concerned himself with not getting hurt instead of trying to win. McGoogan claimed that Moore did little more than cover his face with his arms, and reported that when the fight was called off Moore walked to his corner, apparently relieved to be done for the night. Archie groused about the article for years. What he'd been practicing in the fight, he insisted, was the cross-arm defense Harrison had taught him.

On May 18, 1936, a team of St. Louis amateurs won five out of eight bouts against a Kansas City team at the St. Louis Coliseum. Moore defeated Thurman Martin by a three-round decision in a middleweight match, and his mentor, Monroe Harrison, pounded out a hard-fought decision over Charlie Neaves.

With that, Archie decided it was time to make professional prize fighting his full-time occupation. He needed a job, having quit his WPA job over a dispute with his boss. Moore and his crew were working on a levee one cold day and took a brief rest period.

As they gathered around a fire to warm up, their foreman came on the scene and threatened to fire them if they did not immediately get back to work. Moore stood up, grabbed his shovel in frustration and heaved it into the air. "This is not for me," he announced to his co-workers. "Next time you see me, I'll be in a professional boxing ring and you'll have to pay to see me."

But there was one final hurdle to surmount before going pro. Archie had to face Aunt Willie Pearl, who wasn't much for fighting and still thought her nephew would be a knockout in a pulpit. But Aunt Willie Pearl loved her boy too much to stand in his way, and she gave her approval contingent on three conditions: Archie was to never smoke, drink, or do anything shameful in the ring, such as throw a fight. It was a done deal.

A former bantamweight boxer called Kid Bandy owned a boxing gym and managed fighters. He became Moore's first manager of record and booked his early professional fights, the first of which, as reported in the *St. Louis Argus*, officially took place on July 17, 1936, in Quincy, Illinois. Under a headline announcing "Archie Moore scores K.O. in Pro Debut," the article reported that Moore impressively out-boxed and out-hit more experienced Murray Allen of Chicago, sending him to the canvas five times before a right cross ended it in the fifth round. Both of Allen's eyes were badly cut and a tooth was knocked out.

Poor Allen was also Moore's second professional opponent, on the undercard of a bout featuring former world heavyweight champion Max Baer at Keokuk, Iowa.

Max Baer's barnstorming Midwestern tour had drawn standing-room-only crowds, and a sellout was expected at the Hi-Life Garden. Baer's younger brother, Buddy, a future two-time challenger for Joe Louis's heavyweight title, was also featured on the card. Madcap Max clowned throughout his four-round exhibition with Babe Davis of St. Louis, and the crowd booed heartily. Buddy also failed to impress in knocking out Pete Gibbons in the third round of a boring mismatch. The unheralded star of the evening was Moore, who weighed 153 pounds and made Allen quit in the third round of their match.

Hometown fans got their first look at the young rising professional when Archie defeated former Chicago Golden Gloves champion Sammy Jackson by a unanimous five-round decision at the St. Louis Coliseum on October 9, 1936. Two months later they met again. This time Archie was held to a draw.

Archie's first fight of 1937 was on January 5, against Dynamite Payne of Salt Lake City. Moore went right on the attack, peppering Payne with stinging left jabs and a strong right cross that sent him to the canvas. When he got up, Dynamite was defused for good by another vicious right-hand that floored him for keeps.

Less than two weeks later, Archie fought his first main event, knocking out veteran Johnny Davis in the fourth round of a scheduled 10-rounder in Quincy, Illinois.

Joe Huff was a hard-punching St. Louis veteran who was no match for Moore in their main event at the St. Louis Arena on February 5, 1937. He lasted three rounds.

George Wilsman, the manager for whom Archie had dumped Kid Bandy earlier that year, also handled a South American heavyweight, Vincent Parrille. Wilsman arranged a main event for Parrille in Ponca City, Oklahoma, against popular local Indian Junior Munsell. Moore was on the undercard against Hamm Pounder, another local boxer. An article published March 23, the day of the fight, in the *Ponca City News*, described Moore as a stiff puncher. But most of the attention went to Parrille, who had seen a picture in the paper of Junior Munsell purportedly displaying a "scalp" of a previously vanquished opponent. To prevent the same thing from happening to him, Parrille went out and got his noggin shaved. "No Indian gets my scalp!" he said.

Parrille's quick thinking didn't save him from a second-round KO at the hands of Munsell. In the semi-windup, Archie knocked out the curiously named Hamm Pounder to keep his unbeaten record intact, but then got sort of scalped himself. When Moore went to Wilsman to collect his promised $35 purse, the manager coughed up only $12. Archie left town looking for an honest manager.

Of those early days, Archie would later recall "long bus rides, bad food, little pay, no sleep, and quick knockouts. Some of the bus rides were much tougher than the fights."

After leaving Wilsman, Moore hooked up with Cal Thompson of Indianapolis, Indiana. Thompson was a wealthy entrepreneur who ran a successful chain of barber shops. Moore was impressed with Thompson and his classy ways and agreed to join his boxing stable in Indianapolis. Archie actually lived with Thompson for a while, but relocated to a boardinghouse after a dispute with Thompson's wife. It was Thompson who introduced Moore to trainer Hiawatha Grey, a onetime bantamweight fighter who would be with Moore off and on for the rest of his career. Grey got to know Moore's fighting style better than anyone else and would quickly correct any incipient flaws he noticed before they could turn into bad habits. After a few quick knockout victories in Indianapolis, Moore fought twice in Cincinnati, defeating Frank Hatfield by a knockout and then meeting tough local prospect Billy Adams. Moore was knocked down by Adams and tired down the stretch in the eight-round bout, which he lost by decision. It was the first time one of Archie's bouts went the distance. He had always counted on his knockout ability to send him home early, but as the caliber of his opposition improved, Archie realized that not everyone would fall and he would need to start pacing himself.

He learned another important lesson against cagey veteran Sammy "Kid" Slaughter. Moore paced himself early in the 10-rounder but then fell prey to Slaughter's psychological tricks. Slaughter cursed and teased Moore in the early rounds, hoping to enrage Archie and cause him to throw caution to the winds. It worked, as Moore eventually lost his head and started punching wildly in pursuit of Slaughter. But then Archie regained his composure, resumed boxing at a steady pace, and earned a unanimous decision victory. But not before Slaughter tried a new desperation tactic. Late in the fight, with Archie in total command, Slaughter grabbed him in a clinch and pleaded for mercy, telling Moore he was just an old man out for a payday and begging Archie to go easy. The forgiving kind, Moore let up and was rewarded for his kindheartedness with a haymaker that luckily only grazed his chin. Moore punished Slaughter for the balance of the bout and would never again listen to a sob story in the heat of battle.

Unfortunately, Cal Thompson began having difficulty landing quality fights for Moore, and they both agreed that it would be best for Archie to return to St. Louis. Thompson gave Moore $10 bus fare and wished him luck. They remained friends and stayed in touch for years.

Eight days after defeating Slaughter, Moore was back in front of his hometown fans, knocking out Charlie Dawson in the fifth round. Two months later, he got a rematch against Sammy Christian, who'd held Archie to a draw earlier in his career.

The rematch was on the undercard of a landmark show in St. Louis. It was the first time that two reigning world champions were featured on the same card in Missouri. The main events featured separate bouts involving world lightweight champion Lou Ambers, who won a decision over Charlie Burns, and newly crowned bantamweight king Harry Jeffra, who stopped Jackie Carter. But there were plenty of cheers for Archie, who displayed lightening-quick speed and clever ring movement to outclass Christian and capture a unanimous five-round verdict.

It was a good year for Moore. He had 14 bouts, losing one, drawing one, and adding 12 knockouts to his boxing resume. Archie wasted no time getting busy in 1938, stopping Carl Lautenschlager in the second round on January 7.

* * *

Moore's pal George Porter had a distant relative named Felix Thurman visiting from California. Porter filled Moore's head with stories of talented middleweights located in the Golden State such as Johnny "The Bandit" Romero and Jack Chase, the state 160-pound champion, and convinced Moore to ride back to San Diego with Thurman. The idea was that Thurman, an auto mechanic by trade, would help manage Moore and introduce him to San Diego's top fight promoter, Linn Platner.

The decision to go West was a tough one. Archie had ventured as far south as Arkansas and east to Indianapolis, but had never been so far away from home as San Diego. But if he wanted good fights and career advancement, California was the place for Moore. So he told Aunt Willie Pearl good bye and then stopped by the Pine Street YMCA to bid farewell to Monroe Harrison before setting out on the long journey to San Diego with Thurman in April 1938, with just $30 between them.

CHAPTER 4

A Near-Death Experience

They almost never made it. Near Bartlesville, Oklahoma, with the road slick from the pouring rain, a car came racing around a corner toward them. Thurman had to decide in a heartbeat whether to hit the other car head on or drive off the road and hope for the best. He opted for the irrigation ditch alongside the road, and the car flipped over and landed on its roof. Felix was knocked unconscious. A dazed Moore attempted to pry open the door, but it wouldn't budge. As he worked on the door, Archie noticed a clear liquid dripping on his arm. Fearing it was gas, he punched out the passenger window with his right fist and crawled through the opening. In the process, Moore slashed an artery in his wrist. With blood spurting uncontrollably, Moore tried to get Thurman out of the car. When another vehicle approached, Moore flagged it down.

Calling what happened next "lucky" would be severely understating the case. The car that stopped contained two medical interns and two nurses on their way to a nearby hospital. They quickly administered first aid to Moore, applying a tourniquet to his wounded arm. Later, they informed Archie that he would have died within 14 minutes had the hemorrhaging wound not been treated. Like the return of his lost boxing gear to the CCC camp, the psychic implications of what occurred near Bartlesville affected Moore's outlook profoundly.

"It is impossible to comprehend our luck that day," he said. "At that time in 1938, it was difficult to imagine an automobile stopping to help two stranded African Americans. However, the first car that saw us stopped and saved my life. At that moment I thought to myself, 'I don't know if God is a white man or a black man, but he truly made us all.'"

The interns also pulled Thurman out of the overturned car and tended to him. Felix was shaken up, but not seriously injured. At the hospital, Moore learned that the broken glass came within one-eighth of an inch of severing the tendon in his right wrist, which would also have severed his boxing dreams.

More good luck: except for the broken window and a dented roof, the car was actually serviceable. It was towed to the nearest gas station. Felix straightened out the dented roof himself with a mallet he stored in the trunk with his other tools. Moore's hospital expenses were waived by a generous doctor who turned out to be a big boxing fan. However, the tow job ate $12 out of their already small gasoline fund, and the trip stalled again in Amarillo, Texas. Nearly broke, Felix phoned his wife and convinced her to wire $10 to Grants, New Mexico. That got them a little farther, and in order to complete their journey, Felix was forced to trade in his expensive mechanic's tools one by one for cash until the tired road warriors finally reached their destination.

On Moore's first morning in California, he instinctively rose early for his daily run. As he jogged on the beautiful beaches of La Jolla, Archie noticed a smoky cloud rising above downtown San Diego. He sprinted back to Thurman's house, where he found out that the San Diego Coliseum, the site of all the city's major boxing events, was on fire. If that was an omen of what was in store for him in California, Archie decided it was outweighed by the positive foreshadowing that occurred on the trip to San Diego. He still had two good arms.

After meeting promoter Platner, Moore was booked for his California debut on May 20, 1938, against talented Los Angeles middleweight Jimmy Brent. It was the semi-windup bout on a card featuring former world light heavyweight champion-turned-movie actor "Slapsie" Maxie Rosenbloom. Based on each fighter's respectable records, the Moore-Brent match would have been a worthy main event in itself, but a card featuring such a renowned character as Rosenbloom was sure to draw a big crowd for Moore's West Coast unveiling at outdoor Lane Field.

One hundred seventy-five-pound champion from 1932-34, Rosenbloom boasted of having a punch as potent "as a rum and coke, minus the rum." He stopped journeyman O'Dell Polee in the fifth round before the loud capacity crowd.

But the highlight of the night was newcomer Archie Moore, who knocked out Jimmy Brent in the first round. Moore used numerous head feints—perhaps learned dodging those tree limbs in CCC camp—to keep Brent confused and off balance and sent him to the canvas three times. Promoter Platner was so impressed that he immediately signed Archie for the main event the following week at Lane Field against tough local prospect Ray Vargas. Vargas was a former amateur star who had become a local attraction as a pro.

In front of another sellout crowd, Archie flattened Vargas in the third round. Vargas was outboxed the entire bout. Moore dropped him for a count of nine in the second round and bloodied his nose in the process. Vargas wildly rushed in, attempting to beat Moore to the punch, but could not keep up with the newcomer's speed. In the third, Moore connected with a solid left hook and then sent over a deadly right cross that prompted referee John Perry to call off the fight to save Vargas from serious harm.

Moore had made quick work of his first two California foes, and Platner decided to test his skills against one of the top boxers in the world, Johnny "The Bandit" Romero. The Bandit had fought such top boxers as former middleweight champion Gorilla Jones and had knocked out Carmen Barth, a 1932 Olympic gold medalist. Romero had recently moved up to the light heavyweight division and would hold nearly a 10-pound weight advantage over Moore when they fought on June 24.

Romero's southpaw style and punching power made him a six-to-five favorite in the betting. Moore's purse for this bout would be nearly $200, easily the largest of his career.

Moore's longtime friend Eddie Frazier recalled, "I first met Archie in 1938. I was boxing as an amateur, but Archie trained at my gym. We hit it off right away. I was only 16, but Archie always took the time to give me a few pointers. I liked his outgoing personality. He became an idol.

"I was at the Coliseum for most of his San Diego fights. He battled all the top-notch area fighters like 'Bandit' Romero soon after coming to town. The promoter, Linn Platner, never gave the black fighters easy opponents and rarely gave them a shot. Archie earned everything the hard way—but he did it."

In a close battle, Romero captured a decision win based on his two knockdowns of Moore in round four. The judges awarded each boxer five rounds apiece, but when the point totals were added up, Archie was on the short end.

Moore had dominated the first three rounds, beating Romero to the punch and bloodying his nose. But in the fourth, Romero caught Moore with a right hook that dropped him. Moore rose at the count of eight, but then Romero landed another blow that put him on the seat of his pants. Archie was up at the count of one this time and fought back hard through the end of the round.

Romero poured it on in the next four rounds, punching Archie's right eye completely shut. The weary Moore actually came back to win the last two rounds, but the verdict came back in Romero's favor. The pro-Romero crowd cheered wildly throughout, but when a dejected Moore finally left his dressing room an hour after the fight, he was amazed at the number of fans who had waited to see him and congratulate him on a great effort.

Platner promised Moore a rematch with Romero, but with the proviso that Archie get right back into action and score a few impressive victories first. Accordingly, Moore was back in the Lane Field ring less than a month later. In the other corner was Johnny

Sykes of Montana, a hard right-hand puncher who had scored four KOs in previous San Diego appearances.

In preparing for the fight, Moore worked hard on improving his own right-hand. He even floored a heavyweight sparring partner in the gym during one workout. But it was his left hook that did the trick against Sykes, who dropped for the count less than a minute after the first bell clanged.

The Coliseum was being rebuilt, with completion scheduled for the fall of 1938. Platner promised that if Moore got past Lorenzo Pedro at Lane Field just two weeks after the Sykes quickie, he would get a rematch with Johnny Romero at the new facility. In spite of giving up 11 pounds in weight to the Brazilian fighter, Moore handily defeated Pedro in 10 rounds. Both boxers fought cautiously for the first half, but then Moore stepped things up, landing solid punches on a consistent basis. Pedro slumped to the canvas twice in the seventh round and was turning away from Moore's powerful punches during the final rounds. The Romero rematch was set for September 2 at the Coliseum.

To guarantee maximum coverage, the weigh-in was held in front of the press. Archie was a Sunday School teacher at the Presbyterian Church near his home in suburban La Jolla, but this wasn't Sunday and it sure as hell wasn't about turning the other cheek. Thus, when Johnny began telling Moore he had no animosity towards him and hoped they were friends, Archie interrupted to declare that, friends or no, he planned on knocking Romero out. Then, in his angriest tone, Moore said he would knock out his own brother if they ever squared off in the ring and then pointed out that since Romero was not his brother, he could count on not being around for the last bell. It was psychological warfare, Kid Slaughter-style.

The 3,000-plus enthusiastic fans at the new coliseum witnessed a masterpiece. In one of the finest performances of his career, Archie floored Romero four times before the referee halted the onslaught in the eighth round. Moore pounded Romero severely, leaving him with both eyes swollen shut and with his nose cut and bleeding. Moore won every round, landing consistently with solid right-hands.

The victory established Moore as a world-class contender, but instead of resting on his laurels Archie was back in action just two weeks after the Romero fight. His opponent in the main event at the Coliseum was light heavyweight Fred Rowsey, who claimed to be the best fighter ever to come out of Powder River, Wyoming. Archie joked that he probably was the *only* fighter ever to come out of Powder River, but Rowsey was a worthy foe with a winning record. He had just returned from a successful tour of Australia, where he defeated some of the best boxers "The Land Down Under" had to offer. World welterweight champion Henry Armstrong was seated at ringside to wish his old friend Moore good luck. "Hurricane Hank" was a fellow St. Louisian, and he and Moore had sparred on occasion.

Moore floored Rowsey with the first punch he threw in the fight. In the second round, he opened a nasty gash over Rowsey's left eye. The target practice lasted until the referee said "enough" in round three.

Nine days later, Moore scored a technical knockout over Irish Tom Henry in Archie's inaugural appearance in Los Angeles. It was his ninth fight since hitting the Coast, and his only loss, to Romero, had been wiped out in the rematch. It was time for the conquering hero to return home to St. Louis.

CHAPTER 5

Suspended from Boxing in Missouri

Back home, Moore hooked up with George Porter and Monroe Harrison. They had followed Moore's success in California through the local papers. Moore planned just a short stay, the main point of which was to see Aunt Willie Pearl and help her out with some of his California earnings. But local promoter Jackie Callahan talked Archie into staying a while and anchoring a few fight cards. On November 22, 1938, Moore appeared in a hometown ring for the first time in 10 months. Ray Lyle was a veteran who claimed that he had never been off his feet in nearly 300 professional bouts. Archie introduced him to the canvas with a left hook to the jaw in the second round.

Moore was thrilled to be back in St. Louis. The winter weather was not as pleasant as the sublime San Diego climate, but to be with his aunt and friends made up for that. Moore scored a first-round knockout over Jack Moran and then signed to fight European light heavyweight champion Domenic Ceccarelli at the Coliseum. Ceccarelli was handled by George Wilsman, who had taken Archie to Ponca, Oklahoma and stiffed him for most of his purse. The day of the fight, the *St. Louis Globe-Democrat* featured a large picture of Wilsman standing with his arm around Ceccarelli. According to the accompanying article, it was Wilsman who'd had a dispute with Moore, which led to their split. Wilsman made it worse at a press conference where he announced he knew of several flaws in Moore's style and had taught Ceccarelli to capitalize on them. Archie grimly responded that his fists would do the talking for him. It took a lot to spur Moore to genuine anger, but Wilsman was on the right track.

The European entered the ring with a 10-pound weight advantage over Moore. The well muscled, shiny-domed Italian looked confident until the bell rang and Moore came out firing.

There wasn't a second round, or even a bell to end the first. After a left hook finished off Ceccarelli, Moore almost put Wilsman in the same state just by glaring at him menacingly. The fast KO moved the St. Louis media to dub Archie the "Joe Louis of the 160-pounders."

He wasn't the only conquering hero in the Gateway City. Henry Armstrong had left town in 1928 penniless, and 11 years later he was returning as one of boxing's greatest champions and the first man in ring history to hold three world titles simultaneously, having won the featherweight, welterweight and lightweight belts.

Like Moore, Armstrong had fought out of the Pine St. YMCA as an amateur, but did most of his professional boxing on the West Coast. When he was in St. Louis in late '36 for a few bouts, Armstrong hired Moore as a sparring partner. "Back in 1936, I was just a beginning professional and Henry Armstrong was the world featherweight champion," recalled Moore years afterward. "I couldn't even pay to get anyone to box me. Henry hired me to be one of his sparring partners for fifty cents a round. We were both training in St. Louis, and I could not even afford transportation to the gym; I had to walk the whole way. I sparred six rounds with Armstrong, but he left town before I had a chance to collect the money he owed me."

Now Armstrong was coming home to defend his lightweight title in front of over 17,000 fans at the Auditorium, and his ex-sparring partner, Moore, was in a 10-rounder on the undercard. Armstrong had knocked out Lou Feldman in a previous encounter and was heavily favored to repeat the feat. Did he ever. Armstrong came out firing punches from all angles until Feldman wilted under the onslaught. It was over in one. Conversely, Moore was extended to the 10-round limit by Marty Simmons, who had 10 pounds on him. But Archie wasn't disappointed because his six-bout KO streak was snapped. He figured himself ready for a shot at the middleweight title.

In the opposite corner for his next fight was someone who figured differently. Teddy Yarosz had once owned the 160-lb. title, and the clever stylist from Pittsburgh owned impressive victories over future light heavyweight king Billy Conn and Ken Overlin, who would go on to win the middleweight title.

Yarosz arrived in St. Louis with his stablemate, Fritzie Zivic, who was starting to make a name for himself in the welterweight division and was scheduled to face Tiger Walker in the main supporting bout. Zivic had an alarmingly bent nose and lines of scar tissue covering his eyes, of which he seemed almost as proud as his reputation as a dirty fighter. Fritzie specialized at using elbows, thumbs, and glove laces. He once stated with a malevolent smile, "Most boxers seem to think that laces are only for tying up their gloves." Zivic also used them to rub against opponents' faces in the clinches.

On April 20, 1939, fans packed the Auditorium for the Moore-Yarosz bout. But St. Louisians and their favorite son were disappointed. The ex-champion put on a boxing clinic, keeping his left jab in Moore's face all night. He put on a tremendous defensive display as well, never allowing Moore to land any solid punches. Yarosz's championship experience paid off as he boxed his way to a unanimous decision. After the bout Moore gestured to his head, indicating that Yarosz had too much knowledge and experience for him.

Although bothered by the defeat, Moore wrote it off as a learning experience and vowed to return to action as soon as possible. Unlike boxing today, when a single defeat can end a fighter's marketability, it was not uncommon for the game's best boxers to have a number of losses on their record. The idea was to learn from your mistakes and do better next time.

Talent in the middleweight division was in short supply in St. Louis, so Moore returned to San Diego. In his first competition there in over a year, Moore faced light heavyweight Sailor Jack Coggins on a card at the San Diego Coliseum. Moore had just recently cracked the top 10 in the middleweight division, but once again found it necessary to engage a much larger opponent in order to book a fight. Less experienced than Moore, Coggins entered the contest with a 10-pound weight advantage and a reputation as a solid right-hand puncher. In fact he had flattened his previous 12 opponents and vowed to add Moore to the list. What shaped up on paper to be a knockout affair ended up being one of the dullest bouts of Moore's career.

The scheduled 10-round event was stopped by the referee in the eighth round because the customers were in a coma. The fearsome punchers had done nothing but swap light, tentative blows. The non-fight was ruled a no-contest and the purses of both fighters were held up. Moore admitted to respecting Coggins's power too much and being too defensive-minded. He promised to do better in a rematch. It happened on September 1, five weeks after their snoozefest. This time Moore gave Coggins a boxing lesson over 10 rounds and took an easy decision.

Several days later, Archie met a kind young woman named Mattie Chapman. They quickly became inseparable and eventually were engaged to be married. However, Archie's career came first, and he set his compass for Phoenix, Arizona, for a two-bout series.

The first bout was billed as a battle of uncrowned champions. Moore's opponent, Freddie Dixon, had been campaigning for a shot at the light heavyweight crown for years and figured a victory over middleweight contender Moore would seal the deal. Dixon was known for his superior boxing skills and a jolting left jab.

It was another controversial ending. Throughout the bout, Moore controlled the action and piled up points with slick counter punching. In the eighth round, an uppercut dropped Dixon, who commenced crawling on the mat, wincing in pain and pointing at his groin area. The blow that felled Dixon appeared to be a legal shot to the midsection, but after much debate the bout was ruled a technical draw. Later, Moore admitted that the blow might've accidentally landed low, explaining that he started to throw the punch before the bell, and as his arm shot upward, Dixon came charging in faster than expected.

The result was yet another instance of the unfortunate luck that seemed to always slow down Moore's march toward a world title. Archie stayed in Arizona and trained for his next bout, scheduled for Phoenix two weeks after the Dixon fiasco.

Extremely proud of being boxing's all-time knockout leader, Archie always insisted that the record books lost a few of his knockouts along the way. His bout in Phoenix on November 13, 1939 is one of those lost bouts. Billed as a power-punching light heavyweight out of North Carolina, Billy Day had just returned from a successful tour of the Orient, where he'd won all but one of 15 bouts. Moore went on the offensive at the sound of the bell, smacking Day with sharp jabs and right crosses. It was a left hook that sent Day rolling unconscious on the canvas. The KO of Day was only recently discovered and is included in the 1997 *Boxing Register*. Moore claims that several other bouts have been left off his record, including those of his "Fourth of July Kid" days in the CCC.

Ten days later, Moore returned to St. Louis for his next bout. His career appeared to finally be headed on the right course, but difficulties soon arose that sent Archie's roller coaster ring career on the downward slide again. While delighted to again be near family and friends, at the same time Moore's heart ached for his fiancee, Mattie Chapman, whom he had not seen since leaving for Phoenix several weeks before.

On December 7, 1939, Moore met Pittsburgh's Honeyboy Jones in the main event at the St. Louis Auditorium. Jones had faced many top men in his career, including then-light heavy-weight champion Billy Conn an amazing five times. Honeyboy went the distance each time to enhance his reputation as a rugged journeyman. But Jones's survival tactics left Moore angered and embarrassed in front of his hometown fans.

Early in the fight, Jones was cut by Moore's piercing left jab. Once Jones saw his own blood, he sought the refuge of clinches for the rest of the bout. Moore won the decision with room to spare, but the bout was tedious and unappealing. The crowd booed lusti-ly, and as soon as Moore was announced as winner, Frank Foss, acting chairman of the Missouri Athletic Commission, ordered both boxers' purses held up pending a hearing on the putrid match.

The December 8, 1939 issue of the *St. Louis Post-Dispatch* reported that Moore and Jones would be suspended in Missouri for a year on account of their lackluster showing. Foss claimed that both boxers deserved it, although Jones had clearly been the insti-gator of the clinches that marred the bout. Moore acknowledged it had not been one of his stellar efforts, but pointed out that it was difficult to box effectively against a purely defensive-minded fight-er. While bothered by the suspension, Archie felt an appeal could take months to resolve and would deplete his savings. Boxing was Moore's sole source of income, and rather than fritter away money and time fighting the ruling, Archie decided to return to California, which did not honor the suspension.

But things did not immediately brighten in the Golden State. In San Diego, promoter Platner booked Moore for a match against Shorty Hogue on December 29. Moore dropped a six-round deci-sion to the slick Hogue and, disgusted, briefly contemplated retire-ment.

At least Mattie was there for him. His fiancee stood behind Moore on all decisions regarding his future. She wanted to be with Archie, and so they decided to get married on New Year's Day, 1940. Mattie and Archie, along with Mattie's brother and sister, headed for Yuma, Arizona, to be married by a justice of the peace. Although his future in the ring was uncertain, Moore was pleased to be married and felt that if nothing else his life outside boxing was at least starting to come together.

After nearly 50 professional bouts, Archie was essentially no closer to a decent payday or a shot at a title than when he started his career. He met with his manager, Felix Thurman, to re-evaluate their game plan. Thurman was a good friend but not a shrewd fight manager. After a long discussion, both agreed that Moore would be better suited with an experienced boxing pilot.

Enter Jack Richardson, who dazzled Moore with visions of title shots and fights in exotic lands. Richardson had developed several successful boxers and had a working connection in Australia who booked fights Down Under for his stable. The prospect of relocating to Australia thrilled Moore and his bride. Richardson arranged to send Moore to Australia immediately.

CHAPTER 6

Boxing Down Under

The contract called for Moore to be in Australia for two bouts against native middleweights. Over the years, plenty of American boxers had crossed the ocean to battle the Aussies, with only limited success. Moore was originally brought down as a boxer of decent credentials to play the role of opponent for highly rated Australian middleweight Ron Richards. Richards had already cracked the top 10 by defeating Gus Lesnevich, who would nevertheless go on to win the world light heavyweight title. The original scenario called for Moore to have a tune-up bout with former Australian welterweight champion Jack McNamee, followed by a match with Richards.

Moore set sail on the 22-day voyage to Sydney aboard the cruise ship *The Monterey*. But before he even set foot aboard the ship there was a dispute with Jack Richardson that cast a shadow over the adventure. Richardson forbade Mattie from accompanying her husband of three days on the journey, claiming the added expense would break the budget. At the same time, Richardson managed to find room on the expense voucher for his own wife and son, which deepened the rift with Archie. Since the contract had been signed, Moore was forced to go to Australia alone.

Richardson, a wealthy car dealer from San Diego who had once been an amateur boxer of little note, had purchased Moore's contract from Felix Thurman for the unbelievably low price of $250. Moore claimed later that the pittance paid for his contract amounted to the biggest steal since early settlers purchased Manhattan Island for only 24 dollars in beads.

Lonely and isolated on *The Monterey*, Moore took solace in the meals served aboard ship. Eating was about the only thing to look forward to on the boring trip. The ship had no adequate workout facilities. Prior to leaving, Moore had never needed to diet and had no problems making the 160-pound middleweight limit. Moore also passed the time writing letters to his bride. He knew Mattie was upset about being left behind, but in the face of Richardson's pig-headedness on the matter, Archie had been left with no choice but to go it alone. Boxing came first.

The ship made several refueling stops in such exotic lands as the Fiji Islands. Moore recalled reaching the point where lost U.S. pilot Amelia Earhart's last message was found. Her disappearance was still fresh in everyone's mind. Finally, the cruise ship reached Sydney, Australia. But there was no welcoming parade.

Sydney is Australia's oldest city, a bustling economic power-house built on a beautiful harbor. When *The Monterey* finally docked, Richardson took Moore to a hotel in the district known as King's Cross and promised that someone would pick him up the next day and take him to the gym. King's Cross was Sydney's sin-city area, alive 24 hours a day with all manner of activity going on in its bars and brothels. The bright lights and fast pace were lost on Archie, who pined for his wife and homeland. Fortunately, he soon ran into American boxers Al Brown and Johnny Hutchinson, who were also touring Down Under. He asked them for a run-down on Ron Richards and was warned that the Aussie was a rugged, hard-nosed slugger who was immensely popular in his homeland. Brown and Hutchinson went on to suggest as delicately as possible that Moore had been imported to lose to the native fighter.

But first up—in Melbourne on March 30, 1940—was Jack McNamee. While training for the fight, Moore attended his first Australian professional bout, which coincidentally featured Richards against another top Australian middleweight, Fred Henneberry. It was a grueling contest, with Richards winning via disqualification in the eleventh round. Moore was introduced in the ring that evening to the Australian fans, and looking out over the audience he recognized no one and was recognized by no one. Archie was determined to change that when he collided with the national hero.

The McNamee fight was an easy night's pay for the American. Moore centered his attack on McNamee's body, and the hometwon boy wilted in the fourth round. When Moore congratulated McNamee on a fine effort, he used the opportunity to sound him out about Richards. McNamee said he knew the style needed to defeat his countryman and would welcome the chance to demonstrate it as Archie's sparring partner. McNamee was hired and worked with Moore right up to the bout.

The American set up training camp on a ranch in the Megalong Valley outside of Sydney. It was an idyllic place located near an ancient rain forest in the Blues Mountains. Archie bunked with the Baptiste family and was treated like a family member. It was Moore's first training camp, and he relished it. He started each morning with seven miles of brisk roadwork. In addition to the usual boxer's routine, Moore employed several unconventional methods of conditioning, such as running behind horses and tossing large rocks around the mountainside. But for all his hard work, Moore was having difficulty shedding the excess pounds he had put on when he sought solace in the feedbag on the lonely Pacific cruise.

That problem was solved for all time, Moore would ever more claim, during a chance encounter in the Megalong Valley. "One morning I was doing roadwork in the valley when I came across an aborigine throwing boomerangs," Archie said. "He was intrigued by my bright red turtleneck sweater." Moore explained to the native—who just happened to speak and understand English—

that he was running with a thick sweater on in an attempt to lose weight. "He explained to me that he had a family secret passed down through generations on reducing weight. The aborigine offered me his secret in exchange for the sweater. He even threw in the boomerang as part of the deal. The aborigine explained how he was capable of walking hundreds of miles in the isolated Australian bush consuming only a sliver of dried meat. He said he got by on the strength he derived from chewing the dried meat." The aborigine explained that he chewed on the meat, but only swallowed the juices and not the meat, spitting out the remains. "He got by on a fraction of the food eaten by most people."

Archie soon parted with the boomerang, but continued to tout his "secret diet" throughout his career as it became one of the most famous bits of Archie lore. When questioned about the authenticity of the diet's origin by skeptical reporters, Moore always responded with a smile and a question of his own: "Have you ever seen a fat aborigine?"

The April 18 bout with Richards was held before a capacity crowd at Rushcutter Bay Stadium. Moore and Richards both gave public training exhibitions to hype it. Back in town, Moore trained at Limutkin's Gym with Jack McNamee, who, as promised, shared secrets about Richards's style and vulnerabilities. Meanwhile, Richards vowed to anybody who would listen that he would knock out the American invader.

He was almost right. At the opening bell, Richards came charging right at Moore. Within seconds, Archie was sent sprawling by the first right-hand that Richards threw. The partisan crowd was in a frenzy as it appeared that the native hero was about to score a huge early victory. But Moore wobbled to his feet at the count of six and survived that round and the next few, waiting for his head to totally clear.

As the contest continued, Moore began reaching Richards with an increasing number of punches. His left jab found a home on Richards's face, and the Aussie's left eye was cut in the fourth round. By the sixth round Richards began to grow weary, and Moore seemed to be gaining strength. In the tenth, Archie was so totally in command that the referee halted the contest and declared Richards unfit to continue. The 10,000 fans cheered even though their homegrown favorite had gone down in defeat. The result notwithstanding, it had been an entertaining affair.

Having fulfilled his two fight obligations, Moore wrote Mattie, promising a quick return home. But he had to renege on that promise, because the Richards fight had made him a box office draw Down Under, and Archie needed to strike while the iron was hot. Moore was booked to fight again only three weeks after the Richards win. Mattie's letters from home expressed her unhappiness about the situation, but for Archie boxing had to come first.

Atilio Sabatino was a Puerto Rican who had recently relocated to Australia and had once lost a hairline decision to Ron Richards. He was an exciting brawler, but Archie went right at him in their fight and cut Sabatino's left eye in round three. Before long it was strictly target practice for Moore, and at the end of the fourth round, the police inspector at ringside asked the used-up Sabatino if he could continue. The gutsy brawler answered the bell for the fifth round, but after a succession of powerful uppercuts from Moore found their mark, the contest was halted. The fans weren't the only ones impressed. In his dressing room, Sabatino called Archie the greatest fighter he ever faced.

Just three days later, Moore punished Australian middleweight Joe Delay for seven rounds until the one-sided affair was halted. Three weeks after that, Archie was in Tanzania, where Frank Lindsay lasted four rounds against him. With a rematch against Richards in the offing, Moore tangled next with former Australian champion Fred Henneberry.

Henneberry had previously challenged Richards for the British Empire middleweight title, but was disqualified for fouls in the eleventh round. A win over a ranked contender like Moore would get his career back on track, and Henneberry took the June 27, 1940 fight to Moore from the onset. But Moore kept the fight at long distance, picking his shots and boxing his way to an early lead. Then, in the sixth round, Henneberry landed a low punch and Moore almost fell to the canvas. It happened near the end of the round, and during the minute's intermission, Moore's handlers did their best to bring Archie around.

Early in the next round, Moore retaliated for what happened to him by drilling Henneberry with a left to the groin. The Aussie doubled over, his face twisted in pain. The referee ordered Moore to a neutral corner while Henneberry's handlers entered the ring and carried him back to his corner. Henneberry was given several minutes to recover, and then the ringside doctor was summoned for an expert opinion. The sawbones ordered another five-minute respite for Henneberry, but even after that he claimed to be hurting too badly to continue the fight. He went so far as to insist that his right leg was paralyzed.

Moore was awarded the victory, but for his own safety he was rushed across the street to his hotel, lest any spectators unhappy about the game of nutcracker tag he'd won tried to tear him apart. Moore returned after calm had been restored, and at a press conference complimented Henneberry for his good effort and apologized for the way the contest ended. He told the press that Henneberry was one of the toughest boxers he had faced and said he wouldn't be averse to a rematch.

Moore had hoped to return Stateside following the Henneberry contest to pick up the pieces of his marriage, but as winner over Henneberry he was contractually obligated to fight Ron Richards again in three weeks. Richards had attended Archie's press conference after the fight and let it be known that he now had the strategy to beat Moore.

For that he could thank Jack McNamee, their mutual former opponent who had prepped Archie for his encounter with Richards. Apparently McNamee changed loyalties like most people change socks, and this time he was in Richards's camp as an adviser.

Thirteen thousand fans packed Rushcutter Bay Stadium for the scheduled 12-rounded and saw Richards take an early lead on the strength of a potent body attack. It didn't help Archie's cause when, in the second round, he landed a solid right to Richards's forehead that fractured Moore's hand. Nevertheless, the American's educated left gradually brought him back into the fight, aided by the fatigue of his opponent.

But just as it appeared that Moore would coast to a decisive victory, Richards gained his second wind and came roaring back to take several middle innings and pull even after 10 hard-fought rounds. He faded in the stretch, though, and Moore boxed brilliantly in the eleventh and twelfth. After the final bell the referee tapped Moore on the head, as per Australian custom, to signify he had won.

Afterwards the fighters traded compliments as lavishly as they'd traded punches, with Moore proclaiming Richards the best man he'd ever met in the ring.

His broken hand forcing an extended layoff from boxing, Archie was free to head for home and whatever was left of his marriage. He sailed again on *The Monterey*, which took a different route going home because of the war clouds amassing everywhere. December 7, 1941, was still a way off, but a Canadian ship had been sunk near the Sydney harbor, and the British were already at war with Germany. *The Monterey* went to New Zealand and Tahiti. Moore enjoyed his brief layover in Tahiti and went on a shopping spree. He purchased a large bottle of perfume for Mattie, but it remained to be seen what kind of homecoming was in store for him when his ship docked back in California.

CHAPTER 7

A Second Brush with Death

Mattie was waiting when Archie walked down the gang-plank in San Diego. She even greeted him with a long embrace. But it didn't mask her resentment at having been left behind for eight months, just days after her wedding. In fact, they might as well have been strangers. For several days, Moore stayed with Mattie and her family, but the relationship was beyond repair. Mattie hadn't exactly spent all her time pining for her husband. While Archie was overseas, she'd fallen in love with an enlisted army man. Soon Mattie left for Los Angeles. A few years later, she became ill and passed away. Archie always felt badly about what happened between him and Mattie and said that she deserved better in life than what she'd received.

Alone again in San Diego and recovering from his hand injury, Archie cheered himself up by sending for Aunt Willie Pearl and his niece, June. With his Australian purse money he bought a house and a new van and prepared to set up permanent housekeeping with the people he loved.

Once his right hand healed, Moore prepared to show his adopted hometown why he was now the third-ranked middleweight in the world. On October 18, 1940, he squared off against hard-punching Pancho Ramirez, a Mexican.

Ramirez wasn't his sole concern. The other was psychological. For some reason, a lot of talented boxers from the United States never got their careers back on track after returning home from campaigns abroad, and in the back of his mind Moore wondered if this strange jinx would affect him.

He needn't have worried. On fight night, the jinx was a no-show, and Ramirez would have been better off as one, too. He got knocked to the canvas in the opening session and got a boxing lesson after that. Ramirez was dropped three times in the fifth round before his handlers tossed in the towel to end the drubbing.

A middleweight title shot didn't seem so farfetched a prospect, and Archie stayed active to keep himself in readiness. He knocked out Clay Rowan in a round, but then dropped a close decision to Shorty Hogue that didn't hurt his career half as much as what occurred after his next bout against hard-punching Eddie Booker.

On February 21, 1941, Moore and the talented Booker went 10 hard rounds. The fight featured many exchanges on the inside, and the judges' verdict was a draw. Booker was an excellent fighter, and a draw with him was almost as good as a win. But two days afterward, Archie was doing yard work while waiting for his new sweetheart, Kathryn Turner, to arrive. They had planned a picnic and a drive up the coast. Suddenly, however, Moore crumpled to the ground, clutching his stomach. An ambulance was summoned, and it raced him to San Diego Community Hospital.

Archie had suffered a ruptured ulcer. He was unconscious for five days, and an emergency operation was required to save his life. Several blood transfusions were necessary to pull Archie through. One of the donors was Eddie Booker. Moore was hospitalized for 38 days, during which time he also came down with appendicitis, which required another operation. His weight fell from 160 pounds to 125. When promoter Linn Platner visited him, he said Archie "looked like a skeleton fitted with a tight ebony skin."

Moore believed the ulcer attack was brought on by stress, worry and sloppy eating habits, and figured that Booker's body punches hadn't helped either.

When the doctors told him that abdominal surgery was necessary, Moore made a special request in the interest of saving his ring career. He asked that the incision be made along the stomach muscles so the muscles could be separated, instead of slicing through them, which Archie feared would permanently weaken them. Legend has it that Moore even directed the surgical team via an overhead mirror during the operation. Archie always enjoyed hearing that one.

Dr. Archie's technique notwithstanding, newspapers reported that Moore's career was finished. Later, Archie even received a clipping from the Baptiste family in Australia headlined, "Archie Moore's Fight for Life in America, Will Never Enter Ring Again." At the time it probably seemed that way to him, too. On top of everything else, Moore came down with pneumonia and blood poisoning. Too many opponents were ganging up on him, and Archie could only pray to go the distance. It wasn't just about boxing again; he wondered who would provide for Aunt Willie Pearl and nine-year-old June.

But Moore had always lived a reasonably healthy life, and as time passed, so gradually did the crisis. When he healed up, Archie realized the need to change his mental outlook to prevent any more ulcers.

Kathryn Turner was a tremendous help during his recuperation, both emotionally and financially. She took him on long relaxing excursions into the countryside. Eventually she and Moore married. Turner was actually Moore's third wife. Prior to her there had been a brief union with Elizabeth Thorton, which produced two children, daughter Elizabeth and son Archie Jr.

While he mended, Moore had to provide for his growing family. He contacted Milt Kraft, a successful businessman and boxing fan he'd befriended earlier. Kraft was overseer of a government housing project under development. Archie hoped to sign on as a laborer, but because he wasn't yet physically up to that, Kraft put him to work as a night shift security guard instead.

A large trailer camp had been set up for the workers. Moore was given the key to one of the trailers, and his only duty was to check the area every hour for intruders. Soon other residents of the neighborhood spoke of seeing a phantom runner in the night. Alarmed by the reports, Kraft himself investigated the alleged apparition one evening and identified his night watchman running among the trailers as he made his rounds. The ghost was in training to get his real career back in gear. "Here was Archie down on his luck, a physical wreck, the doctors telling him he would never fight again," said Kraft. "Yet he was positive in his own mind that he'd become a champion."

A strong mutual admiration developed. Kraft had won the national bait-and-fly casting championship in 1939, a feat that intrigued Moore. Archie would show up early each night and quiz his employer on what it took to become a champion. As Archie's strength returned, Kraft put him to work mowing lawns for more cash. The extra money helped, and the exercise helped round him back into shape for the ring.

His surgeries had left Moore with a tender, hockey stick-shaped scar across his abdominal region. The inventive Felix Thurman devised an apparatus to shield the area from punches when Archie got back in the ring. Felix took a heavy rubber foul protector with a high waistband. He split it down the center with a razor blade, then inserted an automobile license plate and sewed the contraption back up. Although illegal to use in a real fight, the device afforded needed extra protection when Moore began sparring workouts again. As added insurance, Moore practiced his defense, especially picking off left hooks to the body.

After the longest layoff of his career, Moore finally returned to action on January 28, 1942. The bout was at Madison Square Garden—not the famous one in New York City, but in Phoenix, Arizona. The opponent was Bobby Britton. Matchmaker John Contos wasn't giving Moore any leeway on account of his layoff. He announced that if the fighters didn't produce an entertaining match, their purses would be donated to the Red Cross. Britton could have used the Red Cross himself after Archie stopped him in round three.

Around that time, Moore decided to launch a small business venture to supplement his boxing purses. He had always had a fondness for fried chicken and prided himself on his culinary expertise where the tasty fowl was concerned. "Fried chicken has a personality all to itself," he said. "You eat it hot or cold, with a fork or in your hand, and it tastes wonderful."

Using ring earnings and $400 borrowed from a friend, Archie opened a restaurant called the "Chicken Shack" in San Diego. He wasn't the only chicken fancier in town, and the business took off immediately. Within a few months, Moore paid off the loan. The Chicken Shack opened daily at 11 a.m. and closed at midnight.

But boxing was still Moore's main course, and he worked hard to perfect his technique. "I never went out thinking only knockout at the start of a fight," he recalled. "I'd go in there thinking, 'Let's see, how I can hit this guy without getting hit? Can I work on his ribs, his solar plexus? Can I wound him with a punch to the biceps?' A lot of boxers don't understand that a decent shot to the arm can make an opponent back off for a round or two. One of the best punches I ever threw, I hit a guy on the elbow. He had a pulverizing left jab and it was causing me great difficulty. I landed a right hook which landed flush on the elbow. His jab became less effective and then I went to work."

After stopping Jimmy Casino in two rounds, Moore had a crucial test scheduled against Big Boy Hogue, brother of Shorty, who'd decisioned Archie the year before. Less than two hours before the fight at the San Diego Coliseum, Big Boy suffered a deep gash in his leg when he walked into the broken fender of a parked automobile. That put him out of the fight, but the promoter didn't have to look far for a substitute. Brother Shorty agreed to step in, so long as the fight was cut down from 10 to seven rounds as a concession to his lack of notice.

But Moore needed only two rounds to atone for his earlier loss to Shorty, and a week later he also stopped Tabby Romero in the second. Then he outpointed talented middleweight Jack Chase before signing for a return match with Eddie Booker, with the latter's California state middleweight title on the line.

At the conclusion of 12 rugged rounds on December 12, 1942, the result was the same as their first war—a draw. Moore had Booker down early, but Eddie came storming back to even things up. Even worse, in the fight Archie suffered a broken left hand. But at least this time he didn't end up in the hospital. Where Moore did end up was out of the chicken business. He decided to close his restaurant and dedicate himself solely to fighting as soon as his injured hand permitted. Shutting down the Chicken Shack would thin down his bank account, but winning a world title was Archie's main desire. He dedicated himself full-time to training, and the following spring he signed to fight again for the California middleweight title.

It wasn't Booker in the other corner on May 8, 1943, but the other member of the Golden State's trinity of great middleweights, Jack Chase. The scheduled 15-round match was the top attraction of an early evening show at Lane Field in San Diego.

Moore's healed left hand was on the mark early in the fight, and then he began to open up with both hands, scoring with particular effectiveness with left hooks on the inside. With two rounds left, Moore picked up the attack even more to post a comfortable decision win. It wasn't just his sharp punching that was responsible for the victory. Archie used his head, too. On that sunny Southern California day, he maneuvered Chase around the ring so as to keep the sunlight constantly in Chase's eyes. Every time Chase squinted, Moore fired rapid combinations.

After nearly eight years of professional combat, Moore had his first title. But his kingdom ended at the California border, and he was far from a rich man. It was enough to make Archie wonder if racial bias was responsible for his slow progress. But, he reasoned, "If Jack Johnson and Joe Louis could do it, so could I." He considered going East, but since Moore was raising his niece, June, and caring for Aunt Willie Pearl, he decided to give it at least another year in San Diego. Moore had fallen in love with the Southern California climate and hoped to make San Diego his permanent home unless absolutely forced to advance his career elsewhere.

Next up on Moore's hit parade was Big Boy Hogue, who was able to make it from the parking lot to the arena without mishap this time. A week before the July 22, 1943 fight, Moore began exploratory talks with George Moore, manager of Hammerin' Hank Armstrong. The other Moore promised Archie big paydays if he kept winning. Big Boy Hogue promised to avenge his brother Shorty, but Moore made it two in a row against the Hogues, winning every round and ending matters in the fifth with a right-hand. Just seven days later, the svelte 158-pound Archie beat Mexican jumping bean Eddie Cerda, and only a week after that he put his state title up against the man from whom he won it. But this time skies were cloudy, and Moore dropped a decision to Jack Chase. The loss not only deprived him of his state title but also killed the managerial deal with George Moore, another major disappointment.

A still bigger one was in store. Archie's third match with Eddie Booker at the famous Hollywood Legion Stadium ended much more decisively than the previous two. Booker used a determined body attack to wear down Moore and stop him by technical knockout in the eighth round. Referee John Indrisano halted the scrap after Moore had been floored twice. Booker came in several pounds over the middleweight limit, and the added weight may have aided him.

Two months later, Archie gave the Hollywood fans a better demonstration of his true fighting talents. Roman Starr was a steel-chinned local product who prided himself on his invulnerability to even the hardest punch. Moore put a dent in that notion and Starr's iron jaw, hammering the heavily tattooed Starr to the canvas twice before referee Mushie Callahan said enough and halted the fight.

Middleweight contender Charley Burley faced many of the same obstacles as Archie Moore and other talented black fighters of that era, such as Lloyd Marshall and Allen Matthews. He was too good, and the wrong color, in a sport that too often mirrored the segregated society at large. Joe Louis used to call Burley the perfect fighter. He possessed power in both hands and was also a defensive wizard. Burley held two impressive victories over Jack Chase and threw Archie way off stride in their April 21, 1944 bout at Hollywood Legion Stadium in spite of taking the fight on less than 24 hours' notice.

Recalled Eddie Futch, trainer of over 20 world champions, ina 1998 interview: "Charlie Burley was working in San Diego at the time and was called the day of the match as a last-minute replacement to box Archie Moore. In those days the weigh-in was held at noon the day of the bout. Burley had to take the rest of the day off and made the trip to Hollywood just in time for his physical. I was always one of Charley Burley's biggest supporters throughout his career. He is an all-time great and only got his just due years after his career ended."

Burley gave Moore a boxing lesson and earned a unanimous decision victory. Ever after, Archie seconded Joe Louis's opinion of the Pittsburgh boxer. "Burley was the toughest man I ever faced," he said. "If anybody was the perfect fighter, it was Burley. When I fought Burley, I was no greenhorn. I'd had nearly 80 fights at the time. Burley was already a legend. He could feint you crazy with his eyes, shoulders, head, even his pectoral muscles. His balance was uncanny and his timing was wholly unbelievable. If you threw a punch at Charley Burley, you had better hit him; if you didn't, he would counter your head off. Hitting Burley with a solid punch was near impossible. The night we fought in Hollywood, I caught Burley leaning way back. He appeared to be off balance. I did not think he could find any leverage in that position, but he almost took my head off with a counter right cross. He had suckered me in beautifully. Charley Burley was inhuman!"

Losing to a legend was no disgrace, and in any case Moore's earlier near-death experience had given him a different perspective on life and its ebbs and flows. Now he practiced what he called "relaxism," which helped in all stressful areas of Archie's life. Boxing wasn't the only one. His marriage to Kathryn fell apart and they soon divorced. The breakup was painful, but the pair remained friends. Once again, Moore now placed full emphasis on boxing and returned to the winning track by posting a unanimous decision over Kenny LaSalle in San Diego.

Eddie Futch headquartered in Los Angeles in the '40s after an amateur career in Detroit. He and Moore became close friends. "I would see Archie at all the fights in San Diego," recalled Futch before his death in 2001. "I usually had a few of my own boxers on the card. Archie would invite me and my fighters over to his house for snacks after the fights. He had a nice studio set up in his basement for entertaining his guests. Archie would then take me into his kitchen and ask numerous boxing questions. Archie even inquired about me working with him. I laughed and said, 'Archie, get away from me!' I explained to him how there was nothing I could do for him in boxing that he didn't already know or have. I explained to Archie that all he really needed was a guy to put in his mouthpiece and to carry the bucket. I was not that kind of guy. I need to be able to enhance a boxer to work with him. Archie knew better than anyone how to fight his fight. Archie used to fight in such exotic locations like Australia and South America. I'd get a card from him that would say, 'When are you coming?' I always got along great with Archie Moore."

After two more victories in August of 1944, Platner promised Archie a trip to New York if he got by Battling Monroe in San Diego. The big problem with Monroe was getting him into the ring. He had a reputation for canceling fights at the last minute. Monroe honored his commitment to fight Moore, but would've been better off finding something else to do. Moore laid him out for the count with a vicious right-hand in round six. Platner came through, also, contacting Jimmy Johnston, matchmaker at Madison Square Garden in New York, and arranging for Archie to go East to try his hand against the best in boxing's mecca.

CHAPTER 8

Training at Stillman's

On his way to the Big Apple, Moore stopped in Indianapolis to see his former trainer, Hiawatha Grey, and have him evaluate his style in search of flaws. Nobody knew Archie better.

The rest of the trip to New York didn't go so smoothly. Moore's automobile overheated and eventually threw a rod, forcing Archie to catch a bus to complete the last leg of his journey. As soon as he arrived in New York, Moore headed for the Paramount Building in Times Square, where Jimmy Johnston kept an office.

Known as the "Boy Bandit," Johnston had been one of the game's top managers, having led Ted "Kid" Lewis, Johnny Dundee and Pete Latzo to world titles. He had promoted shows at St. Nicholas Arena and Madison Square Garden since 1912. Johnston was a shrewd operator, and before he committed himself on paper to Moore, he wanted to see what Archie could do. So he sent Moore to Stillman's Gym for a workout.

"I thought I might be making a big mistake by signing this veteran, and I asked my brother Charley to see how Archie looked in action before I would agree to handle him," recalled Johnston later. "When I reached Stillman's, I was fit to be tied. Imagine me when I saw Archie enter the ring with Lee Q. Murray as his sparring mate. I nearly jumped over the ropes as I yelled to Archie, 'Archie! Archie! Don't box that big fellow, he'll knock you cold!'

"Of course I feared for the worst. If Moore were knocked out, it would be useless for me to try and get him some fights around New York to start him going in the East."

"Why, Mr. Johnston, don't have no fear," Archie calmly replied, adding with a broad grin, "I used to pay Murray five dollars a round to box with me in St. Louis when I trained for my fights there. I can take care of myself against him."

Johnston was instantly sold on Moore and offered him $25 a week salary plus a membership at Stillman's. It was the most famous boxing gym in the country. Top fighters like Jake LaMotta and Sandy Saddler were training there when Moore arrived. Archie later recalled, "It was a rundown place, but all the greats trained there. Stillman's used to charge 50 cents admission and had over 15 rows of seats for the audience to watch the action in the two rings and on the floor. If a big-name fighter was training, Lou Stillman would up the admission to a buck. Lou was quite a character. He ruled the place with an iron fist and would bark out obscenities at anyone who crossed his path. Stillman snarled like a Doberman pinscher, left no doubt as to who was in charge and made certain everybody paid the price of admission. He permitted no freeloaders. Legend had it he once bit the ear off a steer in a rodeo. An old saying about the gym went, 'Open Sundays, Mondays, and always.' It was nothing to see Joe Louis or Jack Dempsey hanging out, soaking up the atmosphere."

Johnston booked Moore in his first New York City bout at St. Nicholas Arena on December 18, 1944, against talented Chicagoan Nate Bolden. Bolden had tagged middleweight champion Tony Zale with his first defeat in 1939 and had also taken LaMotta and Walter "Popeye" Woods. Years later, Moore recalled what it was like in the days before his New York debut. "About a week before the fight, I borrowed $25 from Mr. Johnston. By the day of the bout, I had spent all my money on food and lodging and was without even subway fare, at that time being five cents. I had to walk from my rooming house at 147th Street and St. Nicholas Avenue to my manager's office on Times Square—a distance of nearly five miles. It was a good thing I didn't have to go to the Boxing Commission offices for the weigh-in. They were way downtown then. Times were sure tough back then, but I do not regret it."

Not so tough was the fight with Bolden. "Archie Moore of San Diego celebrated his local ring debut last night," reported the *New York Times* the next day. "Moore clearly out-boxed his rival through 10 rounds that featured scientific work rather than slugging." It was not only Moore's New York debut, but also his first foray into a higher weight class. Moore scaled 172 pounds for the match. "My body could no longer scale down to the middleweight limit, and this bout represented my official move up to light heavyweight," he said.

Charley Johnston, Jimmy Johnston's brother, became Moore's manager of record, although it was the Boy Bandit calling the shots. But as a matchmaker, Jimmy was barred by New York boxing commission rules from openly managing fighters.

St. Nicholas Arena served as the minor leagues for Madison Square Garden. If you did well there, you graduated to the Garden—the real big time. But Archie's KO of Bob Jacobs in his next outing was deemed insufficient to make the grade, and he was sent out of town for remedial work. In Boston, Moore was paired with Philadelphia heavyweight Nap Mitchell, who outweighed him by almost 20 pounds for their encounter on February 12, 1945. But as the *Boston Globe* reported, "A big difference in weight mattered little to Archie Moore, who made a punching bag out of Nap Mitchell in an eight-round semifinal bout. Referee Rawson finally counted out Mitchell midway through the sixth round."

Next on the traveling road show was Baltimore, where Archie would become a fan favorite. "I appeared in Baltimore 22 times, but they weren't big-money paydays," he recalled, "I had to learn to be frugal. I always arrived in Baltimore the morning of the fight and tried to end the show early to catch the 11:05 train back to New York."

Stillman's was his Eastern base of operations. Moore valued the quality trainers and sparring on tap there. It was like no other in the world. Archie soon became an attraction at the legendary gym, sparring with heavyweights and talented lighter-weight boxers like featherweight champ in the making Sandy Saddler and later 147-pound titlist Paddy DeMarco. But he never did get to trade leather with the ornery Bronx Bull, Jake LaMotta, which Archie thought was lucky for the future middleweight king with the in-your-face style. "LaMotta's people kept Jake away from me, because they knew I would have eaten him up," Moore said.

There was a rematch with Nate Bolden in Baltimore. Despite losing to Moore in Gotham, Bolden was favored to win the 10-round main event at Baltimore's Century Athletic Club. But instead it was virtually a carbon copy of their first fight. "Archie Moore turned out to be everything that Jimmy Johnston, veteran handler of boxers, claimed for him," noted the *Baltimore Sun*. "He displayed fine footwork and moved far too fast for Bolden to keep up with him. When Johnston stated his charge was just about the best boxer he had seen since Joe Gans, it was not a great misstatement."

After defeating former sparring partner Teddy Randolph, Moore and highly ranked Lloyd Marshall treated Cleveland to one of the greatest battles the city ever saw. Marshall, another wonderful African American boxer of that era, had an outstanding record. He had knocked out Ezzard Charles and decisioned LaMotta and Joey Maxim. But Moore bloodied Marshall's face with precision punching and captured the decision.

In just seven months under the direction of the Johnston brothers, Moore's career had made more headway than in the previous 10 years. "Jimmy Johnston was a ballyhoo artist who delivered for his fighters," Archie said. "He knew how to produce. I was starting to make my best paydays, and the victory over Lloyd Marshall qualified me as the number one contender. I let Jimmy call all the shots."

In Baltimore again, a big-mouthed guy called George Kochan tried to rattle Moore with his tongue as well as his fists. "He was a white fighter of Croatian heritage who once spit in a black man's face in the ring," Archie recalled. "He was calling me every racial term in the book. I gave him a six-round beating until he could take no more." The crowd showed its appreciation by showering the ring with coins.

Lloyd Marshall figured if he could get Moore back in a Cleveland ring, the result would be different from their first meeting. It happened on June 26, 1945, and the home-court advantage went for nothing as Moore sent Marshall to the canvas three times and stopped him in the tenth. Moments after referee Jackie Davis rescued the hometown boy, Moore aided Marshall's handlers in getting him back on his feet. "Tough luck, old boy. Too darn tough," Moore whispered respectfully to his victim.

The win underlined Archie's status as the preeminent contender for Gus Lesnevich's world light heavyweight title. Lesnevich hadn't defended the crown since 1941, after which he enlisted in the U.S. Coast Guard. Like that of heavyweight Joe Louis and welterweight Red Cochrane, his title was "frozen" for the duration of his service.

Moore felt his best fighting weight was around 164 pounds, but he knew that the big bucks were in the heavyweight class, and decided to go after some. Eight weeks after defeating Marshall, Archie added six pounds to his frame and embarked on a brand-new mission whose astonishing objective was a fight with Joe Louis himself. Step one was taking on the second-ranked heavyweight contender in the world.

Jimmy Bivins was, understandably, a 12-5 favorite to return Archie to the light heavyweight division when they stepped into the Cleveland ring on August 22, 1945. Bivins's list of victims included Ezzard Charles, Charley Burley, Lloyd Marshall and Lesnevich. But the oddsmakers notwithstanding, the fight was a big draw. Promoter Robert Brickman declared in Cleveland's *The Plain Dealer*, "Customers will be coming in from out of town as they haven't come in since before the war. We're certain of that from the long-distance calls for reservations."

Bivins scaled 188, but the advantage on the scales didn't bother the Moore camp, who thought it might actually work to Archie's advantage. "The more that the arrogant Bivins weighs, the better for us," said Charley Johnston. "The heavier the slower." He wasn't the only one making chin music before the fight. Bivins himself went up to Moore before the fight to object to Moore's treatment of Bivins's friend Lloyd Marshall, which Bivins considered to have been unnecessarily brutal. "Why did you knock out Marshall?" he demanded to know. "The fight was already yours. There was no need to knock him out."

Bivins later explained, "Lloyd Marshall and I went way back. I used to sell newspapers to his house as a kid. Lloyd and I used to work out together. Archie was confident going into our first bout. He figured I didn't have a chance. He was an awesome boxer, but I was prepared for him. I managed to tag him pretty good."

The fight was one of Archie's worst. He was knocked down a total of seven times and was actually counted out twice. In the second round, Moore, outweighed by almost 20 pounds, went down on one knee. According to *The Plain Dealer* account of the fight, Moore then fell over backwards for the first 10-count, and Bivins put on his robe and made his way out of the ring. Some in the crowd booed and yelled foul. Jimmy Johnston climbed through the ropes and protested what he called an illegal blow. A five-minute rest was ordered for Moore, and on the instructions of boxing commissioner Stanley Cofall, referee Jackie Davis took the round away from Bivins and the fight resumed.

After that, Archie was effective only in the fourth, when he stung Bivins with left jabs and opened a small cut on his face. But Bivins laid more heavy leather on him in the fifth and dropped Moore for the full count—again—in the next round.

Seated at ringside was Lou Diamond, manager of light heavyweight champion Lesnevich. Diamond told reporters that the only man who might defeat Bivins was Joe Louis. It would take more than two years, but Moore would settle the score with the Cleveland boxer. Years later, Archie confessed that out of all the men he fought, Bivins was the only one he sincerely disliked.

"Bivins hit me while I was on my knees," he said. However, added Moore, "The grudge wore off after some time. Hate is a wasteful energy."

Archie returned to friendly Baltimore against Puerto Rican Louis (The Keed) Cocoa at the Coliseum on September 17. Cocoa was a middleweight, and heavily favored Moore laid him out in the eighth with a right-hand.

Next up was Holman Williams, who had been instrumental in the development of Joe Louis. Williams coached Louis early in the Brown Bomber's career at the Brewster Center in Detroit. Eddie Futch recalled those lessons: "Holman Williams was a stylist; he was fun to watch just shadowboxing," said the venerable old trainer. "Williams never made silly mistakes. Louis learned a lot of his early boxing knowledge from him, especially how to properly throw the left jab and hook. Louis liked Holman and always looked out for him after his career had finished." Louis himself gave credit to Williams in his autobiography, calling him "a beautiful boxer. He told me I had the stuff to be a champion, and I knew he was serious."

Williams had over 150 professional fights when he squared off against Moore on October 22, 1945, in what the *Baltimore Sun* tabbed the nation's top boxing matchup of the week. A win for Moore would give Archie first dibs on a shot at the light heavyweight title. The biggest crowd of the year was expected at the Coliseum, including reporters from four New York papers. The odds at fight time went off at 6-5, pick-em.

Ahead going into round eight, Moore lost the next two innings on account of unintentional low blows. When it was over, one judge called it even, but the other two gave it to Williams. "Holman was slick as grease and hard as lard," said Archie. "You couldn't hurt him. Holman beat me the first time. He gave me a lot of confusing action in our fight. I was always missing over the top on him."

Low blows would figure in Archie's career on more than one occasion. He often boxed out of a crouching position, and therefore many of his punches started near the ground. This unique style of fighting led to numerous inadvertent low punches that cost him points, but Moore stuck with it nonetheless. "My defense couldn't be penetrated by an uppercut," he said. "I began using it because I found the unique defense frustrated opponents and threw them off."

After dusting Odell Riley in six rounds in Detroit two weeks after the Williams fight, Archie met Holman again, and this time there was no controversy about the decision, because there wasn't one. During the rematch Williams wasn't so slippery. Moore sent him to the canvas three times before the contest was halted in the eleventh round. It was only the second inside-the-distance defeat of Williams's career.

In 1997, Archie recalled his battles with those largely forgotten boxing greats. "I was also fighting the establishment. I had to fight mostly black ranked contenders. It was a process of elimination. The rated white guys wanted no part of me, or Holman Williams, Lloyd Marshall and Jimmy Bivins. So we had to fight each other. Those guys would all be champions today. We only had eight divisions then with one champion in each class. I kept my determination not to let anyone stop me, be it a white man, black man or green man!"

It had been six years since Moore last appeared in St. Louis. His position as the number one contender helped fill the Kiel Auditorium for his match with journeyman Colion Chaney, who had developed into something of a local hero himself. But Chaney's three-bout win streak in St. Louis ended when Moore sent him sprawling to the canvas for keeps in the fifth round. Promoter Hans Bernstein immediately offered champion Gus Lesnevich $30,000 to risk his crown in St. Louis against Moore. Lesnevich's management just as promptly turned it down.

While in town, Moore paid a visit to his mother, Lorena. They had never been close, but Archie loved her unconditionally. Years later she would move to Pittsburgh and reassociate herself with her son after he became world champion.

The homecoming was brief. Moore returned to Baltimore to face power-punching heavyweight Curtis "The Hatchetman"

Sheppard in what the *Baltimore Sun* called Moore's biggest career test. He passed, but only after some dicey moments. A capacity crowd at the Coliseum—2,000 fans were turned away—saw Moore twice pull himself off the canvas to outpoint Sheppard in the most thrilling heavyweight contest in Baltimore in years.

Seven days later, his body still aching from the Sheppard war, Archie stepped in the ring at Turner Arena in Washington, D.C., to fight local heavyweight Georgie Parks. Parks told the *Washington Post* that he would squelch Moore in two, but Moore was in an even bigger hurry and put Parks to sleep in the opening session.

After KOing Verne Escoe in May of '46, Moore listened to Johnston lay out his master plan for the future. "Jimmy told me he was going to create his own light heavyweight champion because I wasn't getting my shot," Moore recalled. The plan was to arrange a bout with British champion Freddie Mills at Ebbets Field, and the hope behind the plan was to force Lesnevich into fighting the winner. But before it even got off the drawing board, Jimmy Johnston died of a sudden heart attack. Charley Johnston became Archie's sole braintrust, and the chase resumed.

Ezzard Charles was the one man who truly had Moore's number. Charles had an undefeated amateur career that he capped by winning the 1939 national Amateur Athletic Union middleweight title. He started his professional career in Cincinnati but was headquartered in Pittsburgh when he faced Moore. Charles was on an eight-fight win streak in the Steel City, including impressive victories over future Hall of Famers Charley Burley and Joey Maxim. He made it nine in a row against Archie, using his left jab and slick skills to post a 10-round decision over Moore.

Charley Johnston recommended that he take a few months off, but Moore returned to the friendly confines of Baltimore and posted two knockout victories before heading back to the West Coast. He rounded out his '47 campaign with two draws in Oakland, the first against Billy Smith and the second against old rival Jack Chase. Moore felt especially slighted by the verdict in the Chase bout and successfully campaigned for a rematch, held the following March 18 in Los Angeles. It was the sixth and final confrontation between them. Chase had actually been in semiretirement the last two years, operating his own landscaping business. But he went for one final shot at ring glory against Archie. He should have passed. Moore blasted him out in the ninth round at the Olympic Auditorium.

*   *   *

All the while he was gone from San Diego, Moore had sent portions of his ring earnings to Aunt Willie Pearl and June. Nothing could beat the chance to see them again, if only for a few weeks. Moore signed to box heavyweight Rusty Payne at the San Diego Coliseum for a purse of $1,458. More than 3,500 fans saw Archie, fighting out of his semi-crouch, outbox Payne for 10 rounds. The bout wasn't without its anxious moments for Moore, who was blasted to the canvas briefly in the sixth session. Archie contemplated staying in San Diego, but a lengthy phone conversation with Charley Johnston convinced him his best chance of obtaining a title shot required him to return to the East Coast. A rematch with Ezzard Charles was arranged for Charles's hometown of Cincinnati.

A record live gate for Ohio was guaranteed at the Music Hall, where Charles was a 2-1 favorite to win and 5-6 choice to score a KO. Now the top contender among the light heavies, Charles hoped to challenge Joe Louis if he couldn't get at 175-pound champ Lesnevich. Moore told the *Cincinnati Inquirer* that he rated Ezzard one of the game's greatest fighters. On the day of the fight, Archie walked three brisk miles and rested at his hotel.

With Lesnevich taking notes from a ringside seat, Charles was awarded the victory by a slim margin. One judge had it even and the other two gave "The Cincinnati Cobra" a slight edge. The deciding factor may have been the body punch that sent Moore down for a brief count in the seventh. The give-and-take affair featured three exchanges after the bell.

After Archie signed for a rematch with Curtis "The Hatchetman" Sheppard in the nation's capital, *The Washington Post* declared that his time as a top-notcher was "fast drawing to a close." At or at least near 30 years of age, Archie was considered a graying veteran. Little did anyone know at the time that Moore still had another 15 years of prize fighting left ahead of him.

Unlike their first bout, Moore-Sheppard II was a one-sided victory for Archie. Although outweighed by nearly 25 pounds, he outboxed and bloodied The Hatchetman throughout, and dumped Sheppard to the canvas in the eighth round. It was so uneven that Moore actually pleaded with referee Harry Volkman to stop the fight. When Volkman refused, Moore showed mercy and only threw body punches for the remainder of the bout. Sheppard was another unsung '40s gladiator, called by Moore "the hardest puncher I ever faced. When he hit you on the arms, you felt it."

Archie kept busy, defeating Bert Lytell a few weeks later and then heading to Oakland for a shot at the vacant California light heavyweight title against Bobby Zander. The title had been held by the dangerous Billy Smith, but *The Oakland Tribune* reported that it was declared vacant after Oakland Billy was slapped into the pokey for practicing his right cross on Mrs. Smith.

In a brilliant display of boxing, Moore took a 12-round decision over Zander in Oakland to claim the title. Then it was back across the country for a rematch with Jimmy Bivins in Baltimore.

Thanks to his earlier victory over Archie, Bivins entered the contest at the 5th Regiment Armory as a slight favorite in the fight that got underway only after the fire department was called out to unseat anxious fans who'd come early and grabbed ringside seats they didn't have tickets for. The crowd set a local indoor boxing attendance record.

After everybody was finally properly seated, Moore scored an upset over his heavier foe. After taking a heavy pasting in the ninth round, Bivins signaled to referee Eddie Leonard that he was unable to continue, giving Archie a technical knockout victory. Recalled Bivins, "I never held a grudge after Archie beat me. I just figured

I'd get him the next time. He knew all the tricks of the trade. Every time I tried to do something I wanted, Archie had the opposite reaction [of what] I had hoped for. He was a master."

Moore closed out his '47 campaign with a KO over George Fitch, and then prepared for another go at his toughest opponent, Ezzard Charles. This time the bout was held in Cleveland. Charles predicted in *The Plain Dealer* that he would make Moore a "Fallen Arch" in the scheduled 15-rounder at the Arena. Nearly 10,000 fans turned out to see if he could.

Charles was a prophet. He shook off Moore's early onslaught to knock Archie cold in the eighth round. Promoter Larry Atkins declared afterward that Charles deserved recognition as world champion, since Lesnevich had already rejected his offer of $50,000 to fight the winner. Covering the fight at ringside was popular Pittsburgh sportswriter Harry Keck, who wrote, "Charles's whole body seemed to coil like a huge snake about to strike. Moore was near the ropes, just above me, and his instinct told him that he was in real danger. But before he could climb into a shell, Charles struck with a sweeping right that seemed to travel a complete circle before landing with a sickening thud on Archie's jaw. I was sure that something broke either in Archie's head or in Ezzard's right hand, maybe even in both places." When questioned about the knockout blow, Archie confessed that he never even saw it.

Moore took a few months off before KOing Dusty Wilkerson, and then added a few more victories before risking his California state title against rising contender Leonard Morrow in Oakland.

Morrow was at least 10 years younger than Moore and had developed a reputation in the Bay area with two recent victories in Oakland. Archie was the favorite going in, but some ring analysts suggested the challenger could pull off an upset.

In the quickest defeat of his career, Moore was sent to the canvas three times in the opening session and the fight was stopped before the round ended. Archie had started out moving and landing sharp jabs, but then Morrow landed a short devastating right that caught Moore squarely. *The Oakland Tribune* reported that "Moore sunk to the canvas with a startled, almost incredulous look, on his face" for a count of six. When he rose, continued the newspaper account, "Morrow swarmed all over the then-light heavyweight champion, and in his eagerness to land the payoff blow he missed several punches. He didn't miss a left hook to the button, however. Again Moore hit the deck. Archie, still wearing that expression of, 'it couldn't happen to me,' listened to referee Frankie Brown's count on his knees. He even rested an arm casually on the shoulders of the arbiter. He rose when the tally hit nine. It was all over a few seconds later."

Morrow put Archie down for good with a right-hand, and the loss was so devastating that the *Tribune* foresaw one dire consequence for Moore's career: "The loss has washed Moore out of a prospective fight with Gus Lesnevich, world light-heavyweight champion. It probably will result in cancellation of a proposed Australian tour. It could send Archie into retirement."

Cleary, Archie needed a convincing major victory to regain stature in one fell swoop, and four weeks later he went for it by signing for a rubber match with Jimmy Bivins.

The gamble paid off. The third installment in their series saw Archie pull out a close 10-round majority decision in a fast-paced battle in a Toledo, Ohio. The ring was left standing after the fight because the following evening former world boxing heavyweight champion Primo Carnera was to be featured in a wrestling match.

Five weeks later in Baltimore, granite-jawed journeyman "Tiger" Ted Lowry occupied the corner opposite Moore. Later, Lowry would claim the honor of being the only man to ever twice go the distance with undefeated heavyweight champ Rocky Marciano. Forty-four years after tossing his last professional punch, Lowry vividly remembered his 10-round decision loss to Moore: "We had a terrific fight. He hit me harder than anyone I ever fought. I couldn't eat for a week; it was soup from a straw only. In his prime he would have knocked out Rocky Marciano. Archie was always a classy gentleman. Years after our bout I used to rib him that if it had been my best night I would have beaten him. He busted up laughing from ear to ear."

A new light heavyweight champion was crowned just days before Moore's triumph over Lowry. On July 26, 1948, Gus Lesnevich lost his title to Freddie Mills in London. The champion's name was different, but his attitude was the same. Mills was in no hurry to give Moore a chance at his title. "Moore was too good for his own good," said Eddie Futch. "No manager wanted to risk the title against him."

If nothing else, Archie saw a lot of the country. After stopping Billy Smith in Baltimore, he went to New Orleans to fight local favorite Henry Hall. There, to Moore's everlasting embarrassment, he fell for a trick so hoary most adolescent playground battlers laughed derisively when it was tried on them. "Your shoelaces are untied," Hall told him during the fight. Inexplicably, Moore looked down at his feet, whereupon the New Orleans man clocked him with a roundhouse right. Archie recouped, but kept looking to retaliate with one hard shot, and in the later rounds had a couple points deducted for low punches. It all added up to a decision loss for Moore. He admitted it was not his best showing and promised to make up for it in a rematch already scheduled for a month later. Meanwhile, Moore planned to join his stablemate Sandy Saddler at training camp to help prepare Saddler for his upcoming title challenge in New York for Willie Pep's world featherweight crown.

In Peter Heller's book, *In This Corner: 42 World Champions Tell Their Stories*, Saddler said, "Archie Moore had a lot to do with me winning that fight. I was the number one contender and Pep had to fight me. I would box Archie. Archie was very clever. He taught me quite a bit. He taught me how to slip and how to get inside and how to, in case you're hurt, to cover up so that all your vital spots are covered up. Archie taught me how to punch correctly. That gave me my punching power. Archie taught me quite a bit how to punch, punching from the balls of my feet. That was very important." Saddler stopped Pep in the fourth round to claim the title.

Exactly two weeks after losing the decision to Hall, Archie faced Lloyd Gibson in Washington, D.C. New featherweight champion Saddler was in attendance to show his support. Gibson hadn't lost a fight in four years, since Marcel Cerdan won a decision over him in Rome in '44. If he got past Gibson, Moore was promised a crack at Mills's belt; but once again low punches were his downfall. Archie was well out in front when he was disqualified for fouling in the fourth round. Gibson was carried to his corner by handlers and examined by a ringside physician. He was granted the customary five-minute recovery period, but, suffering from a bruised groin and nausea, he was unable to continue and the fight was his by default. It was frustrating for Archie, an inherently fair fighter whose concentration on body punching was costing him fights and now a title match.

There was some consolation in Archie's clear-cut decision win over Henry Hall in their rematch in Baltimore. But after two more victories at the end of '48, his frustration at his inability to land a title fight after 13 years in boxing led Moore to ponder retirement. In fact, when he stepped in as a last-minute replacement for Bob Satterfield against the Alabama Kid on January 10, 1949, in Toledo, Ohio, Archie looked at it as his boxing swan song. "I took the bout because it was west on my route back to San Diego and I needed money for a new car to get me back home," he recalled. But in fact the only thing that changed was his address.

CHAPTER 9

Relocating to Toledo

Before going to Toledo, Moore picked up Hiawatha Grey in Indianapolis. In Toledo, they bunked at Mother Jennings's boarding house on Indiana Avenue. Moore managed to squeeze in a few sparring sessions at the Police and Fire Gym before boxing the Alabama Kid—real name: Clarence Reeves—at the Sports Arena. The Kid was an aging but crafty veteran out of Columbus who many thought would trouble Moore. But Archie starched him in round four with a two-handed barrage.

The next morning, Moore met with promoter Pat Thurkettle to collect his $300. "I gave Hiawatha $75 and took care of some other bills with much of the rest. I had $100 left over and planned to buy a secondhand car with it," he said. Thurkettle sent him to see automobile dealer Bob Reese. A fight fan, Reese was excited to meet Moore. Recalled Archie: "Bob Reese and I hit it off from the beginning. He said talk of my fight the previous evening was all over town. Reese cut me a deal on a '41 business coupe for $100. He even threw in new tires and a paint job. I was only concerned that the vehicle would get me back to San Diego. Reese misunderstood me, thinking my next fight was there. When I explained to him that I was finished, he couldn't believe it. Eventually, Reese convinced me to stay in town. I did and I fought Bob Satterfield three weeks later in Toledo."

One of the characters Moore befriended in Toledo was Papa Dee, self-proclaimed "medicine man of boxing." A onetime bantamweight fighter and trainer, Dee operated a barbershop in Detroit and often came to town to help publicize local shows. "Once Dee heard of my victory over the Alabama Kid, he came to Toledo to sell tickets for my bout with Satterfield," Moore said. Dee took Archie all over town. "We visited cigar shops and pool parlors, waking up the fistic dead of Toledo," Archie recalled.

Cheerful Norman, who eventually helped train Archie, owned one pool hall they visited. But their initial meeting got off on the wrong note when Norman told Moore he thought Satterfield would knock him out because Archie fought with his hands too low. Even after Moore stopped Satterfield in the third round, Norman needled him about leaving his chin exposed.

Archie was paid $1,500 for the Satterfield contest, enough to get him back to San Diego with money to spare. Moore wanted to make it home by Christmas to see his aunt and niece. June was attending San Diego State College by then.

But when he went to Bob Reese to say goodbye, Reese argued that he should stay in Toledo and continue fighting. Local fans were excited, he said. "I've had them excited in the past and it didn't last," Moore argued. Besides, said Archie, he was tired of being without a steady income. When Reese offered a salary of $75 a week if he'd stay, Archie agreed. "It wasn't the $75 a week that got me so excited," he explained later. "Instead it was the belief that Reese had in me."

Reese was one of the Midwest's leading automobile dealers. He lived 10 miles outside of Toledo on a six-acre spread in Washington Township. Moore used to mow the lawn for extra cash and enjoyed spending time with Reese's children. Eventually, Reese completely took over Moore's finances, getting him to bank his fight purses and live off his weekly salary. Moore was well known for giving away every extra penny he had to the needy.

After again knocking out the Alabama Kid and then Dusty Wilkerson, Archie signed for another fight with Jimmy Bivins. Bivins was then the fifth-ranked heavyweight, while Archie tipped the scales at just under 170 pounds. An impressive win for Moore could mean a title match, or at least a high-profile fight with undefeated Philadelphia 175-pound contender Harold Johnson.

The Bivins fight was held in Toledo, and by knocking the Clevelander out in the eighth round, Archie not only impressed his growing legion of local fans but finally won over Cheerful Norman. "You look easy to hit, but you're not," Norman said. "I was wrong."

The fight grossed $4,000 for Archie, but even more important was the National Boxing Association's call for a light heavyweight elimination tournament matching Archie with Harold Johnson and Gus Lesnevich with Joey Maxim.

On April 26, 1949, Archie and Johnson faced off in the latter's hometown of Philadelphia. Moore knew the dangers of boxing in an opponent's back yard, but a victory would again qualify him as the top light heavyweight contender. Besides, although Johnson hadn't lost in 24 fights, his opponents weren't very noteworthy. The only exception was Arturo Godey, who'd fought Joe Louis twice for the heavyweight title.

Before the match, Johnson's handlers tried to get Archie's goat by going after his goatee. They appealed to the Pennsylvania commission to force Moore to shave off his facial hair. Moore stood firm, and the goatee stayed. In the ring he made it hairy for Johnson. The artful Archie not only won on all three scorecards, but sent Johnson to the canvas twice in the seventh round.

The following month Archie drove to Cincinnati to catch the other elimination bout between Maxim and Lesnevich. It was there that he got his first glimpse of Jack "Doc" Kearns. Kearns had led Jack Dempsey to the heavyweight throne in 1919 and now piloted Maxim with the same bravado and genius for self-promotion. Instead of this bout being billed as an elimination contest, Kearns had it advertised as being for the "American light heavyweight title," with the winner to meet Freddie Mills for the world title. Archie greeted the combatants in the ring, telling Lesnevich "it was about time we were in the same ring together." Maxim won a decision and went on to beat Mills for the world light heavyweight title.

Six weeks after defeating Johnson, Moore was up to his foul cup in controversy again. At the Indianapolis Sports Arena, Archie had a huge lead against Chicago's Clinton Bacon going into the sixth round. But then a Moore punch landed low, sending Bacon to the canvas. As he was falling, Moore caught him in the head with another punch—a double foul under Indiana rules and another loss by disqualification for Archie. But two weeks later he atoned by stopping Bob Sikes in the Hoosier capital.

Archie continued to stay busy throughout '49, winning four more contests, and then signed for a December rematch with Leonard Morrow. Morrow told the press that he would reprise his previous knockout victory over Moore. The fight took place on what was announced as Archie's birthday, and he provided Toledo fans with a Hallmark moment. Starting fast, he had Morrow bleeding from the nose before the opening session was over. Moore was the aggressor throughout the contest and dumped Morrow to the canvas for a seven-count in the eighth. But triumph almost turned to tragedy in the tenth round. Moore smacked his groggy foe with a right to the chin. As he fell, Morrow's head hit the bare wooden floor outside the ropes with a thud that echoed through the Arena. Morrow was carried from the ring on a stretcher and was taken to the hospital by ambulance. Moore was stunned and upset, and a picture in *The Toledo Blade* the next day showed him kneeling next to the unconscious Morrow in the ring.

A belated birthday wish came true the next day when Morrow's condition improved. "I always prayed that I would never kill or injure another man," Archie said. "When Morrow's head hit the outside of the ring where there was no padding, I got real scared. I visited him in the hospital every day until he left."

In an article by W.C. Heinz in the *Saturday Evening Post*, Moore told of his feelings toward his opponents. "I like the men I fight more than they probably think I do. In fact, I've felt sorry for more fighters than I disliked, because of the position I have put them in during a bout. I feel I would hate to hurt a man permanently because hurtin' a man, period, and hurtin' him permanently are two different things.

"There's a common feeling between all fighters, especially those who fight one another. It's a common sympathy, unorganized, but in general, if men felt the way fighters do, with deep-seated admiration and familiar with the sacrifices and hunger and hard work of one another, there would be no more trouble in this world."

A fight with Maxim was not forthcoming, and to get his mind off the situation Archie began visiting and speaking to underprivileged and handicapped people whenever possible. It was a timely reality check. "The blind made me realize it wasn't so important that I couldn't see a path to a title shot—not when they couldn't see at all," he said.

It was a perspective that came in handy in 1950, when Archie fought only twice, defeating Bert Lytell and, in his Chicago debut, Vernon Williams. By then Maxim was the champion, but he wanted nothing to do with the top-ranked Moore. That also went for the other rated 175-pounders and even the heavyweights. "The $75 weekly salary from Bob Reese was predominantly my only source of income," Archie said. "I pulled some tricks with a pool stick, but times were tough again."

But the year wasn't a total wash, thanks to jazz saxophonist Lucky Thompson, with whom Archie became fast friends. "Lucky was the greatest saxophonist," he said. "You can ask any student of modern jazz. Lucky wouldn't compromise his art by playing the rhythm and blues circuit. That surely hurt him." Moore had always been fascinated by the sax and type of music Thompson played. He even ended up joining Lucky and his band for a few tours, and composed the lyrics to the song "Stay in There" for Lucky. Archie's friendship with Lucky helped him fight the boxing blues.

Another way Archie took his mind off his career difficulties was reading. He spent a great amount of his free time on the road in local libraries. "I didn't find time to read when I was a kid," he said, "but once I discovered books, I really began living."

The early part of '51 saw Moore triumph over Billy Smith in Portland in a bout with a bizarre conclusion. For the first five rounds Moore held an edge. In the sixth, Archie picked up the tempo and sent Smith to the canvas. In round eight, Smith went down twice. When he got up the second time, instead of resuming the fight Smith jumped over the ropes and ran back to his dressing room. Smith's purse was held up, and he was suspended. Later he told reporters that he was having difficulties with his cornermen, although to everyone else it looked like all his problems were coming out of the opposite corner.

Moore's next fight took him overseas to Panama City, Panama. John Thomas held a win over Joey Maxim, but he lasted less than a round with Archie at the Olympic Stadium.

Moore was now famous all over the world, but in New York City he couldn't even fight at Madison Square Garden. His February 21, 1951 fight with Jimmy Bivins was held at St. Nicholas Arena, still the Garden's farm club. For the fourth consecutive time, Moore handed Bivins a major-league whipping. When Bivins was floored just before the bell ending the ninth round, his handlers carried him back to his stool. Bivins told the commission doctor he was unable to see out of his left eye, and the physician signaled for the end of the bout.

At Lucky Thompson's suggestion, Moore launched a letter-writing campaign to the press, TV and radio stations and all the boxing commissions in an effort to get Maxim in the ring. The champion had fought in several nontitle affairs and made an unsuccessful challenge for Ezzard Charles's heavyweight title. But in spite of Archie's PR campaign, Maxim chose to defend his title against long-shot Bob Murphy instead of Moore.

Charley Johnston told Archie that it had been a long time since Kearns had a champion and that Doc would take as many safe paydays as possible. In his autobiography, *The Million Dollar Gate*, Kearns admitted to avoiding Moore.

"Now that I was back in business with the light heavyweight champion of the world, I began to move Joey around pretty good, meanwhile ducking a fellow who had been around for years and was screaming for a shot at everybody or anybody. Nobody wanted to fight him, and that goes for the heavyweights, too.

"I'm talking about Archie Moore, who has to go down in boxing history as one of the greatest champions of them all, and in any division.

"As I say, we ducked him just like everybody else was doing. Moore was too smart, too skillful, too experienced, and carried too many blockbusters in his arsenal to take him on before we were forced into it."

Abel Cestac was the South American heavyweight champion, and the huge Argentinean came to Toledo to enhance his reputation in America by beating Moore. But Archie, outweighed by 40 pounds, disabused him of that notion by pummeling Cestac for 10 rounds at the Mercury Athletic Club.

When comebacking Joe Louis came down with the flu and canceled out of a bout with Cuba's Omelio Agramonte, Archie tried to substitute for the ex-champion. But he was turned down then, and a subsequent effort to get Toledo backers to bankroll a light heavyweight elimination tournament also went for naught.

Three weeks after defeating Cestac, Moore went to Flint, Michigan, and kept his skills sharp by stopping Herman Harris in four in a fight whose proceeds went to the local cancer fund drive.

After Moore stopped Art Henri in Baltimore, Charley Johnston decided that hounding Maxim was getting them nowhere. The manager accepted an invitation from Argentine dictator Juan Peron and took Moore and Sandy Saddler on an extended tour of South America.

CHAPTER 10

Befriending Juan Peron in Argentina

The point of heading south of the border to the politically incorrect location of Argentina was to pick up some easy work and decent paydays. Saddler and Moore were each signed for a series of matches at Argentina's famous boxing arena, Luna Park, as well as other venues in the country. But from the moment Archie landed in Buenos Aires, something unexpected happened. He immediately fell in love with Argentina, a country with no overt racial segregation. "There is no color barrier in Argentina," Moore explained. "Most white people can't understand how I felt, moving freely as I pleased."

When they landed in May 1951, Argentina was thriving after an economic slump. Markets all over the world were open to Argentine products. The country was flourishing under controversial leader Juan Peron and his glamorous political partner and wife, Evita. General Peron was a dictator, controlling the radio stations, newspaper, police and the military. But he had made it possible for women to vote for the first time in the upcoming election.

Peron's relationship with the United States had been shaky for several years, and the upcoming presidential campaign wouldn't make things between the countries any better. The U.S. media said that Peron had successfully used United States Assistant Secretary of State Spruille Braden as a whipping boy. At Peron's behest, Buenos Aires was decorated with posters calling the Yankees "the greatest criminals and thieves in history." They weren't referring to the New York ball club, either.

All that notwithstanding, Peron literally rolled out the red carpet for Moore, Saddler and Johnston. The president set them up in a luxurious apartment and gave them a Mercedes Benz and a chauffeur. Peron was a boxing fan, going back to his days in military school. The biography *Peron* mentions that the sport was relatively new to Argentina when Peron enlisted in the early '20s and that he was quickly enamored by it. As a young officer, he helped found a boxing club. In order to raise funds for his school club, Peron organized a match between one of his teammates and a visiting British sailor. Peron's mate took sick on the day of the fight and Peron agreed to take his place. He had a height advantage over his foe, who boxed out of a crouch. The future president's first punch landed on his opponent's head, breaking Peron's hand. Peron ended up taking a beating, but lasted the distance. Peron never had the injured hand properly set, and it healed with a slight deformity. The dictator boasted to Moore that when former heavyweight champ Gene Tunney visited he noticed the deformity and announced that it looked like a boxing injury.

Archie didn't share his own government's disdain for the Argentine leader. "People in the States looked negatively at my friendship with Peron, but the man treated me much better than many people back home had," he said.

A few days before Moore made his Buenos Aires debut in a rematch with Abel Cestac, Saddler fought before a capacity crowd at Luna Park against Argentine lightweight champion Alfredo Prada. The fight broke all boxing attendance records in the country, and Saddler easily disposed of Prada in the fourth round. The week after, Moore stepped into the same ring. Juan and Evita

Peron were at ringside as Moore, again over 30 pounds lighter than Cestac, kept his left jab in Cestac's face for 10 rounds. In the tenth, the local hero's corner threw in the towel. The next day's paper showed photos of the fight as well as one of Archie presenting flowers to Evita at ringside. She probably appreciated them more than the Cestac blood that splattered her during the fight.

Archie and Evita became friends. Moore related to her difficult upbringing and concern for the underprivileged. Born Eva Ibarguren in a one-room home to Juana Ibarguren and Juan Duarte, a married landowner, Evita was illegitimate. Her mother worked as a cook at the Duarte farm in Chivilcoy. Juana was an attractive lady, and soon an affair blossomed between her and the head of the household, Duarte. It lasted 15 years, until Duarte's death. Evita and the rest of her family were forbidden to attend their father's funeral.

Two weeks after defeating Cestac, Moore fought to a draw in Buenos Aires with former European heavyweight champion Karel Sys, who was also training in South America. Next, Archie faced heavyweight Alberto Lovell at Luna Park. After he blasted out Lovell in the opening session, an article in *The Ring* magazine declared that there was no worthy opponent for him in South America. Archie validated the claim by knocking out heavier Victor Carbajal and Rafael Miranda in two rounds each, and, in his final joust, Alfredo Lagay in three.

The Argentine people loved Moore, and the feeling was mutual. In each town Archie visited, he chose a needy youngster and dressed him in new clothes. In his autobiography, *Any Boy Can*, Archie recalled one such episode: "There was a little boy named Adolfo Batto in a little town called Sunchales. I went to his school. The teacher asked for some of her best dancers to perform a native dance for me. This was beautiful, and Adolfo came out to dance, but he was reluctant as his shoes had holes in the sole and his toes kicked out. I asked the teacher to bring Adolfo to my hotel room during the noon hour. He came over and I took him to a tailor shop. The shop was closed because of siesta time, but I knocked on a window and a man came out. I bought the boy two suits of clothes. I also arranged for a trip for him to the dentist. Adolfo and I kept in touch for many years. I enjoyed helping out children like him."

President Peron invited Moore, Saddler and Johnston to his residence, the Casa Rosada, as guests of honor. He gave them each a gold medallion that had his and Evita's picture on one side and their initials on the other. Peron also readied a yacht for their use and even took Archie on some campaign stops. "I didn't drink, but everyone else at the rally was drinking wine out of a goat bag," Archie recalled of one such stop. "I didn't know what to do because I didn't want to offend anyone, either. I took a small sip and spit it out when no one was looking."

It was, both professionally and personally, an idyllic sojourn that actually helped improve relations between the U.S. and Argentina. "I only judge people by their relationship with me," Moore said. "Juan Peron was a huge boxing fan and respected my abilities. I even received a letter from the United States Embassy thanking me for helping with our relationship with Argentina."

Years afterward, Moore rhapsodized about his stint in Argentina in an article in *Boxing Scene*. "My love for South America is almost idealistic, since the attitude down there is what I would love to experience in North America. It's like having a beautiful wife you love who is cold to you, and then finding a plain mistress who adores you. The United States is my home, and I love it dearly, but every once in a while I wink slyly at South America and she winks back."

*   *   *

Michigan KO artist Embrell Davidson was Archie's homecoming opponent at Olympia Stadium in Detroit. He had 35 pounds on Moore, but Archie knocked him out in the first round of the nationally televised fight and then helped Davidson back to his feet.

Walter Smith, an assistant to trainer Emanuel Steward at the famed Kronk Gym in Detroit, was in Davidson's corner that night.

"Embrell was only 22 at the time and was scared going into the fight against a guy with Moore's reputation," he recalled. "He froze! It is nearly impossible to prepare anyone to face a style like that."

Nineteen days later, Moore returned to Philadelphia for a rematch with Harold Johnson. It had been two years since their first bout, and Johnson had won nine out of 10 since then, his only loss coming at the hands of Jersey Joe Walcott. Moore had little trouble winning another decision over Johnson, and then went to St. Louis for a match with Chubby Wright at the Auditorium. The *St. Louis Post-Dispatch* noted the next day that Wright looked scared from the start and bent forward with his hands alongside his head to present as small a target as possible. Moore toyed with him throughout before referee Harry Kessler halted the one-sided event in the seventh.

A third bout against Harold Johnson took place in Milwaukee, Wisconsin. Making things a little more difficult this time was the fact that Charley Johnston entered town a marked man. About two months before, when Saddler fought Paddy DeMarco in Beertown, Johnston got into a dust-up with the boxing commission that was ignited, *The Milwaukee Journal* reported, when referee Julius Fidler had to change his scorecard because he'd gotten the fighters confused. Johnston accused the commission of engineering the change and was quoted as saying, "You can't win in Milwaukee if they don't want you to."

Before the Moore-Johnson bout, Johnston was hauled before the Wisconsin commission to account for his conduct. He suggested that he'd only been trying to "put on a show" and "get the fans stirred up," but the commission demanded an apology. Johnston complied and promised to be on his best behavior. That lasted until the decision for Johnson was announced. Two judges actually would've scored the competitive match a draw, but the deduction of a point from Archie's total for a low blow in round five gave Johnson the win. "I'll never bring Moore back to Milwaukee!" barked Johnston.

Six weeks later, Moore-Johnson IV broke all records for advance ticket sales in Toledo. Both fighters trained at the Police and Fire Gym. Harold Johnson pounded his sparring partners, while Moore battled a cold instead and decided against sparring. Trainer Hiawatha Grey said he was satisfied with Moore's condition despite Archie's indisposition. Meanwhile, another development almost caused a postponement. Charley Johnston was at it again, this time threatening to pull Moore out at the last minute if the commission insisted on using an outside referee for the main event. "What's the matter with local referees?" he asked. "I have always gotten a square deal before, and with a Toledo man as the third one in the ring, I wouldn't worry. Why all of a sudden go out of town to get somebody else? There's a lot of money bet on this fight. Archie has to win to regain his spot as the top contender for the title. Nobody talked to me about making a change of officials."

Nobody listened, but it didn't matter as Archie won a unanimous decision for the third time in four bouts with Johnson. However, that didn't put him any closer to Maxim, who had no plan to defend the title until later that year. So Moore went to St. Louis to fight Jimmy Slade, and beat him handily.

Moore was reported to be 36 years of age, by which time in that era most boxers were ex-boxers. He had been a ranked contender for 12 years, but had never fought for a world title. In frustration, Archie penned a letter on July 11, 1952, to the chairman of the New York boxing commission, Robert Christenberry.

"I am sure that you have been made aware, through a variety of sources, of my attempts during the past five years to fight for the light heavyweight championship.

"Because this matter has grown beyond the scope of my personal acquaintances and followers, and is now a matter of public discussion in the press and elsewhere, I feel that the time has come for me to indicate to you directly my feeling that I deserve to be considered the foremost challenger in this division.

"I understand that there are circumstances which often delay arrangements for logical contenders having the opportunity to meet the champion in any division.

"However, it becomes increasingly difficult for me to understand why the Commission has not taken some action in regard to my challenge of Joey Maxim for the title.

"Similar questions are arising in the public's mind, too. So indicates the mail I have been receiving from all over the world, which questions the purpose of a Commission that takes no steps to correct an obvious inequity within its sphere.

"My interest must be considered in some part selfish. Of course, fighting is the only career I know. I have endeavored to follow this career with honesty and sincerity.

"Nevertheless, it seems apparent that my future now is tied in with a wider matter. Public judgment of the integrity of boxing commissions now becomes part of the picture. It is my hope that you will consider my request that you take some action on the light heavyweight champion's choice of opponents.

"Not only will such action influence my future in the ring, but it will, as well, clarify the public's thinking in regard to the legitimate activities and purposes of the Commission."

Commissioner Christenberry responded that he was in sympathy with Moore's aspirations, but was at a loss to understand his failure to accompany his letter with the required forfeit check of $2,500, payable to the New York State Athletic Commission, in order to make his challenge official.

"The Commission is definitely concerned with maintaining the integrity of boxing, and believing that you are serious in your expressions, we look forward to early receipt of your formal challenge and check," wrote Christenberry to Moore.

Bob Christenberry was widely known to be a forthright man of integrity, whose intentions were no doubt as honorable as his earlier service in the U.S. Marine Corps, during which Christenberry lost a hand in a training mishap with a live grenade. But for him to argue about the "integrity of boxing" bespoke either a stunning naiveté or an unwillingness to face up to the reality of the situation in boxing so staggering that it took "escapeology" to a realm not even Archie himself could have imagined.

Since the retirement of Joe Louis as heavyweight champion in 1949, professional boxing had not been directed by the New York boxing commission nor even the National Boxing Association, the putative ring governing body to which most states belonged since its inception in 1921. Rather, the director was an outfit whose nickname, "Octopus, Inc.," was more descriptive of its operations than its corporate moniker—the International Boxing Club.

The IBC had started by taking over the heavyweight division, organizing a tournament to crown a successor to Louis after making Joe an officer in the corporation and having him, in effect, sign over the rights to his title to the club.

Big Jim Norris was the honcho of the IBC. He was tall and urbane, a wealthy Chicago businessman who had, wrote Barney Nagler in his seminal 1964 book on the IBC, *James Norris and the Decline of Boxing*, a "strange devotion to ruffians who were beneath his economic and social level. He chose his companions as he found them, without regard to their antecedents or their criminality, and in the rowdy world of sports he was unto himself as the arch democrat."

Norris and the IBC eventually controlled the biggest boxing venues in the United States, including Madison Square Garden, and until the courts dissolved it in 1956 on the grounds that it was a monopoly in violation of U.S. antitrust laws, the IBC promoted most of the big fights held in America. Norris was the big, double-breasted IBC front man, but the "ruffian" who was the real power in the organization and in boxing was named Frankie Carbo, whose long list of past crimes included murder and who controlled either directly or through minions many of the top boxers of the late 1940s and '50s.

Carbo was known in fight circles as the shadowy "Mr. Gray." Congressional investigator Jack Bonomi told David Remnick, author of *King of The World: Muhammad Ali and the Rise of an American Hero*, that Carbo hooked up with Norris "because Norris had Madison Square Garden and Chicago Stadium and all that money, and Carbo had the fighters and the managers in his pocket. They needed each other, and together they had absolute power over boxing."

The involvement of hoodlums in boxing was hardly a new development. In the 1930s, Primo Carnera, a giant, generally peaceable native of Italy, was barnstormed to the heavyweight throne by gangsters who fixed fights for him and, once he had served his purpose of fattening their coffers, cut him loose to make a living as a professional wrestler.

But with the advent of television and the money involved in broadcasting fights during prime time up to three nights a week, the Carbo-loaded IBC exercised virtually total sway over the sport. They decided who got to fight for the titles, how much they got paid, and often, in the case of the winners, who would call the shots in their careers.

The corruption wasn't just at the promotional and managerial levels. When Senator Estes Kefauver launched his federal investigation of boxing in 1960, after Carbo had finally been sent to jail for extorting a share of the purses of welterweight champion Don Jordan, Bonomi was his chief fact finder. What he discovered was not only the extent of mob control of boxing, but also that many of the top newspaper boxing writers were on the take.

For all that, columnist Red Smith called Carbo "the more or less benevolent despot of boxing's empire." Decades later, as a new century turned and boxing was plagued by numerous "alphabet" governing bodies and its major players included Don King, the numbers runner-turned-murderer-turned high-profile fight promoter (eventually voted into the International Boxing Hall of Fame), some observers even declared that by comparison the IBC days were a tiptoe through the tulips.

Archie Moore had long outgrown his hoodlum period (which actually hadn't amounted to much, anyway). But to get what he wanted it became increasingly clear that it would be necessary to accede at least some degree to the powers that be—in this case as represented by the IBC-connected manager of champion Maxim, Doc Kearns, who was not a mobster, but rather a pirate. But Kearns's fascinating bit of skullduggery would come later, and in the meantime Charley Johnston continued to beat the drums for his boxer. In the November 1952 issue of *The Ring*, Johnston said that in fact he had sent a $2,500 forfeit check to the New York boxing commission to back up Moore's challenge of Maxim, and took the opportunity to expound on the fistic attributes that made Archie as popular among his fellow light heavyweights as what was primly referred to in those days as a social disease.

"To begin with, he is a fine two-handed puncher," said Johnston. "And with that punch he has consummate skill. He is the killjoy, the spoiler. Let a boxer of his pounds, or heavier, stick his nose above the rest of the field, and Moore comes in and clears him out of the field. But, as for getting a big fight for himself— Big Poison.

"I call Moore 'The Gypsy.' You know how most of the fighters are. You tell Joe Dokes that he fights Joe Smokes in Los Angeles on December 1, and Dokes arrives in L.A. 48 hours before the argument and holes in at some hotel. Moore moves into town just as soon as the match is made. He shows himself. He helps in the publicity. Sometimes if he runs into a string of matches in one city, he will move in and stay there. He developed Toledo into a $20,000 town from a $2,000 stop."

An article in *Look* noted that Bob Reese and some associates tried to lure Kearns and Maxim in Toledo with a sweet deal for a title match. Their plan was to underwrite the first 25 rows of the Toledo Arena at $100 a seat and price the other seats at $10 apiece. They could therefore guarantee Maxim $50,000. Kearns countered with a request for $75,000, and Reese agreed. Typically, then Doc inquired about $100,000, and the deal came apart. "What my friends in Toledo tried almost worked, but there came a financial limit," said Moore. "None of us relished a career in the poorhouse."

After defeating Bob Dunlap in San Francisco by knockout in six, Archie fought heavyweight contender Clarence Henry in Baltimore on one of the hottest nights of the year. Moore recalled, "I fought Henry the night after Sugar Ray Robinson fought Joey Maxim at Yankee Stadium in New York and collapsed in the heat.

It was even hotter in Baltimore the night I fought. Henry was sucking oxygen, but I was bouncing on my toes after 10 rounds and took the decision."

The KO defeat of Harry Matthews by Rocky Marciano prompted another outburst from Johnston, published in *The Ring*. "Why do they keep shoving Moore aside? Take that Harry Matthews fight with Rocky Marciano. Moore could stop Matthews twice in 10 rounds. But it was Matthews, a blown-up light heavy, who got the match with Rocky, and it was Matthews, stopped in two rounds, who collected $51,000 for the five minutes. Moore is forced to campaign from coast to coast, and when things get slack here, to go down to South America and wherenot, in order to clear $12,000 a year.

"Honest, it's pathetic. I mean the way that guy accepts the snubs of Fate and promoters, and goes through life smiling."

As for himself, Johnston said, "I have hollered, I have written letters, I have begged promoters and cajoled matchmakers, I even went to Montreal to present Moore's case before the National Boxing Association officials, but got nowhere. The situation reminds me of the old days, when great fighters like Jean Jeannette, Sam Langford, Battling Jim Johnson, Harry Wills and Sam McVey could not get shots at the heavyweight championship because they were 'too good.'"

Whether on account of Johnston's bluster or Archie's patience, the wheels finally started to grind their way. But leave it to Doc Kearns to introduce his own unique spin. In *The Million Dollar Gate*, Kearns described the meeting and machinations that finally put the deal together. "There was no question that Charley Johnston was certain he had me over his hip this day. 'Sit down Doc,' he waved expansively. 'This visit has been ages getting here.' Charley and I went back a far piece together. My difficulty was that, after Maxim's win over Ray Robinson, it became increasingly evident that the days in which we could avoid meeting Archie Moore were definitely limited. The National Boxing Association began to prod me to defend against him, and a number of the more important state commissions became insistent, too. Now as we sat in Charley's office it was obvious from his manner that as Moore's manager he figured he was home free. So I gave him a little loose line to start the ball rolling. 'Well, Charley, I guess it's about time to put this thing together.' Johnston agreed, then I stated the matter of conditions. First I requested a return clause, to which Johnston agreed. Then I demanded a hefty $100,000 guarantee. And my final request about gave Johnston a heart attack. 'If you win the title, I want a piece of Moore.'"

Using the technique that got him nowhere with boxing commissions, Johnston ranted and raved and threatened, in response to which Kearns only yawned. Then Doc said, "You know damned well that I can figure out something that will keep Moore sitting on the doorstep until he's 110 years old."

It was no contest. Johnston had to accept Kearns's terms or forget about the match. What Kearns wanted wasn't even that unusual in those days, recalled Moore. "Doc Kearns and Charley Johnston were friends. In those days managers would strike up deals. 'If my boy beats your boy, give me a part of him.' Doc Kearns was the best at striking deals. Kearns knew I could beat Maxim."

He was finally going to get his chance.

CHAPTER 11

Finally a Shot at the Title

The world championship fight involving hometown hero Archie Moore had St. Louis buzzing. The advance ticket sales of over $60,000 broke the old record of $56,905, set on January 16, 1950, when featherweight champion Willie Pep fought local boy Charley Riley. In addition, radio and TV rights would bring in an estimated $50,000 more. Archie would get 10 percent of whatever was left after the champion got his guaranteed 100 grand, which the *New York Times* figured might be enough to cover his training expenses. But Moore was finally getting his shot, and the money was secondary.

Born Guiseppe Antonio Berardinelli in Cleveland, Ohio, Joey Maxim took up boxing as a boy to defend himself in his tough neighborhood. In 1940, he was a national AAU champion, turning pro a year later. In spite of his boxing ability, he wasn't exactly a crowd pleaser. Maxim couldn't punch, and he often tied up his opponent in a clinch. Only purists could appreciate his flairless style. But once Kearns took him over in 1945, Joey started to move right up.

Kearns originally set his sights on the heavyweight throne. In due time Doc made Maxim the fifth-ranked heavyweight, but then two decision losses to Jersey Joe Walcott convinced Kearns that the 175-pound class was best for Maxim.

Maxim amazed people with his knockout of Freddie Mills for the title. Not so surprising was Kearns's decision to keep him away from the toughest challengers around, especially Moore. Maxim even briefly moved back up to heavyweight, but lost to Ezzard Charles. His most noteworthy 175-pound title defense was against one of boxing's greatest, Sugar Ray Robinson, then the middleweight champion. Robinson was going for world title number three (he'd originally won the welterweight belt), but due to the intense heat, 104 degrees at ringside, Sugar Ray came up short. He collapsed in the eleventh round, suffering from heat stroke, after building up a lead in the bout.

Against Moore, Maxim was listed as a slight underdog. Still, Archie was 36, and some wondered if he was up to a 15-round battle against a man who'd been stopped only once (by Curtis Sheppard) in 125 bouts. But old-time fighter Harry Trendell saw Moore in training and told the *St. Louis Argus*, "There's the finest piece of fighting machinery in the world today." Archie himself told *The Argus*, "This is my big fight, and I am going to win it. Maxim can run all he wants to, but I am going to catch him."

Maxim sounded cautiously optimistic. "I respect Moore and will be in there fighting all the way," he said. "When it is all over, I expect to still be the champion." The champion added that the only way to make money in boxing was to hold a title, and he needed the money to pay off his new home.

At the official weigh-in, Johnston was at it again. Moore came in at 172 pounds, three under the class limit. Maxim hit 175 on the head when he stepped on the scale slightly after noon. But Johnston then loudly protested that the promoters had failed to have the scales officially checked and sealed beforehand. "I guess we have no chance to win here," he shouted at Commissioner Charley.

He finally won an argument. Two officials of the city's Bureau of Weights and Measures checked the scales again, and Maxim was forced to weigh in a second time. He made the weight, but Johnson's ulterior motive—annoying and inconveniencing the champion—had worked. Like Kearns, he looked for any edge for his fighter.

Moore spent the last few hours before the fight relaxing to jazz music in his dressing room. "It was like preparing for an exam," he said later. "I was confident because I did my homework, but was not sure what questions would be asked." The radio announcers for the Pabst Blue Ribbon broadcast remarked that Maxim looked nervous before the fight. The near sellout crowd cheered wildly at Archie's introduction, as Moore stared beneath the monk's hood of his black silk robe across the ring at Maxim. Johnston and Cheerful Norman stood beside him rubbing his shoulders and giving last-second advice.

At the bell the two warriors circled each other. The Old Mongoose struck first with a stiff left to the chops. Moore fought out of his customary crouch position, while Maxim tried tricky head movements to avoid the challenger's shots. Maxim attempted his own left jab, but brought it back low, and Moore countered over the top of it with a booming right-hand to the champion's exposed jaw.

As the fight progressed, the champion began to grab Archie whenever he was stung. The referee, Harry Kessler, had his work cut out for him. He had to break apart the boxers each time Moore landed a telling blow. When Kessler instructed the fighters to step back from a clinch, Moore usually obliged. Maxim, on the other hand, held on for dear life. The only problem Moore had, he caused for himself in round four. Moore again staggered Maxim with a booming right-hand, but three follow-up left hooks all landed south of the border. Kessler immediately awarded the round to the champion and warned Moore to keep his punches up.

Maxim's blows lacked authority, but he gained respect from the St. Louis fans for his doggedness. Archie landed pulverizing rights, but the champion would not go down. In the seventh, Archie switched from a body attack and sliced up the champion's face with pinpoint punches. Maxim bled from cuts on both cheeks and a gash at the corner of his left eye. Large red welts covered his midsection from the challenger's brutal body assault.

In the tenth, a huge right-hand from Moore sent Maxim staggering into the ropes. More of Joey's blood spilled on Moore and the canvas. Archie hammered him until the final bell, and at the close of round 15 the crowd stood and applauded both men.

Judge Howard Hess scored 82 points for Moore, 58 for Maxim. Judge Fred Connell saw it 87 for Archie, 63 for Joey. The scorecard of referee Kessler gave it to Moore by only a deuce, 76-74, which he later explained in his autobiography, *The Millionaire Referee.* "The decision was unanimous, of course, although my scorecard was closer than that of the two judges. I wondered years later if they subconsciously had tried to reimburse Archie for the fourth round, which I had taken away [for] the low-blow fouls. Not that it mattered. I scored the fight the way I saw it, and so did they."

It took the new champ more than 25 minutes to make it back to his dressing room. The radio announcers interviewed Moore on the air before he exited the ring. "I feel great," said Archie. "It was a hard fight; Maxim stayed in close at all times." Then he greeted Aunt Willie Pearl over the airwaves, acknowledged San Diego promoter Linn Platner and called for a fight with heavyweight champion Rocky Marciano, whose style, Moore said, "is geared for me." Asked by the announcer if it was OK to address him as "Champ," Archie said, "Sure you can. They have been calling me that for years!" Finally, he dedicated the victory and offered his boxing gloves to his friend in Argentina, Juan Peron.

Over 100 reporters from around the world jammed Archie's dressing room. Also there were St. Louis sports announcer Harry Caray and Nat Fleischer, editor of *The Ring*, to whom Moore had given a big smooch in the ring after the decision was announced. Fleischer told the new champ that he had 11 rounds for him, gave two to Maxim and scored two a draw. Archie stated he begged

Maxim to make a fight of it from the sixth round on, but gave him credit for riding with the punches. "He's a good fighter who carries a fair punch, but he didn't hurt me. I didn't coast at all during the fight and tried to knock him out several times, but couldn't."

During all the commotion, Moore's birth mother, Lorena Reynolds, burst into the locker room and kissed and hugged him repeatedly. She told the press that she was never worried and knew her son would win the fight.

A 1989 article in *Sports Illustrated* described the reunion between Moore and his parents the night he won the title: "In his corner, just before he was introduced as the challenger for the light heavyweight crown, Moore searched the crowd. He spotted them: an older black couple sitting together in the ringside seats. Moore had paid to have them brought to St. Louis for the fight. A police car had picked them up and, sirens blaring, had sped them to the St. Louis Arena. The two people were Moore's parents. The ring announcer stepped out and the bell rang, but Moore kept staring down, because for the first time in his life, he was seeing his mother and father together. 'Reconciliation was highly unlikely,' he says, 'I knew that, but I just wanted my father and my mother to see me win the title, together. I wanted to look down on them, next to each other, at that moment. And I did.'"

Maxim was gracious with reporters in his dressing room and extolled his successor. "Those guys don't grow old; they just get better as they go. Look at Walcott. Moore is a better fighter than Ray Robinson and boy, that sneaky right-hand that he throws is murder. I knew he was good, and that is why I worked to get as much of the money as possible. We knew he was good. I thought he would weaken in the late rounds, but he got stronger as the fight went on. Boy, is he tough!"

As Cheerful Norman entertained locker room guests with his victory dance, Archie promised his faithful followers from Toledo that his next fight would be there.

Manager Johnston disclosed that he had inked an agreement with Argentine promoter Ismael Pace for Moore to engage in two non-title fights sometime in the next year.

Two days after the fight, a telegram sent by President Peron to Moore was printed on the front page of *The New York Times*. "I am very thankful for your kindness in offering me your great triumph last night. Your Argentine fans and myself as your friend had full confidence in your victory. On behalf of everyone here, I am sending cordial felicitations and the wish that the crown so brilliantly conquered may be yours for a long time, together with all the honors that your recognized prestige as a great sporting gentleman entitle you. With my best wishes for your personal happiness, I send you a great and affectionate embrace," the telegram read.

After spending an extra day in St. Louis, Moore boarded a plane to spend the holidays with his aunt in San Diego. A week later, he returned to Toledo. Archie received a hero's welcome in both cities. Only five weeks after claiming the title, Moore kept his promise and squared off against Toxey Hall in Toledo in a non-title match.

Hall had won the Chicago Golden Gloves title in 1951 and had only 15 professional bouts. He was best known as the chief sparring partner of heavyweight champion Rocky Marciano. The fight provided little more than a workout for Archie, who stopped his foe in the fourth round, but it convinced Hall that there was nobody trickier in the ring than Moore. "In the second or third round," Toxey recalled years later, "Archie clamped his arms down against his body. His hands were free, and when we came in close he'd grab on to me real tight. The referee said 'Quit holding!'— only he was talking to me, because it looked like I was holding when it was that old dude doing it on the sly."

Now that he had the title, Moore wanted to start making big money. He gathered with his Toledo backers and brainstormed ways to get heavyweight champion Marciano into the ring. Bob Reese headed the team of local advisors that included Mayor Michael LaSalle, who became Archie's legal advisor, and psychologist Nicholas Dallis, author of the comic strip "Rex Morgan, M.D." Before Archie even claimed the title, Dallis had created a fighter in his comic strip named Archer Moran, who won the light heavyweight crown. Moore's cabinet also included Fred Folger, who owned Folger Packing Company, restaurant owner Bert Schoonmaker, architect Karl Becker, and bank president Clinton Ewell.

While they went to work on a plan for Marciano, Archie had another non-title bout in San Francisco, stopping Leonard Dugan in eight on February 16, and then signed up for four more non-title bouts in four different cities in the following month. It would get the champ a few extra dollars and keep him in condition for the return bout with Maxim, set for June of '53.

Moore's fight-of-the-week tour first took him to Sacramento, where he iced Sonny Andrews in five. Then he was back in St. Louis to fight heavyweight Nino Valdes. While training for that, Archie caught up with hometown amateur sensation Charles "Sonny" Liston, who had just won the Midwestern Golden Gloves tournament in Chicago, under the guidance of Archie's old mentor, Monroe Harrison. Liston was now training for the national tournament and posed for a picture with Moore for the *St. Louis Argus.*

Nino Valdes packed a big wallop and caught Moore with several flurries that brought the crowd to its feet at the prospect of an upset. But Archie eventually closed one of Valdes's eyes and took a unanimous 10-round verdict. On to Spokane, Washington, for a match six days later.

The Empire City loved him. Archie's workouts drew a full house at the Al Morse gym. Moore sparred with a few amateurs before holding court with the media. One reporter asked whom Moore would face after the Maxim rematch. "I want Harry 'Kid' Matthews right in his hometown of Seattle," he answered. "Matthews begged for a shot at the title when Maxim wore the crown. Now since I'm the champion, I hear he plans to move up to heavyweight." With a big grin Moore added: "I wonder why?"

Oakland heavyweight Al Spaulding never laid a glove on Moore in their fight. Archie laid a third-round KO on Spaulding, pocketed his $2,500 purse and caught the next plane out of town.

Next stop: San Diego, where opponent Frank Buford proved resilient until Archie finally sent him home in the ninth round.

Even more fulfilling was his reception by the fans. "San Diego had no professional teams at that time, but they backed their home-town athletes," he recalled. "Guys like Ted Williams in baseball and Billy Casper in golf. These individuals became leaders in the community. When they performed in other cities they acted as goodwill ambassadors for San Diego. I remember people approaching me asking for an autograph or handshake, telling me they saw the fight on TV or heard it on the radio. I feel it meant a great deal to the community to see a black man receive so much positive publicity."

San Diego sports editor Jack Murphy had come to town in 1951 from Oklahoma as a 28-year-old journalist. Murphy instant-ly took a liking to the sleepy naval town of 350,000 people. He also developed a lasting friendship with the city's top boxer. "Jack was a visionary with moral values," said Moore. "He led the brigade in bringing the Chargers to town in '61, and later the Padres. He brought San Diego into the big time. He was always a good friend to me." Over the years, Moore was one of Murphy's favorite topics, and he chronicled Archie's fistic achievements in the San Diego area. Said Archie: "Jack was San Diego sports edi-tor for 29 years until his death. He grew with the town of San Diego and became a journalistic giant. Jack used to joke, 'After nearly three decades at the paper, I haven't made much progress through the years; I still have the same job!'" By the time of his passing in 1980, Murphy was an institution in San Diego and even had the Padres' stadium named in his honor.

Ogden, Utah, had never played host to a title fight, and the city embraced the Moore-Maxim rematch. The Chamber of Commerce declared the day of the fight an official holiday. All businesses closed early that afternoon to allow everyone to attend. Recalled Archie: "Jack Dempsey had fought in Ogden a few times, but since then the town had seen little fight activity. For publicity they broadcast the weigh in on TV from a theater stage. The refer-ee, Ray Miller, gave Maxim and I our instructions then. The refer-ee got a bit carried away in front of the cameras, overstating his point along with the rules. I kindly pointed out to him that Joey and I had indeed fought before and had a familiarity with the rules. Miller wasn't too pleased with my comment, and I fear I spoiled his televised debut."

Kearns, still working Maxim's corner but getting a share of Moore's action, told the *Salt Lake Tribune*, "Joey has been in secret training, and if there is a KO, I'll bet Maxim does the damage."

He did plenty in the first six rounds of the fight, winning them all on the judges' scorecards. But then the champion started to slip past Maxim's crisp left-hand and work inside. Moore dominated the middle rounds, but Maxim came on again at the end to make it close. It was a tight decision on all the scorecards, but Archie's hand was raised in victory. Forty-six years later, Maxim still questioned the verdict. "Archie Moore was the greatest I ever fought," he said, "but I won that second fight. No doubt about it!"

After relaxing a few weeks, Archie had his second Argentine adventure. He and Juan Peron had kept in touch through letters. Since Archie's first visit, Evita had passed away at 33, after a long battle with cancer. After easily dispatching Reinaldo Ansaloni in four rounds at Luna Park on August 22, 1953, Archie appeared with Juan Peronon on the cover of the Buenos Aires newspaper *Noticias Graficas*. Moore accompanied the president on several outings over the next few weeks and engaged in a few exhibitions to stay in shape for his final South American fight, a non-title bout against Dogomar Martinez in Buenos Aires.

Archie easily won a decision in what would be his last actual fight in Argentina, although he returned many times to visit. "I didn't go to Argentina as a politician, only as a boxer," he said. "I didn't defend Peron or condemn him. Politics is a profession in its own right. I was neither a Republican or a Democrat, only a diplomat."

While in Argentina, Moore's marriage to Alice Travis fell apart. Archie never went into great detail on his four failed marriages, but said only, "I blame no one for my past failures. Marriage was like a job; it had to be worked at. At that time in my life boxing was my lady. I never thought of leaving my lady. She was forever."

As a third title match against Maxim loomed ahead, Archie had plenty on his mind. In addition to his impending divorce, he was now having difficulty melting down to the light heavyweight limit of 175 pounds. Three days before the Maxim fight in Miami, he weighed 182 and was forced to sweat off the surplus poundage in a sauna and by taking an early run the morning of the fight. News of his battle with the scale spread, and Moore was listed as a slight underdog.

But the fight was even easier than their first one. Joey twice visited the canvas, in the eighth and eleventh rounds. Moore thoroughly outboxed him and prevailed by a wide margin on all scorecards.

Archie took home his biggest payday—$16,375. But the money didn't last long thanks to the divorce settlement reached after the fight, which left Archie nearly broke. The *New York Times* reported that Alice Alberta Moore had divorced her husband on the grounds of willful desertion.

Once again, Moore was brought out of his own troubles by the bigger ones of someone else. He saw a story in the paper about a four-year-old Miami girl named Cora Lee Hunter. Later he recalled: "Cora Lee was blind. I saw the headline in the paper that she needed $800 for an operation. My first impulse was to put my hand in my pocket. But I had just lost a divorce and all I had to my name was $700. I set out to Second Avenue with hat in hand. Before darkness fell I had $400 in it. One thing I'll never forget is a wino giving me his last 26 cents—that he was going to use to buy a pint." The media picked up the baton, and Archie's efforts helped raise more than enough for the operation. Cora Lee's vision was restored. "It was a one hundred-to-one shot, but we pulled it off," Moore said. Years later, Cora Lee would reunite with Archie on the *This is Your Life* television show about Archie.

Only a shot at Marciano would bring the huge payday Moore needed, and he began campaigning for it heavily. But after two non-title tune-up victories, Archie was forced to defend his belt against mandatory challenger Harold Johnson, a man Archie had already defeated three times, or risk being stripped of the crown.

CHAPTER 12

Bring on Marciano

Before Archie would defend his title against Johnson, he would first have to fend off his weight. Just a week before the fight, Moore weighed 190 pounds—15 over the division limit. But at the weigh-in on the day of the fight, Archie scaled a svelte 173. He gave reporters the explanation they wanted to hear: "It was the Aborigine diet I picked up in Australia that helped me lose the weight!" The fight was Archie's first in boxing's mecca. "I wanted to look good for my initial appearance at the Madison Square Garden," he later recalled. "I had been a rated fighter for 14 years, and a number one contender as early as 1945, and I'd now been a champion for over a year and a half. Yet this was my first showing in the Garden. When Mike Jacobs ran boxing there, he said I didn't fit in his plans. I've never quite fitted into the plans of the International Boxing Club."

Archie's training camp was at Greenwood Lake, N.Y., and in an article in *Look* he recalled how he fought boredom there. "One of my fellow campers was Tommy 'Hurricane' Jackson, a wild-swinging kind of television heavyweight with a personality to match. 'Hurricane' had a guitar and harmonica in camp, and when Lucky Thompson came up with his quartet for a visit (Lucky often plays sax accompaniment to my bag punching), 'Hurricane' insisted on joining them as guitarist. Lucky let him in for one number. I love music. I take my tape-recorded arrangements by Lucky and DeLloyd McKaye, a top pianist, everywhere I go. But I just couldn't go on taking 'Hurricane' Jackson's guitar and harmonica, or his yodeling at 5 a.m. So I shifted to Ehsan's to complete my training."

While the champion was slightly favored, Johnson had won 12 in a row, including a decision over Ezzard Charles, and figured to give Moore a difficult time. A licensed union drummer, Johnson goaded Archie by claiming the champion was not a true musician and couldn't even play a comb.

Tickets were priced from $2 to $10. CBS carried the bout on live television. Archie was down for 40 percent of the net receipts. If Johnson won, Moore was guaranteed a return bout within 90 days.

Harold Johnson used his slick counterpunching skills to outbox the champion over the first 13 rounds. Time was running out on Moore, but in the 14th Archie stunned the Garden audience by landing a solid right to Johnson's jaw that staggered the challenger.

Moore tore into Johnson, landing a barrage of punches that sent the challenger to the canvas. Referee Rudy Goldstein counted to four, and Johnson regained his feet. No mandatory eight-count was called for by the rules, but Goldstein administered one anyway. It only delayed the inevitable. When the action resumed, Archie played a solo on the drummer's head, and Goldstein stopped the fight.

Archie once again took aim at Rocky Marciano's heavyweight title and huddled with his Toledo backers to devise a plan that would not only achieve that goal but also put him in the black financially. "One trouble with Archie—but you have to bless the lovable guy for it—is that if he gets hold of any money, he gives it to someone less privileged than himself," financial advisor Bob Reese told *Life* magazine. "If you get on him about it, he just says, 'I can't give away any more than I have.'" At this point in his career,

Archie owed Reese $20,000. According to published reports, Archie's gross income for 1954 came to $98,152.84. But expenses ate up $77, 349.86, and the balance of $20, 802.98 went for taxes and repayment of debts.

A shot at boxing's grandest title would be a shot in the arm financially and the fulfillment of a lifetime dream for Archie. "When Archie told of dreaming of winning the heavyweight title since he was eight years old," wrote Don Wolfe in the *Saturday Evening Post*, "tears actually came to his eyes. Here was an old fighter and a good one, and a respectable and intelligent man, and I was deeply impressed."

The Toledo braintrust decided on an unprecedented public relations blitz to get Moore into the ring with Marciano. It was launched on November 17, 1954, when 427 letters were sent to writers and sports editors around the country. Eventually the mailing list grew to almost 500 newspapers and magazines. Explained Bob Reese, "My business is not prize fighting but merchandising, and I was out to merchandise Archie. I knew I had a good product. He had ability and confidence, and he'd take on any fighter, bar none. We knew we couldn't do it with one or two shots. Maybe seven, eight, or ten might have to go across a sportswriter's desk before he'd find one he liked. We kept it up three times a week."

Not one professional advertising or publicity person aided the campaign. Archie himself wrote as many as 150 letters and postcards daily. When illustrations were needed, Walt Buchanan, *Toledo Blade* cartoonist, lent his talents without charge. Archie also made appearances on radio and TV, and attended banquets and luncheons. He even popped up unannounced to pester Marciano when Rocky was refereeing at Turner's Arena in Washington D.C. Reese got Moore on a plane out of Toledo late in the afternoon, and at 10 o'clock that night Archie was challenging Marciano at ringside.

Mike DiSalle, who would one day become governor of Ohio, went to New York and appeared before the executive committee of the National Boxing Association. DiSalle also traveled to Washington D.C. and spoke with his senator about a possible investigation of boxing if Moore did not receive a heavyweight title shot.

Just as the campaign was switching into high gear, it and Archie's career itself came to a screeching halt. Archie was scheduled to box Frankie Daniels in San Diego on April 17, 1955 when a routine physical exam disclosed a problem with his heart. The Daniels bout was to have been a tune-up for a battle with highly ranked Nino Valdes. It was canceled, and Archie was confined to a hospital bed for further tests.

Although Charley Johnston was his official manager of record, Doc Kearns was now calling the shots for Archie. In Kearns's autobiography, he recounted what happened. "A heart specialist appeared and, after numerous tests, he gave us the crushing news. 'I'm sure the trouble is organic,' he asserted. Archie wanted it straight and asked, 'What's that mean Doc?'

"'Well, if I had to make the decision I'd say you should probably never fight again.'

"Archie turned his head to the wall and his lips quivered, 'This is really cruel,' he whispered, close to tears, 'I've been fighting all these years and I've never made any real money. Now I've got a chance to cash in and this happens.'

"'Goddammit,' I told him, 'we're certainly not going to accept the verdict of two local doctors. I'm gonna get you the hell out of here and see some real experts.'"

Kearns checked Archie out and flew him to San Francisco to see another specialist. The diagnosis was unchanged—a heart murmur. The doctor also seconded the recommendation that Moore never fight again. Kearns and Moore flew East in search of a different opinion, but in Chicago they received the same one.

As a last resort, Kearns took Archie to Detroit to see Dr. John Keyes of the Ford Hospital cardiology department. After hours of tests, Dr. Keyes offered the first glimmer of hope. Rather than something organic, he suspected a fibrillation, or irregular heart rhythm. He wanted to see how it would respond to medication. So for the next five days, Moore remained in the hospital taking medication every two hours. Then he had another electrocardiogram, and the fighter and his manager were on tenterhooks waiting for the results.

When Dr. Keyes entered Archie's room with the results, they were almost afraid to look at his face. But the news was good. "He's as good as new," the doctor said. "The heartbeat is as regular as clockwork. And, Kearns, I wish you'd get him out of here. We need the bed!"

They didn't waste any time complying. "Doc," said Archie as they exited the hospital, "God has been wonderfully good to me."

Only six weeks after getting clearance to box again, Archie kept his date with Nino Valdes in Las Vegas. Some felt he was foolish for fighting so soon, and Moore's physical appearance fueled their doubts. A few sports writers even hinted that Archie risked death by going through with the fight. According to an article in *The New Yorker*, "Sports writers arriving in Las Vegas a couple of days before the fight found Archie exercising before a paying audience in a ballroom above the Silver Slipper gambling casino. He looked terrible. Free to enter the ring at whatever his weight happened to be on the day of the fight, he had allowed himself to balloon to 200 pounds, and he was in such poor shape that he had difficulty lasting three minutes with a sparring partner. He spat out his mouthpiece after 30 seconds in the ring, because he could barely get his breath. The Valdes fight itself was scheduled for 15 rounds, and when it began Moore looked like the winner of a pie-eating contest."

Archie was up to his usual tricks. He carried a flask over his shoulders wherever he went. Moore would discreetly take a swig as reporters looked on quizzically. Finally one of them asked, "What is that stuff you are always secretly sipping?" Archie's reply was typically mystical: "I'd rather not talk about it. It's a secret strength extract—a kind of a goose juice—that I got from the natives while I was boxin' down in Argentina." In fact, it was only beef broth Archie drank to build his strength for the 6'3", 210-pound Cuban giant.

The bout with Valdes was one of the biggest fight shows ever staged in Nevada up to that time. Kearns was the official promoter, and he told *The Las Vegas Sun*, "This battle is for the 'real' world's heavyweight championship." Former heavyweight champ Jimmy Braddock was named referee and sole arbiter.

Nino Valdes had won his last 11 contests, including a victory over Ezzard Charles. It was that victory that sent Valdes to the top of the heavyweight rankings. Nino was in the best shape of his career and aimed to reverse his earlier loss to Archie and secure a shot at Marciano.

Valdes started strong and took the first two rounds. Archie had tipped the scales at a career high of 196 pounds and paced himself for a long battle. Moore gave away the early rounds and then picked up the tempo, using pinpoint jabs to swell and eventually close Nino's left eye. Still trailing after six rounds, Archie opened the middle rounds with rapid combinations.

Archie's punches weren't the only thing bothering Valdes's eyes. The bout was outdoors at Cashman Field, and the crafty Moore made sure that his back and Nino's face were facing the desert sun as much as possible. By the twelfth round, Archie was in command, and after the final bell referee Braddock called him the winner by a score of 8-5-2.

Only six weeks after defeating Valdes, Moore signed to defend his 175-pound crown against middleweight champion Carl "Bobo" Olson. He would need to drop 21 pounds, although cynical reporters noted that Kearns had been in charge of the weigh-in for the Valdes fight and may have added as much as 10 pounds to Moore's weight. Whatever the case, Moore was still overweight, and *New York Post* sports columnist Jimmy Cannon fingered gluttony as the culprit. Responded Archie: "No, I am not a glutton—only an explorer of food."

Archie's weight concerned others more than it did him. "Fat," he said, "is just a three-letter word meant to confuse people!" To drop excess weight hurriedly took willpower and discipline, he said. In actuality, Archie's secret to losing weight was simple. He ate a low-calorie diet and stepped up his workouts while lowering his fluid intake a few days before the weigh-in.

An article in *The New Yorker* described Archie's regimen for Olson: "Moore did his training at Ehsan's Training Camp, a dreary, unpainted sweat pit in Summit, New Jersey. His trainers closed the doors and windows of the gymnasium early every afternoon, quickly transforming it into a steam cabinet, and in this suffocating atmosphere, Moore, swaddled in a tightskin rubber costume, went through his ritual of shadowboxing, sparring, bag-punching, and rope skipping, giving off sprays of water like a revolving lawn sprinkler. The close air was almost unbearable, but he drove himself furiously, and during the last 24 hours before the weigh-in had nothing to eat or drink except a half lemon. The method seemed extreme, particularly for a middle-aged athlete, but it was effective."

On the morning of the weigh-in, Archie was a mere half-pound over the light heavyweight limit. He ran the excess off. Dehydrated and thirsty, he could barely restrain himself as he jogged from tearing leaves from trees he jogged past and licking the dew off them.

The fight was a no-lose situation for Olson, since his middleweight crown was not at stake. Although a considerable underdog, Bobo's earlier victory over Joey Maxim led many to believe an upset was possible. Olson had given Maxim a solid trouncing, knocking down Joey on his way to a decision victory. The 26-year-old Olson was a non-stop puncher whose plan was to wear down the aged champion.

Moore, of course, had considerably more at stake. He had to win impressively to further the possibility of a shot at Marciano. A loss to the middleweight champ would ruin any hope of that.

Archie entered the ring of New York's Polo Grounds wearing an extravagant robe designed by Marie Hardy, the mother of his new love interest, Joan Hardy. The luxurious outfit cost Moore $250. It was made of a white baby flannel imported from England and was lined with gold satin and trimmed with braids that contained 10-karat gold. Understandably, the elegant garment went right into storage after the fight.

Bobo went into cold storage in round three. "I set him up with a couple of jabs, and he was right there," the champion told the *New York Times*. "Then I hit him with a double right-hand. When he tried to evade a third, I caught him with a left hook. That did it." Archie continued: "It took a while to get warmed up. The canvas was slow and I couldn't catch up to him at all until near the end of the first round. He gave me some trouble in the second, too. In fact, he shook me once with a sneak right-hand. But by that time I was moving well and it was nothing to worry about."

Olson later recalled his version of the fight in the book *In This Corner*. "I was beating him [Moore] for three rounds. I had three cuts on his face already and he was a hard guy to box, but then he conned me right into a left hook. He saw me pull back when he led off with a right-hand, caught me right on the tip of the nose and really stung me, so at the end of the round he did the same thing. He faked with a left hook, and when I pulled back he caught me with a left hook, right-hand, left hook, and when I got up the referee said it was over. It was real disappointing, because in my mind Archie was an old man and I was going to fight Marciano."

The impressive victory started the drums beating again for a shot at the heavyweight title for Moore. "I'd like to meet Rocky Marciano next," said Archie. "I believe I can beat him or any other fighter alive."

The public relations campaign orchestrated by Moore's Toledo braintrust was rolling at full steam again. Newspapers in cities with more than 50,000 residents received a letter or press release three times a week arguing Moore's case for a heavyweight title fight. One of the gimmicks was in the form of a sheriff's poster offering a reward for the capture and delivery of Rocky Marciano to "Sheriff" Archie Moore. The "reward" would be a great fight and the crowning of a new champion. The press releases were often signed, "The Father Time that Marciano wants no part of."

As 1955 rolled around, Archie also wrote Marciano himself, wishing him a Happy New Year and urging him to make a resolution to fight Moore. Classified ads were taken out in 40 U.S. newspapers saying, "Information WANTED on how to make Rocky Marciano defend his world title." Archie tried everything, offering to fight Rocky for charity, on a winner-take-all basis, or even in a four-round exhibition match with 16-ounce gloves, and with a gentlemen's agreement that Archie would not hit Rocky's nose, which had a tendency to bleed a lot.

The Moore ballyhoo cost the Toledoans $45,000, but it was money well spent. Not long after the Olson fight, Marciano's manager, Al Weill, agreed to a Moore bout on September 20, 1955, at New York's Yankee Stadium.

Archie was grateful, and thought the champion and his faction should be, too. "Weill and Marciano ought to thank me," he said. "Without me, they wouldn't be getting ready to pick up the champion's 40 percent of the biggest gate they've ever had. I hear it could go more than a million, counting television and movies and everything. It's the heavyweight championship I cherish just as strongly as Rocky Marciano does. That is why this will be a great fight. I have trained for it as I have trained for no other in my life, and with peace of mind I've never known before. It's the fight of my life."

Prior to leaving for training camp, Archie was asked by a reporter if he felt resentful about being ignored for so many years. He responded, "There isn't a person on earth who hasn't had problems of some kind, but resentment in itself could lick a man more destructively than another man's fist." Moore knew what he had to do in the ring, and he knew whose efforts were responsible for getting him there. "For this fight," he declared, "I shall be announced from Toledo."

Training camp for Archie's heavyweight title challenge was in North Adams, Massachusetts. Moore had fallen in love with the town in 1946 when he knocked out Esco Greenwood there. Archie liked the greenery and mountain air and had made a mental note to return to the small town when the opportunity presented itself. A manufacturing town of 22,000, North Adams totally embraced the heavyweight title challenger in turn, advertising itself as "the home of the training headquarters of Archie Moore."

When Archie arrived there in early August, he was met at the airport by 2,000 fans, including a delegation of city officials. The Chamber of Commerce granted the challenger and his entourage all-expenses-paid residence in a children's summer camp called "Camp Kenwood." The Chamber even converted an old arena into a gymnasium with a boxing ring for Archie and reclaimed a portion of its outlay by charging $1 admission to the public.

Archie returned the kindness by speaking at area Rotary and Kiwanis meetings, often preaching about juvenile delinquency. He recounted his own brushes with the law as a youngster, and when asked how he conquered his delinquency, he told his audiences, "I grew up."

In what was left of his free time, Archie rode around North Adams in a large red Thunderbird and took up a new hobby that gave his promoter a case of angina. When Jim Norris, president of the International Boxing Club, heard that Moore was taking flying lessons, he wired Archie immediately. "I learn with considerable dismay that you are doing quite a lot of solo flying," said Norris. "I do not want to interfere in any way with your training, but surely this is not a necessary procedure for getting into shape. You and I have waited a long time for the Marciano fight, Archie, and I think you owe it to yourself, to the people who worked so hard to help you get this match and to me as the promoter to do nothing to jeopardize this great contest. I request most urgently that you abandon solo flying for now. You will have a long time to enjoy that hobby. Best wishes." Archie appeased Norris by not flying solo, but he still shared the controls with a co-pilot on flights.

Some in the media were more concerned about what the challenger was up to on the ground. Some days he sparred only two rounds. Archie reassured them with a reminder that "I've been fighting almost 20 years as a pro. I know what to do in a ring. Knocking the stuffing out of sparring partners doesn't improve my condition." For the most important fight of his career, Archie promised he would be in the best shape of his life.

He elaborated in an interview with the *New York Times*: "People that called me Archie when I was struggling, I don't like for them to call me 'Champ' now. That's just a title. What I like is for people to call me Archie. I'm naturally placid. I'm so happy I'm a fighter, I don't know what to do sometimes. When things stack up on me, I can always go down to the gym and take it out on the bag. Go down filled up to my neck. Come back and I've got it off. In fighting I find complete freedom. I'm faced with a foe equipped as I am—two arms, two legs, and a heart. I don't dislike Rocky; that's all talk. His personality is none of my concern. I've never said anything left-handed either. When I said I could beat Rocky, I meant it. If I didn't believe it, I'd be content to make the light heavyweight title pay off."

A few days before the fight, Moore was visited by Jack Murphy of the *San Diego Union*. Murphy's printed analysis started out favoring Rocky, but ended up in the corner of the man Murphy dubbed "Childe Arch" on account of Moore's disposition. "Marciano should win because he is younger, stronger, possesses a fearful punch and has an extraordinary capacity for punishment," Murphy wrote. "Marciano offends the purists because he is a fighter without style. He is graceless, frequently clownishly awkward, and it is embarrassing to see the champion of the world sprawl across the ring after missing a punch. Yet he can punch, and take a punch. In this day, and often in times past, nothing more is required. Logic—cold logic—points to a Marciano victory.

"But what is logic when Archie Moore is involved?" Murphy continued. "The point I seek to make is that Moore, in a figurative sense, is about as easy caged as a tiger. Sometimes I get the uneasy notion—call it hunch or superstition—that this is a man who can do anything he sets his mind to and hand. Absolutely anything."

At the Madison Square Garden weigh-in, Moore tried to get under the champion's skin, "Marciano is a slow, lumbering ox, who couldn't hold a glove to a scientific wizard," Archie said. "I understand that Rocky has started to take dancing lessons at his training camp, Grossinger's." The good-natured champion didn't take the bait. "I can't dance and I never could," he said. "If you don't believe it, you can ask my wife." Marciano's trainer, Charley

Goldman, was thinking baseball, not dancing, "The Rock is like Yogi Berra," he said. "He doesn't look too classy, but he hits the ball out of the park and he does okay on defense, too."

Archie cracked back, "I guess Charley knows Rocky will do the catching in Yankee Stadium on the night of September 20."

Both boxers scaled 188 pounds. They didn't shake hands and avoided direct eye contact. But when Rocky stepped on the scale, Moore whispered something that drew a laugh from Marciano. Later on it was reported that Archie had said, "My, Rocky, you have such beautiful brown eyes."

A surprise at the weigh-in was the appearance of Jack Richardson, the manager who took Archie to Australia. Richardson wished his onetime charge luck and produced the rabbit's foot Moore had carried with him Down Under. Richardson predicted to *The San Diego Tribune* that "Moore will win, and win big. They make a lot of the difference between ages of the two fighters, but that's nonsense. I happen to know that Marciano is really 34. They list him at 31, but he is cheating by three years. I'm absolutely sure he's 34. And I'm sure Archie is not more than 38. When I took him to Australia he had to produce his birth certificate. I saw it. He's 38. So what's four years between two fighters? Archie not only has a wonderful chance, he'll win."

Moore ended up waiting an extra 24 hours for his chance at boxing's greatest title. Threats of a hurricane in New York forced Jim Norris to postpone the fight for a day. The delay was generally seen as something else in the champion's favor. Former world champion Ezzard Charles, who had thrice defeated Moore and was the only man to go 15 rounds with Marciano, told reporters, "I don't think it will bother Marciano, but it can't do Moore any good. This is Archie's big chance; he's steamed up about it. The delay may flatten him out somewhat. I know it didn't help me when I had to wait 48 hours through two postponements for my second fight with Marciano. [Moore's] like a pitcher getting warmed up in the bullpen, then being told to sit down and forget about it. It takes something out of a man."

Archie waited out the delay at the Warwick Hotel, on 54th and Sixth Avenue in New York, seeing only close friends. Bob Reese and Cheerful Norman acted as security guards, turning away all requests for pictures or interviews.

The night before the fight, a special air of excitement filled New York. This was the biggest bout since Joe Louis defeated Billy Conn in 1941. Most major hotels were filled to capacity. There was a line a mile long waiting to get into Jack Dempsey's steakhouse.

Undefeated in 48 professional fights, Marciano was a 3-1 betting favorite. But Archie had the sartorial edge, entering the ring in a beautiful black robe with, as promised, the word "Toledo" inscribed on the back. The striking outfit would have made Liberace envious. Archie was introduced as out of San Diego and Toledo.

At the opening bell, both warriors came out circling. Archie started pumping left jabs at Rocky and made the champion miss several times. Moore continued to outbox Marciano and ended the stanza with a left hook to Rocky's head.

Later, Moore recalled for Jack Fiske of *The San Francisco Chronicle* his impressions. "From watching all of Rocky's fights, he'd come out swarming like a bee, but in this fight he came out hands high, and it was almost comical, this raging bull trying to box. I said to him, 'I thought you came to fight,' and it made him mad. I'm trying to make him mad, understand.

"In the second, he came out swinging. I feinted him, he threw the right...I knew it was coming...I pulled back half a step and *pow!*—a short right-hand uppercut. Rocky fell on his knees and face."

The crowd of over 50,000 at Yankee Stadium exploded in unison, sensing a historical upset. But true to his nature, Marciano did not stay down. Up at the count of two, Rocky walked to the ropes as referee Harry Kessler counted to five. Wrote A.J. Liebling of Marciano, "A man who took nine to come up from a punch like that would be doing well, and the correct tactic would be to go straight in and finish him. But a fellow who came up on two was so strong he would bear investigation."

When the action continued, Archie resumed his attack, blasting Marciano with another solid right to the jaw. The challenger then pumped repeated stiff jabs into Rocky's face that drew blood as the round came to a close.

Archie's clever feints, superior footwork and slick counterpunching also gave the challenger the third session, but then Marciano began to take over. In the fourth he shook Moore with right-hands to the body and uppercuts to the head. A flush left hook staggered Archie, but the old warrior gamely fired back. At the bell, both boxers traded powerful rights. But it was Rocky's round, and the Brockton Blockbuster now had momentum on his side.

Rocky was checked slightly in the fifth by Moore's jabbing attack and some solid body punches. But in round six, after catching Rocky with a counter right coming in, Moore was on the taking end of things. Marciano landed a right-hand that dumped Archie on the seat of his trunks. Moore arose at four and traded bombs with the champion. Archie managed to get in a few rights, but ate plenty in return. Rocky eventually dropped the challenger again. The bell rang and Archie staggered back to his corner.

In his autobiography, Harry Kessler recalled, "Round seven was Archie's last hurrah, although both boxers battled all the way through the eighth round with a viciousness never before seen in the ring. Marciano kept coming at Moore in spite of the aging foe's weakening capacity for everything but the ability to absorb punishment. There must have been moments during the first two minutes of that round when Rocky was asking himself how much this guy could take! The answer was: Plenty! Marciano did the only thing he knew: he stepped up the attack and simply submerged Moore in unceasing punches for the last 54 seconds of the round. Rocky included a ponderous right hook in his everlasting assault, and it sent Archie to the floor for the third time. On this knockdown, I had reached the six count when the bell gave Archie the brief respite between rounds.

"His right eye was puffed and purple from blows he had absorbed in the sixth round; his panting revealed that his stamina was gone. He was almost sagging in his corner when I went over to him.

"'Archie, do you want to quit now?' I asked him.

"He looked at me, haggard, and said, 'Mr. Kessler, I'm the world's light heavyweight champion, and if I go out, I wanna go out like one!'

"No one ever questioned Archie Moore's courage; they would not get the opportunity to do so now. When he came out for the ninth, it was with a resolve to fight back with all he had left. Battered, bruised and badly drained, he closed with the Rock, who slugged home combinations like a cyclone, hammering—by actual count—53 whirlwind punches before he caught Moore in his own corner and deposited him on the floor. Archie, his left arm draped on the middle rope, was conscious, but the will to fight had been beaten out of him. He was still sitting there, exactly where his stool would have been, staring at nothing, when I reached the count of 10!"

It was one of the most exciting fights in heavyweight history, and 45 years later the outcome still surprised an inside member of the Marciano camp. "I don't know how in the world Rocky ever beat that dude," said Toxey Hall, "but he did." Archie's cross-arm defense had been a major concern in the champion's camp, allowed Rocky's chief sparmate. "He talked to me about it a lot," said Hall, who, it was hoped, had gleaned special insight into the puzzle in his losing effort against Moore two years earlier. Alas, when Marciano asked, "How could you break through the defense of Archie Moore?" Hall gave an honest answer: "That one I don't know."

The answer, Rocky learned for himself, was sheer brute force, by punching Moore on the arms, shoulders and anywhere else he could to wear the old fellow down.

On his way to the dressing room, Archie seemed groggy but waved to his supporters. He told reporters, "Maybe I followed him too close. I think Rocky fought a great fight. I'm not making any excuses. I enjoyed the fight myself. If the people are happy, then I am happy. Rocky is the strongest man I ever fought. He consistently overpowered me." Unnecessarily, Archie apologized to his handlers for not pulling off the upset.

Archie said he planned to defend his light heavyweight title and in between defenses would continue boxing heavyweights. "I've got some thinking to do," he said. "I've got to go fishing. You fellows know where I live. You can come see me." Where exactly is that, a reporter shouted. "The USA." Moore answered to general laughter. "I have many hometowns."

Archie didn't go into hiding. From Yankee Stadium he went right to a jazz club in Greenwich Village where his friend Lucky Thompson was playing. He was keeping a promise, as he explained in *The Archie Moore Story*: "I had helped Lucky get a booking by promising to show up at the club. Lucky greeted me sourly. He was angry because he had bet some money on me and lost. But even in the face of his surly and ungrateful behavior, I felt fine. I felt I had done the best I could." Archie also did a pretty good job playing the fiddle until nearly five o'clock in the morning.

Moore had been guaranteed 20 percent of the net profits, which topped the $1 million mark. Since Kearns had been instrumental in obtaining high-profile fights for Archie against Harold Johnson, Bobo Olson, Nino Valdes and Marciano, his cut of the purses had been raised. Meanwhile, putative manager Charley Johnston was also in for a cut. It would be his last. Problems with Johnston had surfaced before the Marciano fight. "Charley wanted too much financially out of Archie," said Joan Moore, then known as Joan Hardy. "There was bad blood forming. He wasn't allowed in training camp before the fight." The bad blood boiled over immediately following the fight. Archie later recalled that a writer met Johnston in the corridor leading to his dressing room and asked him if he was going to see how his fighter was. Johnston's reply, Moore said, "was my moment of truth. He said he didn't care how I was; he was going to see how much we had gotten on the losing end." But because of their contract, Archie was legally stuck with him for a while longer.

Another major player was also out for good. Champion Rocky Marciano retired from boxing, the only heavyweight king in history to finish undefeated.

CHAPTER 13

A Final Crack at Heavyweight Glory

In his courageous defeat, Archie won over many new fans. One of them was President Dwight D. Eisenhower, who invited Moore to a luncheon at the White House along with 32 other representatives of the sports world. Their mission was to discuss ways to reduce juvenile delinquency.

Archie was the only invitee to have a game plan prepared for the president. This came out when Eisenhower requested that the visitors gather on the White House steps for photos. First, Archie respectfully asked for a moment of the Chief Executive's time. The president and the other guests listened in amazement as Archie outlined a detailed plan for how five world boxing champions could raise a million dollars for the purpose of fighting delinquency. When he was done, *The Saturday Evening Post* reported that the president told Moore, "You ought to be elected to Congress."

Photographs of Ike, golfer Barbara Womack and Archie covered the newspapers nationwide the next day.

Moore enjoyed the limelight, and the press loved him for his unique outlook and colorful quotes. Requests for speaking engagements came flowing in at an overwhelming rate. A better boxer than secretary, Archie inadvertently booked appointments for the same date. Finally, to keep everything straight he started his own company, Archie Moore Enterprises, Inc. His first employee was Joan Hardy. "Archie was surrounded by clutter," she recalled. "I became his financial manager and business manager before we were married. Archie would sleep in and I would open up the mail. I would read it to him and then give him my advice on it. I then took over all the finances and put him on a salary. Archie trusted everyone and would lend out money he'd never get back, but I had bigger eyes than he did when it came to that."

Managing the CEO's weight was a different matter, however, and in the months following the Marciano fight, Archie ballooned to hefty proportions. Later he remembered, "During my fighting career, I owned three sets of wardrobes. One set for when I defended the light heavyweight title, another when I was competing as a heavyweight, and my final wardrobe came in use when I pressed the heavyweight limit." Kearns often remarked that Archie had only two enemies during his career—a knife and a fork.

Because of his increased poundage, Moore had to postpone a 175-pound title defense against Yolande Pompey from March to June of 1956. His weight was rumored to be around the 220 mark, and while his fabled Aborigine diet might whittle him down, a barnstorming tour against modest competition would do the same and also put some money in Moore's pocket.

The first stop was San Francisco, where on February 20, fleet-footed Howard King was in the other corner. King had looked impressive in several recent Bay area victories, but insiders felt King would be fortunate to hear the final bell. They were almost right. Archie floored King in the first round with a right to the jaw. King barely beat the count, but managed to last the whole 10 rounds. Moore weighed 197, *The San Francisco Examiner* noted, "with plenty of blubber around his middle."

Seven days later, Archie returned to action in San Diego against former victim Bob Dunlop. The homecoming didn't last long, as Moore starched Dunlop in the first. In an interview afterwards, Archie told the *San Diego Union*, "They've been saying my reflexes have slowed up and that I'm slow. I guess this will show them." Around this time the press starting referring to Moore as "Ancient Arch." He not only didn't mind, but stopped dying his hair to visually live up to the billing.

A few weeks after disposing of Dunlop, Moore was in Hollywood to battle former California champion Frankie Daniels in a televised bout at Hollywood Legion Stadium. It was his first appearance there in over 10 years. The bout proved to be little more than a sweat breaker for Archie. Notwithstanding the rolls of fat hanging over his trunks, Moore was fit enough to coast for 10 rounds, and Daniels lacked the know-how to press him. Some thought Archie was actually shaken by a punch in round five, but he assured *The Hollywood Citizen-News*, "I wasn't hurt in the fifth. I don't hurt that easy."

Blasted for allowing Daniels to go the distance, Archie gave some of the credit to his opponent. "When a man is fighting strictly on defense, it's hard to put him down. I was trying to go for a knockout, but the guy was so fast…he's got good legs."

Ten days later, the Moore Tour landed in Sacramento for a rematch with Howard King. The record books list Hollywood as the venue, but newspaper accounts confirm Sacramento as the location. King again lasted the distance, although he visited the canvas twice en route to losing the decision. Archie appeared to be at least 20 pounds over the light heavyweight limit, but when pressed on the weight issue would only comment, "I wish I could fight every night!"

With nine weeks to go before the mandatory defense against Pompey, Archie was in Richmond, California, against muscular Willie Bean. Bean had previously been California's heavyweight champion and had beaten a lot of good fighters. His strength and aggressiveness led some to believe an upset was possible. A large crowd filled the Richmond Auditorium, which a year earlier had been the site of the closed-circuit broadcast of the Marciano-Moore bout.

There was no comparison between that and the Bean fight. It was a one-sided drubbing, with Moore dumping Bean to the canvas five times before the referee halted the fight in the fifth. Noted the *Richmond Independent*: "The Los Angeles giant seemed nearly paralyzed with fear at the very onset of the bout, and made only token gestures of trying to make a fight of it."

Bean himself told a different story—with the same ending—recalling the fight in a 2000 interview. "I think I was handling him quite well," Bean said. "But I wanted to knock him out. I told my corner that, and they were cursing at me and telling me, 'Don't get close to the guy!'" In the fifth, a punch sent Archie to the ropes covering up, exposing the ample and amply scarred Moore midsection. "Archie had all those operations…and everybody made the mistake of going for his body," recalled Bean, who promptly fell into the same trap. "I could hear my corner yelling 'No!' as I dropped my left hand to throw a right to his body—and the lights went out."

Contrary to expectations, at the same time Archie was fattening his record, his waistline was also expanding. Somehow, in spite of the steady activity, he had managed to actually gain five pounds, and the press began to roundly criticize Archie's roundness. It was time to go Aborigine. Archie vowed publicly to lose 20-plus pounds in several weeks, and also announced he was close to publishing a deal that would reveal his secret diet to a hungry world.

In April of 1956, Moore scored three more knockout victories over subpar competition. Marciano's heavyweight title was now vacant, and Moore was in line to challenge for the empty throne. But Archie kept his contractual agreement to meet Pompey on June 5 in London. In spite of his weight problems, Archie never considered parting with his light heavyweight title.

A few days after knocking out Gene "Tiger" Thompson in Tucson, Arizona, Archie boarded a plane for London. It was his first visit, and the British press were anxious to meet the flamboyant world champion.

After eliminating his jet lag with a 12-hour snooze, Archie attended a press conference on Fleet Street and faced questions about Pompey and the possibility of facing Floyd Patterson for the vacant heavyweight crown. Of course the media also needled him about his weight, but Archie was more than up to the challenge and regaled reporters with fanciful tales from Down Under. He told *The Daily Mirror*, "I was given a secret recipe by a dying Aborigine under a gumtree in a desert near Woorawoorwoorowwoora. At least I figured he was dying—he looked mighty sick. And he made me promise I would never tell the secret of this semi-vanishing oil until he died. Well, how do I know he's dead? I ain't taking no chances."

Archie stayed at the Star and Garter Hotel, only a block from Windsor Castle. He ran daily in Windsor Park and complained that the cold, damp weather affected his ability to shed excess weight.

British boxing writer Reg Gutteridge described Archie's weight-reducing difficulties in his book, *The Big Punchers*: "While making drastic efforts to come to scale at 12 stone 7 pounds [175 pounds] to defend against Yolande Pompey at Harringay Arena in 1956, Moore dined daily at Isow's Restaurant in Soho. He infuriated waiters, carefully placing chewed meat in a napkin and whispering that it was too tough. Jack Isow, the roly-poly owner who could not punch his way out of a paper bag, threatened to throw Moore out. Every day the champion would heavily overtip waiters as a form of apology, until they tumbled to his act. He also kept a small pharmacy of laxatives in his bathroom. One way or another, he never failed to make the required weight."

On the day of the fight, Gutteridge needed a story for his afternoon column and sought out Archie. Gutteridge caught up with the champion in a Turkish Bath, where Moore was sweating himself down to 175 with just a half-hour until the weigh-in. Embarrassed to be caught using such a mundane method of weight reduction, the quick-thinking Moore tried to convince Gutterridge that he was there having the wrinkles steamed out of his trousers.

Pompey hailed from Trinidad and had modest ring credentials. In seven years he had suffered only two defeats, but his opposition was unexceptional. Yolande wasn't regarded as much of a puncher, and his fighting heart was considered his best asset.

Still, the challenger began piling up points early against Moore. Archie started so slowly that referee Jack Hart called a timeout in the second round and warned him that he expected more action. "The referee was rude to me," Archie sniffed later in an interview with *The Boxing News.* "Surely a champion is allowed a few rounds to get to know his opponent's style."

In the fourth round, Archie finally picked up the tempo and landed several hard shots while backing the challenger to the ropes. But Pompey again provided most of the action over the next few rounds.

Archie came alive again in the ninth, pounding Pompey at will. The challenger answered the bell for the tenth, but Moore ended it seconds later, and after his hand was raised, Archie took a bow and handed over his shiny robe to J. Onslow Fane, president of the Boxing Board of Control.

It had been no day at the races for Archie, but the following day was. He went to Epson Downs horse track, where Moore was approached by heavyweight contender Ingemar Johansson. The Swede had been at the Pompey bout and told Archie that a match between them in Sweden would draw a $70,000 gate. It was not a lucky day at the track for Ingo, as Moore declined on the grounds that he was after a heavyweight title bout that would earn him $70,000 for himself.

By the time he returned Stateside, Archie had decided to award himself the heavyweight title. In a letter titled, "I'm no challenger, " Moore told Jack Fiske of *The San Francisco Chronicle,* "Once when I was a kid back in St. Louis, I managed to get hold of some candy. Another fellow, who hung out in my block, found out about it, and right away he wanted to know about *our* candy. That sort of reminds me of this young boy Floyd Patterson and his crowd. They're talking about how we're going to fight for the title. That's really funny. I've already got the title.

"It's like I told that kid back in St. Louis: 'It's my candy—not ours—and the only way you are going to get any of it is to take it away from me.' Well, that's about the way I feel about Patterson, if he wants my title he'll have to fight for it. By the way, that kid back in St. Louie never did get his mouth sticky—just bloody.

"If I hadn't been around this business so darn long, I'd have probably blown my top when the alleged promoters of the nation decided to stage a huge 'elimination series' to determine the successor to the heavyweight throne when my pal, Rocky Marciano, got too fat to fight any more.

"When old Rock decided to quit, he told the press that I was the best man around. That shouldn't have been news. I was the top man before Rock retired—it doesn't take any genius to figure out who was next in line.

"Naturally the buck chasers cooked up the so-called eliminations to fool the public. They trotted out Bob Baker and Bob Satterfield, both of whom I KOed; and Nino Valdes, whom I'd thumped twice; and a couple of raw novices named Johnny Summerlin and Harold Carter. They also beat the drums for Tommy Jackson and this kid Patterson. Nobody said anything much about the new heavyweight champ, Archie Moore. They were too busy trying to con the public with these silly matches.

"Of course, the contestants weren't top fighters, and neither were the fights. The public didn't go for the counterfeit contenders, and when I whipped Pompey in defense of my world light heavyweight championship, the promoters began to remember old Archie.

"They told me they were going to give me a chance to fight Patterson for the heavyweight title. That's really a laugh—the candy deal all over again. Well, I'll give Patterson the same chance I gave that kid who wanted my goodies. I'll give him the same kind of licking, too."

While Archie was in England, Doc Kearns was in Toronto, Canada, negotiating Archie's next fight. It was a Kearns classic—"a con job, plain and simple," wrote Doc in his 1964 autobiography.

"I lined up a bout against a pleasant young fellow named James J. Parker, who was billed rather attractively, if extravagantly, as the 'Canadian heavyweight champion.' Now understand, I'm not putting the knock on Canadian fighters, but Parker had as much right in the ring against a man who had floored Marciano as did maybe Shirley Temple. At the outset, ticket sales hinted that the customers probably thought so, too. Which is when I turned on the ballyhoo."

Kearns arranged to fly in British fight impresario Jack Solomons, ex-champ Marciano and even Dr. Joyce Brothers, who'd gained a reputation as a boxing expert on a TV game show. He further dressed up the promotion by insisting that reporters covering the fight and all patrons in the first 10 rows dress formally. Archie himself added luster to the occasion by wearing a sequined dinner jacket into the ring.

A lumberjack by trade, Parker quickly learned what it was like to be on the other side of the ax. Archie battered him all over Toronto's Maple Leaf Stadium. Parker's left eye was split two inches along the eyebrow, his nose was not quite in the same place it was 24 hours earlier, and his lips were swollen to twice their normal size. The referee mercifully halted the contest in round nine, and afterward Archie told the press, "I hated having to go on hitting him, but you don't leave a job half done. I was glad for everybody's sake when it ended."

As negotiations for a Patterson fight wore on, Archie aired his views to *The Ring*. "If Patterson is not ready for me by the end of the fall, I will lay claim to the world crown," he said, apparently forgetting that he'd already done just that. "I have accomplished everything asked of me. I've fought 10 times this year to keep myself in proper condition for the Patterson test. I whipped Pompey in a light heavyweight title fight on foreign soil, and I stopped the Canadian heavyweight champion on his own ground. Now I'm to do the same with Patterson, if given the opportunity. But the cards appear to be stacked against me.

"I'm not getting any younger. If I have to wait much longer, I may never get the chance to prove conclusively my right to the heavyweight crown. I'll wait a few months longer. But I'm certain the public and the various boxing commissions will agree that if Patterson is unfit physically to face me in a title bout, I should be declared the champion, or the National Boxing Association, the New York Commission, the European Boxing Board and the World Championship Committee should name another top challenger and have him fight me for the world title with the stipulation that the winner must meet Patterson in his first defense by next June.

"That, it seems to me, would be the best way out of this dilemma. Without a heavyweight champion, boxing is in the doldrums. I am the best man and should be recognized as the champion, or I should be given the chance to face the man, who all commissions think is, next to Patterson, the best in the field."

Moore did most of the bargaining on his own. Still, Archie's manager of record, Charley Johnston, materialized to remind Moore that he was still under contract and so Johnston would be collecting his manager's fee regardless of who was steering the ship. Terms were finally settled, and Moore-Patterson was signed for November 30, 1956 in Chicago.

But three months before that, Archie was involved in another big match. "He came by my house in New York and asked me to marry him but to keep it a secret," recalled Joan Moore, who became Archie's fifth and final wife. "He wanted me to live in San Diego, but he knew I wouldn't relocate unless I was married. He promised me if I didn't like San Diego we could move to New York. I should have known better; he had no intention of ever leaving San Diego!"

Seven years after their introduction, Archie and Joan were married in Ensenada, Mexico, on August 20, 1956. Reported the *New York Amsterdam*: "World's light heavyweight champion Archie Moore was married to curvaceous New York model and designer Joan Hardy after a thrilling coast-to-coast race between cupid and a United States airliner DC-7.

"The beautiful Mexican civil ceremony was witnessed by the bride's mother, Mrs. Edward D. Hardy, Mrs. Evelyn Cunningham and news reporter Betty Granger, who flew with the couple after being sworn to secrecy. Betty Granger and Mrs. Cunningham served as matrons of honor for her."

The wedding party slipped out of Idlewild Airport at 4:15 Saturday afternoon for a fast flight across the nation to San Diego. Archie and Aunt Willie Pearl joined the group on the journey to Mexico. Joan wore a gown designed by her mother and made of white embroidered satin and Chantilly lace, which Archie had purchased in London.

After the wedding, Archie purchased 120 acres of land in Ramona, a town located 40 miles northwest of San Diego. There, at the foot of Mt. Woodson, he established his training camp, "The Salt Mines." The rugged terrain afforded Moore the chance to train in seclusion, discounting snakes and a few mountain lions. Once the site of a nudist camp, the Salt Mines was like no other boxing camp. It consisted of five lodges, two swimming pools and an outdoor and indoor gym. Large rocks had been painted red and stenciled with names of such boxing legends as Sugar Ray Robinson, Joe Louis, Stanley Ketchel and Joe Gans. Archie even spelled out his own name in huge letters on the ground, large enough to be read by planes passing overhead. The property also had marked trails for roadwork. Archie did his preliminary training there before heading to Chicago in late October for his final month of preparation for the Patterson fight.

The brisk Midwestern weather didn't agree with Moore, but in his second bid for the heavyweight throne, weight was not an issue. Archie stayed in downtown Chicago and trained daily at a gymnasium set up at the Midwest Hotel. If he won, Archie would be the oldest heavyweight champion ever, supplanting Jersey Joe Walcott, who had won the title at age 37.

Floyd Patterson, on the other hand, was gunning to become the youngest heavyweight champion in history. Just 21, only four years earlier he had captured the Olympic gold in Helsinki, Finland, in the 165-pound division. As a pro, Patterson had compiled a record of 30-1, losing only by decision to Joey Maxim early in his career. However, his only ranked foe up to then was Tommy "Hurricane" Jackson, whom Patterson had decisioned in an elimination bout. A few weeks before the fight, Moore and Patterson appeared on the *Today Show* from their respective training camps.

Archie predicted a knockout victory. Patterson was annoyed by Moore's confidence as well as the questions of reporters about his relative inexperience. "It's possible that I've learned in a short time what it took Moore so much longer to learn," he said.

The San Diego Union sports editor Jack Murphy was alarmed when Joe Louis predicted a Moore win by KO. "If that's not a jinx," wrote Murphy, "I've never seen one. Practically nobody can remember when Louis has tabbed the winner in an important fight."

The official odds were 6-5 pick'em, and many in the press felt Archie would conquer the youthful Patterson. The bout marked the fourth time in history that two leading contenders met for the vacant championship. Archie insisted to the press that he was even sharper than he had been for Marciano. Moore even floored two sparring partners during his final workout. Everything seemed to be peaking just right for the Mongoose, when a figure from Moore's past surfaced to level sensational charges against the boxer.

"Moore Hit by $750,000 Suit," headlined the *Chicago Tribune*. The story reported that Dollree Mapp of Shaker Heights, Ohio, the divorced wife of boxer Jimmy Bivins, had filed separate suits charging that Moore beat her and backed out of a promise to marry her. Archie immediately branded the charges as false. He told the *Tribune*, "If there was a truth in the charges, I would be in real trouble, wouldn't I? These suits are nothing new. She filed them before—in California and in Ohio—always just before a fight. They didn't worry me then, and they don't bother me now."

In his autobiography, *The Archie Moore Story*, Moore wrote, "I had to live with the nightmare for some time. I have told my wife Joan the whole story, leaving nothing out, and she understands. It happened before I met her. [Mapp] was after my money, but the charges were ludicrous and my attorney had the case dismissed."

That disposed of, Moore dedicated his second heavyweight title try to Eddie Booker, Jack Chase, Charley Burley, Lloyd Marshall and other talented black boxers who had retired from the ring before they received their just dues. But his performance in the Chicago Stadium ring left many wishing he had joined them.

Floyd Patterson took charge in the second round and never let up until he was crowned heavyweight champion. A crowd of 14,000 witnessed the one-sided affair. A series of Patterson left hooks in the third round opened a deep cut along the bridge of Archie's nose near the top of his eye. It was the first time Moore had been cut in the ring.

In the fourth, Archie tried to take charge with left leads and sneaky right uppercuts. But Patterson's speed made the difference as he countered with swift combinations to Moore's head. A pile-driving left hook sent Archie to the canvas in round five. Bruised and battered, Archie barely beat the count. Patterson promptly dumped Moore again, this time with a right-hand. Semiconscious, Archie just missed getting to his feet before the count reached 10. Ancient Archie had petrified overnight.

Archie's dressing room concession speech was lyrical and touching. Standing on a bench, he told reporters, "It seems that even I must bow to the thing called youth. Youth and those fast legs. I came to the end of a very hard road, and when I got there I found the gate closed."

Archie's performance was so lackluster that estranged manager Charley Johnston hinted of a dive right there in front of the press and proceeded to engage the defeated challenger in debate until Moore begged Kearns for a rematch with Patterson. As described by Kearns in *The Million Dollar Gate*:

"Newspaper men clamored outside the door and finally I took it upon myself to let them in.

"'What happened?' one asked Johnston.

"Charley's voice cracked when he jerked his head in Archie's direction. 'Ask him.'

"'I don't really know,' Archie told them. 'I think maybe I worked too hard, and I was overtrained and stale. I tried, but I just didn't have it. I didn't seem to have any snap.'

"That was the gist of it, then we were alone again. At this point Charley could contain himself no longer. White-faced and shaking, he walked up in front of Archie and shook a quivering finger at him.

"'I don't know what was going on out there but it didn't look good to me. As a matter of fact, it looked Goddamned funny.'

"Archie's head came up and his face showed shock at the accusation.

"'I did my best. It's all any man can do.'

"Charley wasn't satisfied. His voice was cold and rasping. 'I don't think you did. I don't think you gave it anywhere near all you have.'

"Archie's nostrils flared and his eyes narrowed. He almost shouted. 'I did, I tell you. I did.'

"'Well, I don't think so,' Charley said acidly. 'I got a funny feeling that something wasn't just right. And, frankly, I don't give a damn if I never handle you again.'

"Archie turned to me and his voice trembled.

"'Doc, you do it for me,' he begged. 'Get me back in with Patterson and I'll take him.'

"'Let's all cool down,' I suggested. 'This won't settle a damn thing, bickering like this.'

Former *Los Angeles Herald* sports editor Budd Furrillo recalled, "It's so damn hard to figure out Archie's performance against Patterson. That fight still dazzles me. Patterson had developed quite a reputation. There was a myth that he could really kill because he was so fast. I was a good friend of Rocky Marciano's, and I remember the night Patterson lost the title to Johannson. That night Rocky said to me, 'Why did I leave?' I said, 'Because everyone said that Patterson would have killed you!' That was the reputation Patterson had going into his fight with Archie. I was at the Moore-Patterson fight, and I have watched it on tape several times. Let me tell you, Archie's performance looked worse in real life than on tape, and I'm a big fan of Archie's."

After he returned to San Diego, Moore told the *San Diego Union*, "I'm tired of traveling and I want to rest. I haven't made any definite plans—maybe go up to the Ramona ranch each weekend to punch the bag a little. No boxing." When asked how long he thought he could continue fighting, Archie said, "Can't ever tell. My wife would like me to quit." As for his performance in

Chicago, Archie remarked, "I don't like alibis and I've usually stayed away from them, but I do feel I over-trained for the fight."

In *The Archie Moore Story*, Moore answered rumors that he had gone into the tank against Patterson. "To do so I would have had to have a reason, and the only reason would be that I bet money on Floyd. It takes a minimum of two to make a bet, and if the man I bet with will come forward, I'll be glad to meet him for the first time. If I had won the fight, I would have been the holder of the heavy and light heavyweight titles. I think it would have meant quite a few dollars in the Moore bank account. The odds weren't favorable for a 'killing,' and when you rule money out, there isn't another reason for me to go into the tank. After all, my share of that fight was $118,300.50."

The Patterson fight was devastating, but Archie was still the light heavyweight titlist, and, incredibly, his greatest feat in the ring was still ahead.

CHAPTER 14

Old Man River

Although many in the boxing community wrote off Archie, the veteran fighter still had faith in his own abilities. "I was still a world champion and I knew I had plenty of fight left in me, despite what people said about my gray hair," he said. Anybody else's hair would have turned even grayer with Doc Kearns as a neighbor, but Archie and Joan were more than a match for Kearns when Archie's de facto manager moved to San Diego and rented an apartment upstairs from the Moores. Recalls Joan: "Doc was slick, but we hit it off right away. He tried to negotiate a lower price on a monthly rental agreement with me. I didn't budge, and Doc respected me for it. I told Doc how much we charged and that his wheeling and dealing tactics wouldn't fly with me. He laughed and paid the amount. Although Doc was sly, he was a sweet old man, too. You always knew when Doc was coming—the aroma of toilet water usually preceded him."

Archie enjoyed his six-month respite from boxing. A lot of time was spent in the basement shooting pool with Kearns and mapping out their next move. Moore also enjoyed playing host.

Recalled Joan, "Archie used to throw huge picnics in the back yard and invite friends and media members. He would either have food catered in or cook his own fried chicken. He used to think his fried chicken was the best thing going. He loved to entertain and fill the reporters' heads full of quotes. He was a comedian and he didn't even really know it." Of course, along with the picnics came the pounds. Archie's weight again skyrocketed to over 200.

The National Boxing Association was after Moore to risk his light heavyweight title and imposed a mandatory title defense date of June 7, 1957. If Archie did not comply, he risked being stripped of the belt. He took the chance and instead signed for a lucrative two-bout series in Germany arranged by Kearns.

Just before leaving, Moore learned that Joan was pregnant. That welcome news was undermined when Archie received word that his friend Sandy Saddler's career was in jeopardy after an automobile accident. The taxi that the featherweight champion was riding in had been sideswiped, and Saddler suffered a severe concussion. Saddler was bedridden for three weeks, and it was disclosed that he was in danger of going blind from his injury. Saddler didn't want to retire, but medical experts insisted the risk of boxing was too high. Saddler and Moore had kept in contact since their days together in Argentina. Before leaving for Germany, Archie contacted Saddler, offering to help in any way.

Saxophonist Lucky Thompson, who acted as Moore's cornerman and planned to tour Europe after Archie's fights, accompanied Archie overseas. Just 12 years after World War II, Germany's renaissance was impressive, and the abundance of restaurants was a constant distraction to the champion. As for the natives' treatment of him, Moore saw only "sweetness and light. They treated me as a champion and welcome visitor."

His first opponent was 27-year-old Hagan butcher Hans Kalbfell, a veteran of only 17 fights. While their fight held no surprises (Moore breezed to a 10-round decision), there were plenty of raised eyebrows at the April 30 weigh-in when Archie scaled a whopping 206 pounds. He had agreed to defend his title against Tony Anthony in just five weeks, and although Archie insisted that "bringing down my weight to the 175 pound limit is very easy for me," and said it would take just "a few weeks," rumors of an eventual title suspension swirled.

Archie easily outpointed Kalbfell over 10 rounds. *The Boxing News* reported that "Moore recently signed a 50-day contract with German promoter Willy Knorzer, and is obviously cashing in on his reputation and the fact that he is still a world's champion. And the opponents that are being suggested for him are just not in Moore's class.

"To start with, he outpointed Hans Kalbfell, who had had only 17 bouts. This could be rated as an 'exhibition,' not a genuine contest. Kalbfell was down twice, and Moore seemed very sorry about this. In fact, Archie rarely opened up, but was content to treat the crowd to a display of the 'finer arts' and looked as if he could have stopped his man any time he wanted to."

The day following the May 1, 1956, bout against Kalbfell, the National Boxing Association notified Archie again that he faced suspension and forfeiture of his title if he failed to defend it by June 7. A telegram containing the warning was sent to Archie by NBA president Floyd Stevens.

The National Boxing Association was adamant about the June 7 date with Tony Anthony in Detroit. President Stevens had met with Jim Norris of the International Boxing Club, Anthony's manager and Doc Kearns. After a lengthy discussion, Stevens wired Archie in Germany requesting a response within three days about the Anthony fight.

"Look at me," stated Moore the day after the Kalbfell fight. "I'm 30 pounds overweight. You know nobody wants to see me in a title fight in this shape. If I keep working hard and they give me time to train, I may be ready in a month."

Three days later, Archie pulled the plug altogether on the June 7 bout and was promptly suspended by the NBA. Archie wrote to Jack Murphy at the *San Diego Union*, "I'll comb the hinterlands until I'm ready to come back."

Archie signed to fight Belgian heavyweight champion Alain Cherville in Stuttgart, Germany, on June 2. With his world title in limbo, Archie focused on a strict training and weight-loss regimen and in four weeks dropped 20 pounds, scaling 186 for Cherville. The Belgian champion put up a game effort but was stopped in the sixth round at the Exhibition Hall Arena. A left hook to the body dropped Cherville with seconds left in the round. The bell rang during the referee's count, but Cherville's handlers threw in the towel between rounds.

The next day, Moore returned to San Diego to iron out his difficulties with the NBA. He insisted on a $100,000 guarantee to defend against Anthon, and noted, "They gave me a six-month waiver when I fought Floyd Patterson for the heavyweight title. At that rate I still have six months to go." NBA honcho Stevens, he said, "has no right to deprive me of my livelihood. As for the fight in Detroit, Stevens wanted me to sign a blank contract with no money or no opponent listed. Now, he's a businessman. He should know I wouldn't sign under those terms. In fact, he had a deputy there to handle the matter. He didn't appear."

Looking back, Archie recalled, "I had to wait over five years as the top contender for my crack at the title. When I finally received it, we had to pay Maxim $100,000. I had defended my title against highly rated contenders but not for big money. ...Is it unreasonable that I wanted a guaranteed large purse in the twilight of my career? I almost put together a fight with middleweight champion Sugar Ray Robinson that would have generated some revenue."

As for the suspension itself, it didn't overly concern the champion. "I was never worried. Why would they have taken my title? No one else in the light heavyweight ranks had my box office potential. It would have been a bad business decision for the NBA to strip my title, so I relaxed for a few weeks at home while they came to their senses."

Archie finally signed to defend his title on September 20, 1957 in Los Angeles against Tony Anthony. He was guaranteed a handsome $90,000 for the title defense. Archie also figured the fall date would give him enough time to come down to the light heavyweight limit.

Anthony's trainer, Ernie Braca, once trained Sugar Ray Robinson and openly predicted a knockout for his charge. Twenty-two-year old Anthony had a fair punch but a suspect chin. He had been stopped five times, and in his last fight had been held to a draw by Yvon Durelle. Braca alibied that Anthony had the flu against Durelle and should have postponed the fight, and noted that his boxer, who'd only recently moved up to 175 pounds, had never lost to a light heavyweight.

Archie's training camp was plagued from the outset. A month before the bout, Joan went into premature labor and spent 25 hours in Sharp Hospital. The scare forced Archie to commute daily between home and training camp. A week later, with the fight just 21 days off, Moore's weight struggles caused a big public flap. Noted Jack Murphy in the *San Diego Union*, "With the fight only three weeks away, the champion's struggle with the scales promises to become one of September's liveliest issues.

"The California Athletic Commission already is becoming apprehensive about Moore's plumpness at this late date, and Clayton Frye, an inspector for the commission, plans a personal investigation in the near future.

"Frye has even warned that he'll call off the fight if Moore doesn't buckle down to serious calorie counting. But the inspector, a mild man at best, is in for the fight of his life if he tries to force Moore onto the scales before the official weigh in on September 20. Childe Arch will give him more arguments than a Philadelphia lawyer. By the time Moore finishes his oration, Frye probably will be ready to believe the old champ will enter the ring as a flyweight."

Archie had moved his training quarters to "The Whistle Stop," a second training camp owned by Moore and used by amateur boxers. First thing in the morning, he and some amateurs took a four-mile run through the hills. Hiawatha Grey was back to lead the camp; Cheerful Norman had been dismissed after a dispute following the Patterson bout. Charley Johnston, although still under contract, was not permitted in camp.

Eleven days before the fight, Joan gave birth to the couple's first child. Rena Marie Moore weighed in at almost six pounds. But Archie had precious little time to spend with his wife and healthy new daughter. He was having his own labor pains trying to get down to 175 and pleaded with promoters to postpone the fight two weeks. The answer was no.

Jack Murphy openly rooted for his friend in his column the day before the fight. "I've been wrong on Moore twice [when he lost to Marciano and Patterson] and I'll be wrong again tomorrow night if he drops this one to Anthony. I like Moore by a knockout, probably within 10 rounds, because his extraordinary skill and experience should offset Anthony's speed and youth.

"Anthony is dangerous and deserving of much respect. But I've been unable to convince myself that he's a fighter of the caliber of Marciano or Patterson.

"Moore has described himself as the most powerful man ever to fight as a light heavyweight. The description is probably accurate. In addition, he appears in superb condition and I've never seen him work harder in the gym. The champion has been driving and punishing himself with a zeal that would startle his former trainer, Cheerful Norman.

"It's preposterous, in a way, to place so much confidence in a middle-aged athlete who admits to 40 years and probably gives himself the best of the bargain. But this, surely, is one of the most remarkable men in the history of boxing.

"When the old ones go, they go very quickly. It's quite possible Anthony—young, quick, and eager—will tip Moore into oblivion tomorrow night.

"But I'll have to see it to believe it. Call it stupidity, call it a weakness. But I can't resist picking my favorite fighter one more time.

"Have luck, Childe Arch."

Archie knew if he lost he would be finished as a boxing attraction. If not for the title he held, he would've already been thumbed out of the ring, even in his home state. The California boxing commission had waived its 38-year-old age limit for the bout.

According to one reporter, that wasn't the only favor granted the Mongoose. "It's strange," wrote Dick Lausie, "how Sugar Ray Robinson and Archie Moore can get away with anything they want to. The plan to weigh in at 10 o'clock, not noon, is an out-and-out attempt to make things easy for Archie the Balloon. He'll have all day to recover from starving."

Archie sure didn't catch any breaks on the scale. It took him six tries to make 175, and to get off the final quarter-pound he had to do some laps around the arena and step on the scale completely naked. It didn't help when Ernie Braca informed the California Boxing Commission that he didn't mind if Anthony won the title by forfeit.

Writer Mel Durslag of the *Los Angeles Herald-Examiner* remembered, "Archie was a great spoofer. He loved to create mystique. He did it on his age, his weight, his diet, etc. He was a writer's dream. There was no shortage of stuff with him. Sometimes the suspense on whether he made the weight superseded the fight itself, as in the Tony Anthony bout."

Anthony entered the Olympic Auditorium ring oozing confidence. He had trained daily at the Ocean Park Arena near Los Angeles. Hundreds of fans turned out to watch him work out. Anthony was also in great demand for personal appearances. A local automobile dealer gave him a new sports car to drive to and from the gym and said it was his to keep if Anthony won the title. "Just start getting the papers ready," the challenger said, "because this is the last you are going to see of this car."

Anthony was in the driver's seat for the first three rounds of the fight, throwing a high volume of punches. Moore managed to slip or pick off most, but at the end of the third he took a low shot that made him angry. Referee Mushy Callahan had to separate them after the bell. Archie flashed a lethal stare that drew a reaction from the crowd. From then on the Old Mongoose was in charge.

Over the next two rounds, ringsiders could hear the champion urge Anthony to fight. He tried, but Moore toyed with him.

The end was near as Moore punched Anthony from corner to corner in the sixth. "He must have hit Anthony 20 times as Tony went from one neutral corner to his own and then slid on down the ring ropes," reported *The Los Angeles Times*.

"Finally Anthony was beaten into a stooped position and he keeled over backward on the seat of his pants and rolled over. Timekeeper Jack Smith got to six as the bell sounded and prolonged the match."

Tony not only answered the bell for the seventh, but even took the fight to the champion. Moore avoided the desperate rush and countered with a solid body punch that sent Anthony into retreat. A powerful right-hand dumped the challenger to the canvas for the last time.

"California's most famous fugitive from a rocking chair and carpet slippers put the crusher on 22-year-old Tony after 2 minutes 29 seconds of the seventh," said the *Los Angeles Times*.

"Moore, who claims to be under 41 and more likely is in his mid-40s, thus successfully defended the title he won in 1952 for the sixth time."

After the fight, Ernie Braca fumed that "Moore talked his way to victory." Archie's priceless reply: "Please remind Mr. Braca that I mixed a few punches into the conversation."

After visiting Anthony in his dressing room to comfort the weeping challenger and encourage him to keep fighting, Moore met the press. Asked how long he could continue boxing, Archie said, "Maybe eight or 10 more years, who knows? If this secret diet still brings me down to 175, I'll keep going." His plans included a title defense against Canadian Yvon Durelle, but not until another tour of South America. Moore also expressed excitement over the addition of Rena to the family and said he hoped to spend some time at home before returning to action.

Archie also completed his dream house on the property that had once housed his Chicken Shack restaurant. Joan's father, a mason, flew in from New York to direct the project. The end result was a beautiful red brick ranch-style home complete with a swimming pool shaped like a boxing glove. Next to the pool was a cabana. A separate building contained Archie's clubhouse and music studio. Surrounding everything was a traditional white picket fence. The bathrooms contained gold-plated faucets. The basement den had a huge picture window that looked out to the mountains. Aunt Willie Pearl lived in a small cottage behind the main building.

Moore signed for a three-fight series in the Pacific Northwest. On Halloween of 1957, Archie, scaling 192 pounds, stopped Bob Mitchell in Vancouver, B.C. A week later in Seattle, Archie decisioned Eddie Cotton. Next stop: Portland, where he halted Roger Rischer. "I was again fighting my way into shape," Archie said. "If I had only fought twice a year, I would be training more than fighting, which requires the services of sparring partners. By fighting so frequently, I was the one getting paid to get back in shape."

After spending the holidays at home, Archie, Joan and Rena jetted off to Brazil. When Archie fought Brazilian titleholder Luis Ignacio in Sao Paulo, they drew the largest crowd, estimated at 18,000, to ever see a bout in Brazil.

"Ignacio put up a good fight, but he had no answer to Moore's ring knowledge," reported the *New York Times*. "The big surprise was that Ignacio was able to stay the 10 rounds with the champion."

Two weeks later, Archie fought in Rio de Janeiro against Portuguese champion Julio Neves and stopped him in the third round. After enjoying Brazil for another week, Archie and family returned to San Diego. There, Archie signed to fight Bert Whitehurst on March 3, 1958, in San Bernardino, California.

Archie scaled 198 pounds for the bout with one-time KO victim Whitehurst. He was looking for another shot at Patterson for the heavyweight title. Given his advanced age—Moore told the *San Bernardino Evening-Telegram* he was 47—few considered Archie would ever be able to train down to the light heavyweight limit. But all Moore knew for sure was that he wasn't too old to keep learning. "You know why I can continue on while others fade away? I'll explain why. I am a man who has more faith in himself than others...maybe more pride, too, but pride has an egotistical sound and I'm not a proud man. Every day I do something to improve my skill of the game, whether it is refining an old move or mastering a new one. I never stop learning, and I realize age is just a number."

He had to call on all his resources to stop the much-improved Whitehurst in the tenth round before the largest paid crowd to ever witness a fight in San Bernardino. Whitehurst was actually ahead on one of the scorecards entering the final round. Archie turned up his pace and stopped Whitehurst with a right cross.

Seated at ringside was Henry Armstrong, who was in southern California promoting his autobiography. The old friends headed to San Diego to spend a few days at Moore's home. The only boxer to ever hold three world titles simultaneously had been in retirement for 13 years and was now an ordained Baptist minister. In San Diego, Armstrong paid Jack Murphy a visit at the *San Diego Union*. When Murphy prodded Armstrong on the matter of his host's true age, Armstrong said, "I don't like to say anything about that; after all, I just came from his house." But then Hammerin' Hank told Murphy, "Archie is 45. We're the same age. But he isn't going to admit it. When I was at his house, he reminded me that he was 20 in 1937. If that's the way he wants it, okay, I didn't say nothing."

A week after chilling Whitehurst, Moore was in Vancouver against Bob Albright. According to the record books, the KO win over Albright tied Moore with Young Stribling on the all-time knockout list with 126.

Archie signed to fight Willie Besmanoff in Louisville, Kentucky. Besmanoff gave him a race, providing the Ancient One with 10 competitive rounds. Archie's hand was raised in victory, but he looked overweight and reportedly had only sparred two rounds in training. Among those disapproving of his designs on another shot at Patterson was ex-champion Joe Louis. Joe said that Archie looked so bad the first time against Patterson that he didn't deserve another crack.

Louis was a personal friend, but his comments touched a nerve in Moore. "I suppose that Louis looked good in his first fight

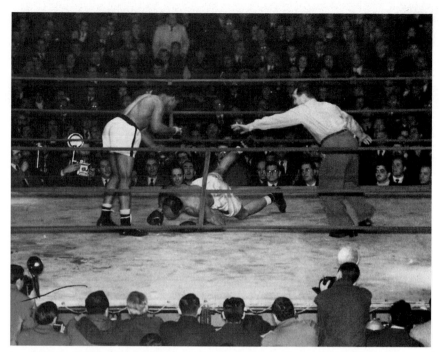

In a 1951 bout at Luna Park Stadium in Buenos Aires, Archie scored a first-round knockout over Alberto Lovell. Photo courtesy of Archie Moore family

Moore poses for a photo with controversial Argentine dictator Juan Peron, standing next to Moore. Also in the photo is featherweight Sandy Saddler, on the right, who accompanied Moore to Argentina. Photo courtesy of Archie Moore family

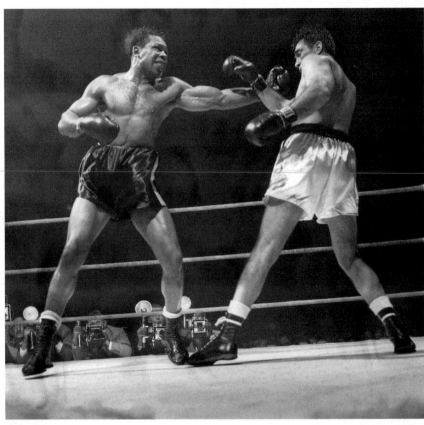

Moore jabs at light heavyweight champion Joey Maxim in the third round of their 1952 15-round championship battle in St. Louis. Moore claimed the title via a unanimous decision. AP/WWP

Moore shakes hands with challenger Bobo Olson, world middleweight titlist, following the weigh-in for their 1955 bout. Notice each fighter's preference in footwear. AP/WWP

Archie shoots pool in his basement with his longtime manager, the cunning "Doc" Kearns. Photo courtesy of Archie Moore family

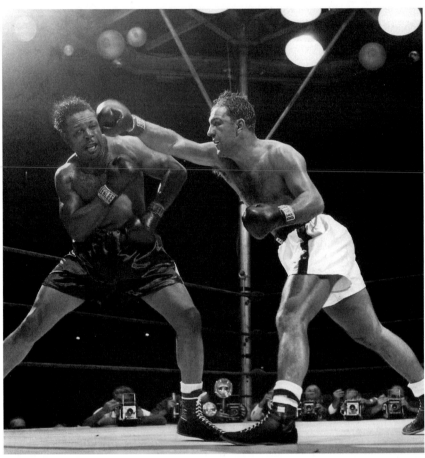

Archie lasted nine rounds in his epic 1955 battle against heavyweight champion Rocky Marciano after sending the champ to the canvas in the second frame. It was Marciano's final bout. AP/WWP

Moore, a self-proclaimed "explorer of food," bulks up for his 1956 heavyweight title match against Floyd Patterson. AP/WWP

Archie, front and center, photographed outside the famed Argentine fight arena, Luna Park Stadium, in Buenos Aires, Argentina with members of the local boxing scene. Photo courtesy of Archie Moore family

Moore left training camp prior to defending his title against Tony Anthony in 1957 to bring his wife, Joan, and newborn daughter, Rena, home from the hospital. AP/WWP

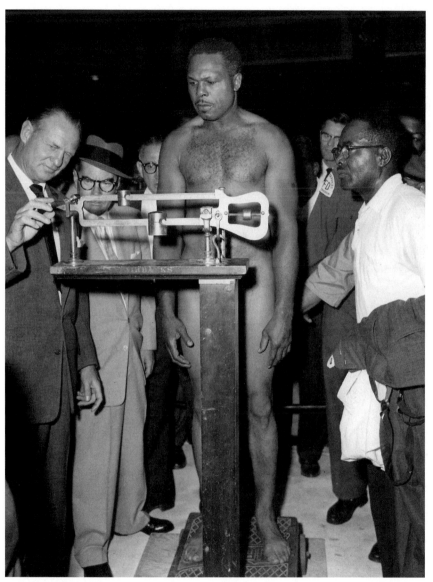

At times, Archie's battle with the scale stirred more press than the actual bout. Here, completely naked, Moore barely makes the 175-pound limit in defense of his title against Tony Anthony in 1957. AP/WWP

A sharp-dressed Archie Moore flashes a fist and a smile with wife Joan from ringside at the 1957 Sugar Ray Robinson vs. Carmen Basilio fight. AP/WWP

Moore battles challenger Yvon Durelle in the early rounds of the spirited 1958 brawl. AP/WWP

Archie survived several near knockouts before finally sending challenger Yvon Durelle down for the count in round eleven of their classic war in 1958. AP/WWP

Archie starring as Jim the runaway slave in *The Adventures of Huckleberry Finn.* AP/WWP

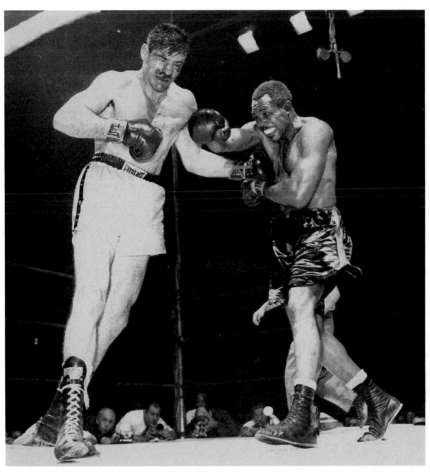

A straight right-hand buckles the knees of bloodied challenger Guilio Rinaldi in the 12th round of their 1961 bout, held at New York's Madison Square Garden. AP/WWP

A young Muhammad Ali, then known as Cassius Clay, pictured outside Archie's home with Moore's daughters, J'Marie on the left and Rena on the right. Ali briefly trained under Moore at the beginning of his professional boxing career.

Photo courtesy of Archie Moore family

The end of a Hall of Fame career draws near: Moore is stopped by former pupil Muhammad Ali (then Cassius Clay) in the fourth round of their 1962 bout. Moore was 26 years older than Ali, whose professional career was just getting underway. AP/WWP

From left to right, Moore's protégé George Foreman, Moore, close friend Sandy Saddler, and Smokin' Joe Frazier photographed in December 1972. Moore led Foreman to victory over Frazier on January 22, 1973, in Kingston, Jamaica, for the world's heavyweight title. AP/WWP

Daughters Rena, left, and J'Marie, right, playfully pull at their father's cheeks.
Photo courtesy of Archie Moore family

Archie with his arm around his Auntie Willie, the special woman who raised Archie from age three. Photo courtesy of Archie Moore family

An elderly Moore sporting his favorite knit beanie. Archie was inducted into the International Boxing Hall of Fame's first class in 1990. Patricia A. Orr/Fightphotos.com

against Schmeling [Schmeling won by knockout in the twelfth round]," Archie said. "For that matter, Joe wasn't the greatest in his fight with Marciano. [Marciano stopped him in eight.] I don't have any quarrel with Louis, but why should he be taking shots at me? Remember this: Joe is only a couple of years older than me, but he folded up quite a while ago. I'm still going. I've outlasted him and I don't have to apologize for my record. When he was going great I was only a middleweight. Who did he fight? Remember his 'Bum of the Month' campaign?

"The difference between Louis and me is that he fought a bum a month and I fought a bum a week, so to speak."

Archie's match against granite-jawed Howard King was his first appearance in a San Diego ring in over two years. Family life had mellowed the champion. Archie replaced his Jaguar, valued at about $30,000, with a beat-up pickup truck worth under $60.

Howard King tried to hype the bout as a grudge match, but Moore took the elder statesman's role, saying, "I don't dislike King, but that doesn't mean I'll vote for him if he runs for governor. This young man should be reminded that I stand on the threshold of the all-time knockout record. I mean to acquire sole possession of that record at King's expense."

But the knockout title would have to be claimed another day, as Archie settled for a 10-round decision. Nine days later, he returned to action against Charlie Norkus in San Francisco. Norkus was a heavyweight of modest credentials who had been away from the sport for a few years and lost 50 pounds preparing for Moore. If Archie was envious, he hid it from Jack Fiske of the *San Francisco Chronicle*. "I got to keep on winning and eventually I'll have to get Patterson again. I'm not too interested in losing weight now because I have a heavyweight title fight, not a light heavyweight bout in mind right now."

The knockout record was put off yet again as Moore coasted to a unanimous decision win over Norkus. Archie won every round but could not halt the defensive-minded Norkus. It was not an impressive victory, and once again the press criticized Moore's pudgy physique and even his boxing trunks. Fiske wrote the trunks looked baggy and ludicrous with a "slit" in the middle. Archie filed a prompt correction: "Man, don't call that vent a slit! I like to wear my trunks loose for comfort. After fooling around with sports cars I learned you need air conditioning, so I designed those vents myself. They're for air."

Moore received another crack at the stout chin of Howard King, and this time bounced the durable journeyman off the canvas three times en route to a unanimous decision win on June 9 in Sacramento. Two months later, in Reno, King held Archie to a draw when Moore was impeded by a hand injury and the flu.

In the meantime, heavyweight champion Floyd Patterson was knocked out in three rounds by Ingemar Johansson. There would be a rematch, keeping Archie's heavyweight title ambitions in limbo. The NBA was also after Moore to defend his light heavyweight title.

On the managerial front, as soon as their contract officially expired in July of 1958, Charley Johnston was history. Commented Archie: "If it weren't for fight managers, a lot of fighters would have been millionaires. I have emancipated myself from the pit of boxing, and I am no longer tied down by managers." Of course, Doc Kearns remained on the payroll as an adviser, but only on a fight-to-fight basis.

CHAPTER 15

A Classic: Moore-Durelle

After 12 consecutive non-title fights for small money, Archie was again forced to defend his crown or risk being stripped. Moore's insistence on a guarantee of a $100,000 purse seemed exorbitant, but after lengthy negotiations and a bit of salesmanship, Archie closed the deal for a defense in Canada against Yvon Durelle.

When it was reported that the champion had "fessed up to being almost 50, the 30-year-old Durelle couldn't believe his good fortune. "Winning the championship from this ancient type will be like falling out of a boat," he said. "Nearly 50! Who would have believed it? Why, he might be my grandfather!"

But then Ageless Archie issued a clarification. The sportswriter interviewing him, he said, "wouldn't believe I was 39, so I told him I was 49. I like long conversations, and that one would have ended if I hadn't kept it going."

Durelle was a strong, brawling fighter compared by some to Rocky Marciano. A native of Baie Ste. Anne, New Brunswick, Canada, where he was born on October 14, 1928, Yvon had been a fisherman from the age of 10. Even working 18-hour days at sea, Durelle had difficulty making ends meet and boxed professionally for added income. That didn't leave much time for training, and *Sports Illustrated* suggested that "when Durelle throws a hook, it is more likely to catch a haddock than an experienced boxer."

Nevertheless, the Fighting Fisherman had netted 79 victories in 98 bouts. He was champion of Canada and the British Empire, and the number-three-ranked contender in the world. Like Archie, Durelle had his problems staying within range of 175 pounds. In his autobiography, *The Fighting Fisherman*, Durelle said, "I knew when I fought Moore I couldn't go 15 rounds even shadowboxing. I'm a big-boned guy, and to get down to 175 pounds I didn't have much to work with. I'd get tired fast. I felt weak all the time. It wasn't natural because days after a fight I'd be up over 200 pounds. My total food for the days in training were two eggs and two toasts, or one egg if I hadn't worked enough off."

"One time," noted Durelle, "in a restaurant I was so hungry that I grabbed food off some guy's plate as I was walking by. I said, 'My friend, I'm sorry, but I got to eat, too.' I never saw the guy before in my life. He just looked at me. It was a piece of meat and I ran out on the street and wolfed it down. I was so starved I had to do something. You go out of your head, you know."

Oddly enough, for once Archie did not have difficulty making weight. He phoned Jack Murphy at the *The San Diego Union* with the good news: "I'm down to 175 and I look sort of funny. It's not that I'm skinny, but I just don't look the way I should."

Some grand new threads fixed that. Moore was the picture of elegance at the weigh-in ceremony, swinging a silver-headed cane and decked out in a long, plush camel's hair coat over a shawl-collared tuxedo with matching Homburg hat. The valet attending Archie was also a nice touch. Durelle, meanwhile, was also resplendent in work pants, rubber boots, an old knit sweater and worn-out felt hat. Irrepressible Archie just couldn't help himself. Leaning over, he inquired of the challenger, "Who is your tailor?" Durelle's manager had to step between them to keep the contest from getting underway prematurely.

Later, Moore defended the propriety of his query on the grounds that, "I wanted to give boxing a touch of class. The game could use some dignity. Durelle showed up dressed like a farmer!"

For two guys known to be hard on a scale, both Moore and Durelle tipped the Fairbanks well under the light heavyweight limit this time. Archie weighed 173 1/2, Durelle 172. It was so unusual that rumors circulated that the scales were tampered with. It all made for good press, and Archie further fanned the flames by penning his analysis of the impending battle:

"I'm aware that many observers tend to regard Durelle as just a rough club fighter with no style or class. I fought another fellow who fit this description—a fellow named Rocky Marciano, to be specific. Rocky gave the impression of being the crudest of the crude in action, but you've got to admit he was pretty successful not only against me but everybody else he fought. Nobody ever beat the guy. Durelle is the same kind of fighter; he has amazing recuperative powers and you only have to look at his past performances to know that he'll get up on you. He'll get up as long as he can. The guy is like one of those pit bulldogs that are bred to fight to the death. He never steps back.

"Now it's no secret that I'm less than a decade away from the half-century mark, a whole lot less than I like to think about. I've developed my style to conserve energy. For every step I take in the ring I try to make the other fellow take a dozen. I have been pretty successful, if I do say so myself, in conning most of my opponents into falling for my system.

"Strangely enough, it's easier for me to fight the orthodox fighters like Harold Johnson and Tony Anthony. They have more poise and boxing ability than a Marciano or a Durelle, but their ring knowledge is the very thing that helps me beat them. I can feint them, get them trying to anticipate me. Marciano didn't know enough boxing to know what a feint was; he never tried to outguess you—he just kept trying to knock your brains out. If he missed with one punch, he just threw another. Physically and mentally he was like an animal once the bell sounded.

"Durelle has the same system, and if he continues too long in boxing he'll probably get hurt. But the important thing to consider, from my point of view, is the fact that he's still in his prime. I expect the hardest kind of fight when we meet. I know that I'll have to be in top shape because this Canadian bull will take a lot of killing. He'll be after me from the opening bell, and I expect it will take more rounds to weaken him than will be comfortable for me. It'll be like a bullfight, remarkably so. I'll have to hit him with some terrific shots to soften him up.

"A fighter like Yvon is out only when the referee counts him out. You can't knock him out with a typewriter or a verbal opinion. December 10 could be the roughest night of my seven-year reign as 175-pound king.

As for Durelle, he was less verbose and put it in terms he knew best: "I know right now what I'll do. I'll go right after him from the start. I'll wear him down. About the seventh round Moore is going to slow down, and I'll still be throwing. If Moore goes into that crab-like shell, being a fisherman I know quite a bit about handling shellfish."

It was the first title bout televised from another country into the United States. But Archie had his mind on a different historical aspect: "Going into my bout with Durelle, the knockout record was given considerable attention. My last four victories had been by decision. I wanted to break the record in a big fight. I went into the Durelle fight thinking knockout."

Always the entrepreneur, Archie jumped into the ring and immediately turned his back to the television cameras. Remembers friend Melvin Durslag, "Archie was always looking for a business angle. For the Durelle bout he had received a sizable payment to display 'Nat Rosenburg's Diamond Palace, San Diego,' on the back of his robe. As soon as Archie jumped into the ring, he turned his back to the cameras, giving Nat Rosenburg his money's worth."

Nobody expected the bout to begin the way it did.

A three-to-one underdog, Durelle caught Moore cold with a wild right a minute into the first round at the Montreal Forum. Archie froze, and then fell flat on the canvas. It seemed impossible for him to beat the count of referee Jack Sharkey, the former world heavyweight champion.

Los Angeles sports writer Budd Furillo recalled, "When Archie went down, I thought he was dead. I still don't know how he ever got up. That was the greatest fight I ever saw."

Later, Moore recollected, "The first thing I heard was the number five and I saw Jack Sharkey's big mouth as he leaned over me, counting. I knew I had to get to my feet. I felt as if the top of my head was blown off. I walked the street of dreams. Whether there was a delay in the count or not I don't know—I was out of it. When I heard the count I rolled to one knee, and I thought I was up at nine. I was surprised a man my weight could hit so hard."

Having barely made it up in time, Archie was beswarmed by the anxious Durelle, throwing nothing but haymakers. As Archie staggered about, a half-punch, half-push sent him back to the canvas. Sharkey ruled it a slip, but then Durelle was all over Moore again and sent the champion down with a punishing right. Once again, Archie somehow staggered to his feet before Sharkey reached double digits, and then managed to finish the round afoot.

In the corner, Kearns splashed ice water all over Archie to shock him back to life. It worked. Moore spent the next round jabbing and staying out of Durelle's range. Surprisingly, it wasn't that difficult, since Yvon was not fighting as aggressively as he had in round one.

But the Canadian shifted back into high gear in the third, landing a higher percentage of punches than the still defense-minded champion.

In the fourth, Archie started to take charge, connecting with solid jabs and left hooks when Durelle marched in. "I needed to start landing some power shots to keep that bull off of me," he recalled later. But in the next round the bull again hit the bull's-eye. Moore came out moving and circling, and Yvon chased him into the ropes and landed a thunderous right-hand that dumped the champion to the canvas. Hurt even more than he was in the first round, Archie still managed to climb to his feet by the count of six. But there were two minutes still remaining in the round, and Durelle pounded him all over the ring. The champion valiantly traded punches, but was on the short end of every exchange. Although nearly out, Moore landed a solid right seconds before the bell. That looked like his final gasp.

That's when Kearns's ingenuity turned things around in Moore's corner. By having Moore stand and wave at his wife, whom Archie was too befogged to even see, it appeared that the champion was gaily signaling to his opponent in the opposite corner that this was the most fun he'd had in ages. The deflating effect on poor Durelle was instant and obvious.

With the recovered Sandy Saddler screaming encouragement from ringside, Moore opened the next round jabbing and moving. Hitting Archie was exhausting work, and Durelle had trouble keeping up. A Moore right sent him down for the first time. Yvon rose at the count of two, but the fisherman's boat was taking on water big-time.

Over the next two rounds, Durelle missed with most of his punches as Archie moved, slipped, and blocked before countering. In the tenth, he dropped Durelle for a seven-count seconds before the bell. Durelle was all but finished after the round, as he recalled in his autobiography. "I just wanted to quit right there. My stomach was paining like hell. We're both tired, but I'm too tired. I was hit good. I wasn't really hurt until this round.

"A fight is momentum. I've seen myself so tired I could hardly stand up, but when I saw the other guy more tired it gave me new strength...It's in your mind. It's your mind and your will that gets beat more than your body. I give Moore credit; he had guts, stamina. But I got no help at the end of the tenth. When I went back to my corner nobody did nothing for me. For 30 seconds nobody touched me. The chair was late to come...They gave up on me. When your'e hit on the head there's a big pressure in your head. You've got to relieve that pressure. But all they gave me was a shot of brandy and orange juice; that's all they had. That was my medicine. You see it on the film. I'm standing up waiting for my chair, and they're all running around but nobody does nothing for me, I was all alone there for 30 seconds. Then a shot of brandy. When I came out the pressure was still in my head."

At the bell for round 11, Archie raced off his stool and floored Durelle again. The brave challenger got up, but he was bleeding from the nose and the mouth and another onslaught from Archie put him down for keeps, ending what Kearns would proclaim, with justification, "The greatest [fight] since Dempsey knocked out Firpo."

After the fight, Archie phoned Jack Murphy in San Diego. "I'm glad I gave'em a good show," he said. "At my age and at this stage in the game I just had to win. A man has got to have drive, he's got to have determination to keep going.

"I had to win for so many reasons. I wasn't fighting just for myself, but for a lot of other people. When I was on the floor I thought about my wife, Joan, my daughter, Rena, and the baby we're expecting in February.

"Durelle knocked me down, and I've never heard so many people yelling in my life. I thought, 'Why don't those Canadians be quiet so I can hear the count?'

"The Canadians are real fans, and Durelle is a dangerous fighter. I underestimated his punch. He hits awful hard. I was lying there and I said to myself, 'This is no place to be resting. I'd better get up and get with it.' Every time I looked up, I looked into Jack Sharkey's face. I got tired of looking at that man.

"Durelle is one of the top light heavyweights I have ever fought. I have to feel sorry he lost. But of course I have to look out for myself."

The following day Archie headed to downtown Montreal to the hot baths to soak his bruises. On his way out of his hotel suite, Moore announced to reporters that he was no longer interested in pursuing Floyd Patterson, Ingemar Johansson or Sugar Ray Robinson now that he had found a suitable challenger in Durelle, who could draw a big gate in a rematch.

In his story the next day, Murphy put what happened in Montreal in its proper perspective: "The Mongoose observes a birthday tomorrow [pick a number between 42 and 49] and I can't think of a nicer present than the prestige he acquired in getting off the floor four times to flatten Durelle in the most exciting fight of the electronic age.

"This was a fight that did more for Childe Arch than any single event, or combinations of events, in his long varied career. Possibly Moore isn't even fully aware of what this enthralling show did for him.

"It was a fight that, for the first time, earned him the sympathy and affection of the public. Instead of bravado and bluster, they saw the more basic qualities of a great fighting heart and craftsmanship of the highest order.

"Moore's rousing battle came across with such emotional impact that a lot of people suddenly began thinking in terms of a demonstration to welcome him home. I don't know if the same thought has occurred to the mayor or the Chamber of Commerce, but it's a subject that deserves consideration and fast action."

After a detour to New York City so Archie could be introduced on *The Ed Sullivan Show*, the Moores were met at the San Diego airport by thousands of ecstatic fans. The mayor himself was on hand to join Moore in a parade through the city's downtown area. "People cheered and tossed confetti as if it was me who had been in outer space instead of that monkey," recalled Archie.

Almost 40 years later, a 1997 article in *The Ring* entitled "The Greatest Light Heavyweight Fight of All Time" featured the reminiscences of both combatants. Said Moore: "I thought to myself, 'I'd better keep from this guy or he's going to hurt me,' and then he hit me again and I thought he'd broken my head. I said to myself, 'Well, I guess this is the end for me, but I'm going to fight this son of a bitch, or I'll die fighting him if it comes to that.' I had really reckoned that I would die fighting this man. He should have followed up in that second round. He should have come out like he did in the first round, but he didn't. He hesitated…and I hit him first. I think it was all the fault of his manager. He told Yvon, 'This guy's a fox, he might be foolin' you.' He tried to pick me off instead of rushing me off my feet, and that gave me a little time to let the fog clear a little bit. As the fight progressed I gathered my senses, and when it was over, I knew it had been a great fight. I never get tired of watching that fight."

Recalled Durelle: "I remember every damn punch I threw in that fight, even the ones that missed. I don't even have to look at the film. They forget about a lot of championship fights after a few years, but everyone still remembers that fight. But I wish I could have won the world championship for my country."

While Moore basked in the acclaim that came his way after the Durelle fight—he was named "Fighter of the Year" by the International Boxing Writers—there was a dark cloud in the form of *The Ring's* selection of Ingemar Johansson as its "Fighter of the Year." Archie finished third behind Johansson and Sugar Ray Robinson.

At the time of the announcement, Archie was in Chicago for a personal appearance for the Woodstock Children's Home. Moore phoned sports editor Sid Ziff of the *Los Angeles Mirror News* to voice his disappointment at being passed over by "The Bible of Boxing." "I couldn't believe it when I heard Fleischer had named Johansson. It saddened me deeply because I realize that time is running out on me as an athlete. My age will put it beyond my reach in the future. Nothing I can ever do in the future will ever approach that effort. I don't see how [Fleischer] could take a novice like Johansson and rate him over me. This has been a heartbreaking blow to me." *The Ring's* selection of Moore-Durelle as "Fight of the Year" was of some consolation.

Another prominent award that Moore received was the Edward J. Neil Memorial Trophy, the boxing equivalent of the Pulitzer Prize awarded by the Boxing Writers Association. Archie flew to New York to accept the honor. It was one of the special moments of his life. But instead of going immediately into his speech, the champion requested consent to make an introduction. Then he asked Durelle, who was in the audience, to rise. "It takes two to make a great fight," said Moore. Until that moment, few in attendance knew Durelle was at the banquet.

A rematch was obligatory, of course, and as negotiations got under way Archie received a letter from *Sports Illustrated* writer

George Plimpton. Plimpton was known for his participatory journalism, and his proposal was to get in the ring with Moore in the cause of literature. Plimpton would train significantly and learn as much about the sport as possible in preparation, and, with luck, would live to regale his readers with a lively account of his brush with greatness.

The champion happily granted Plimpton's request, and the sparring session was scheduled for Stillman's gym in New York. Plimpton hooked up with trainer George Brown (introduced to him by Ernest Hemingway), quit smoking, read numerous "how-to" guides on boxing and worked out religiously. Brown taught him how to jab, and after a month of preparation judged that his protégé possessed "enough skills to take on 95 percent of the population."

The boxing fraternity, however, was reserving judgment. Max Baer, the former heavyweight champion, wrote Plimpton in a letter: "If you get belted and see three fighters through a haze, go after the one in the middle. That's what ruined me—going after the other two guys."

Archie's carefree attitude about the exhibition changed when he dined with Peter Maas, a journalist friend of Plimpton's. Maas told him, with a straight face, that Plimpton had once been an intercollegiate ring champion and possessed the skill and ambition to make the champ look like a chump.

By the time they entered the ring before a packed house at Stillman's, Archie was taking no chances. "Hey, Doc," he said to Kearns before they started, with Plimpton listening in, "you remember the guy who couldn't remember his name after we finished with him?…Just plumb banged that guy's name right out of his skull."

It was quickly apparent as the exhibition got under way that George Plimpton was no Yvon Durelle, and after bloodying the author's nose Archie fought like a candidate for the Nobel Peace Prize. Even so, George Brown cut the third and final round by a full minute as a favor to his man. When Plimpton remarked that the round had seemed short, Brown said, "I suppose you were preparing to finish him!"

Plimpton became an avid Archie Moore fan. They kept in touch, and Archie invited George to his house whenever the writer was on the west coast.

The birth of Archie's second daughter, Joan Marie, came on February 17, 1959, postponing a bout against Sterling "Dizzy" Davis in Odessa, Texas. Three more sons would follow: Hardy, D'Angelo and Anthony. Archie rescheduled the bout for March 9. April Fool's Day would have been more appropriate. Davis was a professional wrestler. Promoter Pat O'Dowdy guaranteed Archie $5,000 for the fight. Dizzy claimed to have had "about 25" previous fights wearing gloves, but his ring credentials were unverifiable and unenhanced by his fat, bald, 40-something appearance.

Texas boxing commissioner Sammy George instructed Archie to make a real fight of it, but even George Plimpton did better than the aptly named Dizzy. The self-described possessor of "the fastest, hardest right-hand in the world" never touched Archie. The referee stopped it in the third after Davis had been down three times and was cut over his left eye. The crowd of 1,700 didn't seem to mind; they were just proud to have someone of Moore's stature fighting in Odessa.

If Archie looked like Superman against the wrestler, that designation automatically belonged to the fellow in the opposite corner in Moore's next scheduled outing. Actor George Reeves played the "Man of Steel" in the popular weekly TV series, and as a publicity stunt, he and Moore were scheduled to box an exhibition. Like Plimpton, Reeves trained diligently, but on the morning of the exhibition, the 45-year-old actor took off for galaxies unknown via a bullet to his brain. Depending on which tabloid account you believe, he either killed himself or was murdered. None of it made sense to Archie, who called the whole episode "bizarre."

Meanwhile, Yvon Durelle kept busy by knocking out Teddy Burns in Maine. Then negotiations began for Moore-Durelle II. The rematch was slated for July 25, 1959, in Montreal. The terms: Archie was assured $175,000, Durelle was promised $15,000 plus 60 percent of the television money. But before the final terms were agreed to, Archie attempted to get crooner Frank Sinatra involved in the promotion. Explained Durelle in his autobiography: "During the winter months Chris Shaban [Durelle's manager] was involved in wrangling over arrangements for a second fight with Moore. In February he got a call from San Diego. It was Moore on the line. 'I'm in the bathtub, I've got a phone in here...Are you tied up with Eddie Quinn?'

"Shaban said, 'No, I'm not tied up with anybody.'

"'I think Frank Sinatra would like to put the fight on. If you're not signed with Quinn, I'll get a hold of Sinatra and see what we can do.'

"'Okay, you let me know,' replied Saban.

"About a week later Saban received a call from New York. He wouldn't say from whom—'I forget who it was'—but presumably it was someone with the International Boxing Club: 'Stay away from Sinatra. If he takes the money in at the gate he'll pay you. If he doesn't, you'll get nothing. He's in with the Mafia. They're the ones you'll have to deal with.'"

Eventually Sinatra and company were left out of the deal, but the fight did not come off without its share of problems. Rumors circulated that Kearns was trying to ink a deal with Durelle's team in case Archie lost the fight. Reports from Yvon's training camp had the challenger in top condition, suffering no weight difficulties. Moore's training at the Salt Mine, was on schedule until the champion suffered a foot injury that necessitated a postponement of the fight.

The Durelle camp charged that the foot injury was just a smokescreen to hide Moore's difficulty melting down to the division limit. By eating and drinking little and constantly sucking on lemons, the challenger was on target to hit 175 himself. But the postponement sent him back in the other direction, and when training resumed, Durelle hired one of the game's top trainers to whip him into shape.

Charley Goldman had been Rocky Marciano's trainer, and since Durelle was a crude brawler in the Rocky mode, maybe lightning would strike again. Goldman entered camp a month before the fight and attempted to improve Durelle's boxing skills, especially his left hand. Several people questioned whether it was possible to alter the challenger's style effectively in only a few weeks. But after several weeks of training, a second postponement was necessary after Joan Moore entered the hospital for emergency ear surgery.

Archie was unaffected by the delays and had no difficulty making the weight. It seemed as if the aging warrior got better with time despite rumors swirling that he was 50 years old for the second Durelle encounter.

A friend of Archie's named Bob Condon trained with Moore at the Salt Mines. When Condon returned to his home in New York before the fight, he told everyone that Archie would take Durelle out in the third round. "He knows exactly what he will do in round one, round two, and how he will finish Durelle in round three," said Condon.

The sequel to "The Brawl in Montreal" was held on August 12, 1959, at the Montreal Forum. One of the new members of Archie's entourage was comedian Redd Foxx. Foxx had known Moore since his youth in St. Louis. Redd even had his hair cut in the shape of a big "M" in honor of his friend. Advance tickets sales for the 12,500 seats equaled $94,000, a Canadian record. Prices ranged between $5 and $25. The fight was aired on ABC-TV in the States and blacked out in Canada.

Durelle protested when Jack Sharkey was named referee again. "Sharkey took his time counting over Moore every time I had him on the canvas in those first five rounds," he said. "And once he not only wiped off Archie's gloves when he got up but he came over and wiped off my gloves, stalling for time."

The second time around, Yvon was in an even better position to critique Sharkey's counting, as the Ancient One knocked Durelle down four times. Durelle was counted out with eight seconds left in the third round. Archie helped him up and gave him a hug. The plan Moore had confided to Condon worked to perfection.

Durelle fought on for a few years, but in the only other significant fight of his career he was stopped in the twelfth round by

Canadian heavyweight champion George Chuvalo. Yvon and Archie were a mutual admiration society ever after. "I think the world of him," Durelle told *The Ring* in 1997. "He's a real gentlemen and we respect each other." Likewise, said Archie. "I love Yvon Durelle like a childhood pal, a buddy. And as the years go by I can enjoy our great fights even more knowing that he's a healthy man who is in charge of his faculties and has the admiration of the people around him."

Before the second Durelle bout, rumors abounded that Doc Kearns was maneuvering behind the scenes to take over the Canadian's contract in case Durelle became champ. But with Archie still on the throne, Doc tried to match him with Ingemar Johansson for the heavyweight title. "I'm the youngest 78-year-old manager of all-time," he said. "And I plan on being around for a while."

As for the light heavyweight champion of the world, Archie was about to participate in another classic, but this match would not occur in the ring.

CHAPTER 16

Stripped of the World Title

While in training for the Durelle rematch, Archie heard from Hollywood producer Sam Goldwyn Jr. about a movie Goldwyn planned to make of the Mark Twain novel *The Adventures of Huckleberry Finn*. Goldwyn wondered whether Moore would be interested in reading for the part of Jim the runaway slave. After reviewing the proposed script, Archie agreed to take on the role, although Joan expressed some trepidation. "At first I was concerned about Archie's character of Jim," she said. "I was afraid Archie might be criticized for playing a slave. At that time, few African Americans were given non-stereotypical parts. My brother-in-law at the time, actor Sidney Poitier, was an exception."

Archie consulted the future Academy Award-winning actor himself about the project and later recalled in *Ebony* how Poitier helped prepare him for the part. "Sidney told me that I could play this role very easily and even offered to give me some pointers on how to handle some of the more delicate lines. One day, without telling Sidney that I was merely acting, I cited to him the lines of a sequence in the film. In this sequence, Jim breaks down, confessing to Huck that once he slapped his little daughter for disobeying an order before discovering that she could not have heard his order because she was deaf from scarlet fever. Since I substituted my real daughter's name for Elizabeth, the name in the script, Sidney thought that I was actually confessing to something that I had done in real life and began to cry. After I told him that I was only fooling, he laughed and through his tears said, 'My God, Archie, don't ever do that again.'"

Moore got his first look at the film script in Montreal, and as he set about memorizing his 16 pages of lines he was dismayed by the repeated use of a too familiar racial epithet. "My main objection was to the constant use of the word 'nigger.' It was a common word in those days, too common, but I felt it unnecessary to use it as often as they did. When Joan arrived in Montreal, I had her read the script and she agreed with me. But she thought the script could be fixed easily enough to overcome my complaint." Joan was right, and the final version contained the revisions recommended by the Moores.

Archie's competition for the role included many actors and his friend and fellow champion, Sugar Ray Robinson. The latter lost out, Moore told *The New Yorker*, "because he was too sleek. They didn't have sleek slaves in those days." In the end, it was Archie's audition that carried the day. When he completed his audition, Moore recalled, "the professionals on the set—electricians, stagehands, and the like—broke into spontaneous applause. Tears came from the director's eyes. Goldwyn was dabbing his eyes and shaking his head in wonder. An electrician told me it was only the second time in 30 years that he had seen such emotion during a test."

Metro-Goldwyn-Mayer production head Sol C. Siegel announced Moore's starring role in *The Adventures of Huckleberry Finn*, and Sam Goldwyn told the *San Diego Union*, "Archie puts onto the screen the warmth and poignancy of Jim so vital to the character of the role."

Shooting started in Beverly Hills. Archie stayed at the Chateau Marmont on the Sunset Strip, where Sidney Poitier was also staying while making a movie called *All the Young Men* for Columbia. Coincidentally, Poiter's filmed also starred heavyweight champion Ingemar Johannson. Poitier spoke highly of Archie's acting: "Sure, he's a prize fighter. But many jobs in motion pictures go to singers who never took a dramatic lesson, other athletes and girl models, whose only claim to acting talent is the fact they posed for swim suit ads. Archie comes into this business with no less talent than 50 percent of the people in it. Moore, as well as Johannson, could go on to be good actors because each of them has a catching personality."

One of Archie's frequent visitors was Doc Kearns. Kearns had done some work in Tinseltown years ago with Jack Dempsey. Kearns enjoyed being in Hollywood again and told Moore that he hoped *The Adventures of Huckleberry Finn* would turn out better than *Daredevil Jack* and Dempsey's other forgettable film projects.

After shooting was finished, Archie gave a special performance for Jack Murphy, who was thoroughly enchanted. "He made me forget Archie Moore, the fighter," Murphy said. "I saw him as Jim, the wise old slave, floating down the Mississippi River in the company of his young friend Huck Finn. As an actor, Moore is a natural. He's been playing one role or another all his life, and boxing has never known a man who could match his flair for theatrics."

While filming one day, Moore was taken to a different studio for "publicity shots." In fact it was a ruse to get Archie on *This Is Your Life*, the popular TV show hosted by Ralph Edwards, on which surprised celebrities were reunited with figures from their past. In addition to being taken aback, Archie was embarrassed because he was unshaven for his role as Jim. But he recovered nicely, joking that slaves couldn't afford razor blades. The biggest surprise came when Cora Lee Hunter was brought in to greet the man who, six years earlier, had helped the *Miami Herald* raise $12,000 for her cornea transplant by literally walking the streets to beg money. Cora Lee raced across the wide stage into Archie's arms, but instead of the long thank-you speech she had planned, she could only utter through tear-filled eyes, "He's great." Back in Miami she had told everyone how excited she was about being reunited with her "boyfriend."

As soon as a rough-cut version of his film became available, the producers at MGM invited Archie and family to the sneak preview. The audience and critics reacted positively, and Archie said, "For the first time I really felt like an actor. A lot of those people didn't even know I was a prize fighter. They just liked me up there on the screen. That was okay with me. I signed autographs and beamed and probably would have stood there until the porter left the theater if I hadn't been dragged away. The excitement was so great that when we left the restaurant after the show I had to pull the car off the road and grab 40 winks before continuing the drive home."

The all-time knockout king floored reviewers with his sensitive portrayal of Jim. "I wanted to prove that I could act without losing any dignity," Archie said. "I don't agree with those who say the role belittled the African American. Slavery was a fact at that time; there's no escaping that. Jim had something to say that was important even for today. He was a man searching for freedom. This man Jim is really every man who is trying to be free. Jim is spiritually free, but he yearns to be free physically, so he can buy his wife and his two children out of slavery. Every man wants to be free in a different way. Jim is just one in the long history of man's struggles to be free."

Moore's acting skills really came in handy when Kearns booked him as a wrestling referee. "Archie Moore remains one of the best drawing cards in sports," Kearns told the *Miami Daily News*. "I have had him on tour as a wrestling referee recently and he's been responsible for record gates. We pulled $37,000 for a date in Detroit. Who else does that kind of business at the box office?"

The tour produced its share of bombastic headlines, such as the one in the *San Diego Union* proclaiming that Archie had been KOed by a wrestler. According to the story, the light heavyweight champion was out cold for five minutes after wrestler Ray Shire tagged him in the course of a free-for-all at Victory Field in Indianapolis. Kearns accused Shire of using brass knuckles and said he'd give Shire and his brother and tag-team partner Roy

$10,000 if either could last three rounds with Archie wearing boxing gloves.

But the National Boxing Association had someone a little more formidable in mind for its light heavyweight champion, and when Moore showed no inclination to give Harold Johnson a crack at the title, the NBA once again threatened to strip him.

NBA president Anthony Maceroni said it wasn't fair to Johnson or other 175-pound contenders for Archie to hoard the title, and told Moore to make up his mind whether he was a light heavyweight or was going after Johansson's belt.

As long as the NBA salon brought up the heavyweight champion, Moore reminded Maceroni via a statement to the *Miami Daily* that Ingemar Johansson hadn't defended his own title for eight months, and that as far as Harold Johnson went, Moore had already beaten him four times.

Kearns defended his position in *The Million Dollar Gate*, "I demanded a $100,000 dollar guarantee every time Archie defended the title. Naturally, at times it is difficult to find someone who will go for that kind of price, and thus it was that on frequent occasions some commission or other, or the National Boxing Association, began yelling for our scalp.

"It always struck me as peculiar that these people never worried about what you were going to be paid for your own property. 'Put it on the line every six months,' they insisted, having nothing whatsoever to lose, 'or we will take it away from you.' I have speculated frequently as to what these same gentlemen would say if the bar association told them that they would have to sell their law practice for $50, or the publishers association advised them they'd have to peddle their newspaper right now for a mess of pottage because they had been in business six months without helping a rival newspaper open up across the street."

Meanwhile, since it was Archie's world championship at stake, Kearns took their case to the world's foremost deliberative body with the following statement:

"I humbly suggest that the high-handed action by the National Boxing Association in depriving Archie Moore of the light heavyweight championship is a matter which probably concerns your organization," he telegrammed Henry Cabot Lodge, U.S. ambassador to the United Nations. "Moore has boxed all over the world for years. He has served as a boxing goodwill ambassador to the sports-loving people in dozens of countries and in hundreds of cities. A well-respected popular American citizen, he is nonetheless a citizen of the world.

"I humbly submit that such a true internationalist should not be subject to personal indignities and loss of livelihood through the petty tyrannies of this organization and its dictator, President Anthony Macaroni [sic].

"In the interest of fair play the world over and the furthering of democratic procedures, will you kindly grant me and my fighter, Mr. Moore, an audience at your earliest possible convenience?"

Whining about both the misspelling of his name and Kearns's attempt to go over his head, Maceroni passed the buck, saying that it was the members of the NBA who voted for Moore's ouster.

Another vote was engineered by NBA vice president Stan Goldberg and New Jersey commissioner Joe Walker—brother of Mickey Walker, Kearns's former welterweight and middleweight champion. This time it went in Moore's favor, with the stipulation that he defend against second-rated contender Ernie Schoeppner on July 18, 1960. Archie agreed and began the road back by fighting a tune-up against Willie Besmanoff in Indianapolis on the eve of the Indy 500.

Getting back into shape—Archie's weight was around 220—was hard enough; but even worse was the separation from his family after such a long homestand. Ten days before the Besmanoff fight, Archie wrote home:

Dearest Darling Joanie,

I had no problem getting here. Thank God. I almost did not leave when Rena began to cry. This is why with God's help in our plans I can retire still light heavy Champ and enjoy our kiddies and home and have a normal family life. I have much work to do. I went to

*church today. Everyone here whom are acquainted with you sends love.
I had a decent workout today.*

Bye for now.

I love you Cookie Pie,
Archie

But retirement, Moore told the *Indianapolis Star*, was not in his immediate plans. "They made me two new mouthpieces out at the Indiana Medical Association Dental Center and each of them is good for five years, so I guess I'll have to use them up," he joked.

He might've briefly reconsidered in the second round when a Besmanoff right put Moore's 206 pounds on the canvas. Archie got up quickly and from then on made the German baker pay, busting Besmanoff's nose wide open and finally forcing the referee to intervene in round 10.

With the Schoeppner fight just eight weeks off, the question, as always, was would the Mongoose be able to whittle down to 175 pounds?

The rematch between heavyweight champion Johansson and Floyd Patterson was booked for June 20, 1960. One hundred sixty theaters all over the U.S. were going to show the fight on closed-circuit screens, and as long as the equipment and lines were leased for 30 days, the idea was to telecast Moore-Schoeppner 29 days later in some theaters. That fell apart when Archie asked for a 30-day postponement, claiming his wife was ill. Piggy-backing the fight on Johansson-Patterson was one thing, but, reported the *Miami Daily News*, "Irving Kahn of Teleprompter, Inc., didn't think the fight [Moore-Schoeppner] attractive enough in itself to warrant additional leasing expenses." Once he pulled out, Moore-Schoeppner was canceled.

Few believed that Joan Moore's health had as much to do with the situation as Archie's girth, and later Moore spilled the beans himself. "The truth is, I wanted to wait and see if Johansson whupped Patterson again. If he had, Doc had it arranged for me to take a shot at the heavyweight crown for $500,000! I didn't want to punish my body getting down to the light heavyweight limit if a career-high payday was in the works."

But that went kaput, too, when Patterson became the first man to regain the heavyweight throne, knocking Johannson out with a vengeance. With the NBA turning the screws, Kearns made a personal appearance before the organization's Executive Committee to ask for more time. A tentative date of September 17, 1960, was arrived at for Moore to defend against Schoeppner, with Mexico City as the venue. But once again the champion pulled out, and instead ended up in Dallas on September 13, fighting a journeyman named George Abinet in an over-the-weight (literally) match. Reported *Boxing Illustrated*: "Archie, aged 47 or more, fat (at 200 pounds), seemed able to end it any time he wished, but he still has to carve, melt or rub 25 pounds off before he can legally defend his 175-pound title. Therefore he took his time and got himself a workout—although he'd probably have done just as well slamming the big bag in the gym." Abinet failed to answer the bell for the fourth round.

As the NBA moguls fumed and fulminated, Archie headed to Rome for a non-title bout against fifth-ranked Giulio Rinaldi. And as long as boxing politics was taking up so much of his time, he decided to try the real thing and announced his candidacy for the California Assembly, to fill the term of George Crawford, who'd resigned to become a judge.

But the campaign ran into difficulty right out of the gate. On his nomination papers, Archie listed his occupation as "light heavyweight champion of the world." Informed that state law permitted only a three-word job designation, Moore settled for "light heavyweight champion." But then it was pointed out that Archie had listed Missouri as his birthplace on one sworn statement and Mississippi on another. His explanation—that he really wasn't sure where he was born and wanted both states to share the glory—didn't fly. Neither did his next brainstorm—"various places." Finally, Aunt Willie Pearl came to the rescue, and Mississippi got the nod. Luckily for all involved, ages and birth dates were no longer required.

For all that, the political arena might be a welcome change, suggested Jack Murphy. "I don't know what prompted the old gladiator to test his popularity with the electorate, but some of the attractions are obvious," he wrote. "As a politician, he won't be forced to make weight; in fact, the registrar of voters doesn't even require him to go near the scales. Further, the campaign won't involve him with the National Boxing Association and the rule which stipulates that a champion must defend his title every six months."

Moore's problems on both those scores followed him to Rome. The NBA announced it was no longer recognizing Archie as light heavyweight champion because of his failure to toe the company line, and Moore had to ante up $1,000 of his $20,000 purse after failing to make the stipulated weight of 185 for the Rinaldi fight.

Of the two, the NBA's action was the least bothersome, at least publicly. "That's a laugh, isn't it?" said Kearns. "They got nothing better to do than going around picking up titles. But it doesn't mean nothing. Titles are lost in the ring, not by somebody sending out a letter. Who's the NBA anyway but a bunch of self-appointed officials?"

Besides, the powerful New York Athletic Commission and the European Boxing Union still recognized Moore as the light heavyweight champion.

As for the weight problem, Moore's trainer Dick Saddler blamed it on their inability to comprehend the European metric system. "I still don't know what we really weigh," Saddler sighed after the weigh in, "and I haven't since we've been there. Everybody says, 'It's about this,' or 'It's about that,' but we've never been sure." Actually, Archie got off lightly, since his contract called for him to be docked $1,000 for every pound he weighed over 185. He could have lost another $4,000, but the generous promoter let the rest slide because Moore's drawing power produced one of the most financially successful gates in Italian boxing history, grossing nearly $65,000.

Fourteen thousand fans filled the Olympic Sports Palace to see their paisano pull off one of the year's biggest upsets. Given little chance going in, Rinaldi generally outhustled the famous visitor. Going into the tenth round, the bout was still a toss-up, but Moore's fate was sealed when he staggered against the ropes. European rules gave the referee the leeway to administer a "standing eight-count"—now standard in the U.S., too—if he thought a boxer was hurt. Referee Marcello Tinelli did just that to Archie. "It was ridiculous," Moore said later. "I wasn't hurt. I was feigning on the ropes trying to draw Rinaldi into a trap, but the referee didn't know my style. I tried to show him I was all right by flailing my arms. I even did a soft shoe dance. No, on second thought, I did a hard shoe dance. But the guy counted eight before he got the message."

The decision went unanimously for Rinaldi. Archie didn't protest, telling the *Boxing News*, "I'd have been more satisfied if it had been a split decision. I would say that the fight really should have been a draw." He was already looking ahead and liking what he saw.

"I now have a real opponent for a title defense, and the NBA won't have to be bothering me anymore," Moore told *The Ring*. "Rinaldi is the one contender who can attract sufficient people at the gate. He's both popular here and actually good. He is a new man, a new energy in the sport. We need new blood and we have it in Rinaldi, who I hope will be my next opponent when I defend—successfully of course—the title I hold. A 10-round bout doesn't mean anything. We need a 15-rounder."

Before departing Rome, Archie took in a movie. "I never knew my Italian was that good!" he remarked, after viewing *The Adventures of Huckleberry Finn* dubbed in Italian.

Arriving home in time to vote for himself for the 79th District Assembly seat, Archie was defeated by George Lapthroen. But a fellow Democrat who fared better at the polls on Election Day sent his regards.

I was most pleased and grateful to have your generous good wishes after the election. It is very encouraging to receive your expression of confidence for the future.

Your words sustained my belief that this country is ready to meet the inescapable challenges of the sixties.

With all good wishes and thanks.

Sincerely,
John F. Kennedy

It was back to the Salt Mines, literally, for San Diego's favorite fistic son. There, Archie was soon joined by a young man ready to start his own startling and remarkable journey into boxing history.

CHAPTER 17

Training Cassius Clay

The same day that Archie lost to Rinaldi in Rome, Cassius Clay won a six-round decision over Tunney Hunsaker in Louisville, Kentucky and launched what would become one of the brightest careers in professional boxing history. Clay—who of course changed his name to Muhammad Ali after he won the heavyweight title in 1964—had won the gold medal as a light heavyweight at the 1960 Olympics in Rome. To guide him in the pro ranks, he signed a contract with a consortium of 11 Louisville businessmen headed by Bill Faversham. They weren't boxing men, and their first task was to find someone who could work with Clay to sharpen and improve his obvious talent in the ring. Who better than the Mongoose?

The Moores were already familiar with Cassius. Earlier, when the San Diego Chargers recruited Archie to go to Louisville to help sign a football player, Clay and his younger brother, Rudy, came to the hotel room where Archie and Joan were staying. The Clays invited the Moores to their house for a party, and Archie and his wife were charmed by Cassius's ebullience and friendliness.

Overseeing the youngster's preparation for the professional stage, however, involved more than a smile and handshake. "Four lawyers came out to San Diego and set up the deal for Archie to train him," recalled Joan Moore. Eventually everything was properly signed and sealed, and Cassius Marcellus Clay duly appeared in San Diego to begin his professional apprenticeship under the master. He was an instant hit with the females in the Moore household. "My sister [J'Marie] and I were real small kids when Muhammad stayed with us," recalled Rena Moore. "We used to joke with him and chase him all over the place. I used to call him my boyfriend although I was only a few years old. Muhammad would baby-sit for us if my parents went out or entertained guests at the house. He was the best sitter we ever had because he was more fun than strict."

While Cassius made an impression on the ladies of the house, he soon butted heads with the head of the household. Recalled Archie in *Muhammad Ali, His Life and Times*, "I admired his stamina when he came to the Salt Mine. I saw him run up a hill that was at a 35-degree angle. He ran up that hill twice, came down, ran over to me, and asked, 'Want me to do it again?'

"He had all the natural talent in the world, but he wasn't always willing to learn. I wanted to teach him the tricks of longevity, so when he was fighting as an older man he wouldn't take the punishment that he eventually took in the ring. I said to him, 'Son, I want to teach you how to punch.' He knocked a lot of guys out, but he did it his way, with a lot of energy and a lot of strain. I said to him, 'I want to teach you how to be a real power puncher so you get your man out of there in one or two rounds. We don't want you to go 15 rounds. We don't want you to go 10 rounds. We don't want you to waste your stamina. Knock these guys out quick, because your body just has a certain number of hard fights in it.' And I thought it would have been nice for him to listen to that, but he told me, 'I don't want to box like Archie Moore. I want to box like Sugar Ray Robinson. Sugar Ray's my man.' I said, 'Son, you don't want to do like that. You want to go out, slide underneath the punch, and whap, knock the guy out, and then you go on to the next guy. You'll fight a lot more fights like that.'"

While Clay learned under the tutelage of Moore, the master had a fight of his own against former sparring partner Buddy Turman in Dallas. Trainer Dick Sadler had the dubious distinction of riding there with Clay by train. Sadler described the crazy ride with the energetic Clay in *Muhammad Ali, The Holy Warrior*: "I rode with Clay from the West Coast down to Texas, where Archie had this fight. We went by train and it was a pretty wild ride. First the kid would be standing, shouting out the carriage: 'I am the greatest. I am the greatest!' He'd shout this at the passing cars and sheep and fields and stuff. Then after a while he started singing this number by Chubby Checker about the twist. He didn't know the words, just kept on and on singing, 'Come on baby, let's do the twist; come on baby, let's do the twist!' And it got to me. It was driving me crazy, to tell you the truth. I said, 'Jesus, son, you done twisted all across California and Arizona.' By the time we got to New Mexico, I told him, 'Look, sing the Charleston or the Boogaloo or any damned thing, but get off the twist!' Seven hundred miles of twisting, twisting, and 'I am the greatest!' It drove me crazy!"

The bout in Dallas against Turman was little more than a light workout. *The Dallas Morning News* reported, "Ageless Archie Moore, never troubled and fighting only enough to win, scored a unanimous 10-round decision over Buddy Turman in the main event of a Memorial Auditorium fight card." Although Archie rarely put his offense in full gear, he looked to be in decent condition, weighing in at a reasonably svelte 189 pounds the morning of the fight.

Although Archie won the main event, it was Cassius Clay who tried to steal the show. "Muhammad was always making a fuss, bragging to anyone who would listen, but what people realized at the time was that in many ways he was talking the truth. Muhammad told everyone he saw in Dallas that he would one day be champion. Coming from a young man with only one professional bout under his belt, many people didn't know how to take him." Shortly after returning from Dallas, Archie and his protégé began to have pronounced differences of opinion.

After Clay had been staying at the Salt Mine for about six weeks, the relationship between him and Archie hit the boiling point. Cassius became tired of what he considered Moore's tyrant methods, and the young phenom challenged his instructor. Archie remembered, "Cassius thought I was bossing him around too much. I was only trying to gain his respect. One day he asked me to spar. I declined, because I was a world champion and he was a novice. I wasn't his sparring partner; I was his coach."

Clay also had difficulties with the chores that were shared by everyone at camp. Archie recalled in *Muhammad Ali, His Life and Times*, "We washed our own dishes and did our own cooking at the Salt Mine. I didn't have the money or the wherewithal like the big-timers to hire people. So I said to [Clay], 'You've got to wash the dishes on Wednesday and scrub floors on Thursday, and you can help me cook on Friday.' I told him how we divided up the chores. We had other men at the camp, and each person pulled his load. And he said to me, 'Archie, I didn't come here to be a dish-washer.' I told him, 'You're not a dishwasher, but you have to carry your own load.' He said, 'I ain't gonna wash no dishes like a woman.' So I said to him, 'Okay, you ain't gonna eat.' And so he said all right, he'd wash dishes, and he looked at me with those pretty eyes and was scowling at me the whole time he was wash-ing. And then the next day came and it was time to mop the floors, and he said okay, okay, he mopped the floors. But just as soon as I thought he was becoming disciplined, he said, 'I'm tired of this; I want to go home.' Christmas was coming up, and he said he want-ed to go home for Christmas. Christmas was a good excuse for him to go. And I said, 'Okay, how do you want to go? Do you want to fly?' He said, 'No, don't want to go on no plane.' I asked, 'Do you want to go on a bus?' He said, 'No, I want to go on a train.' So I put him on a train and sent him home to see his folks in Louisville for Christmas, and he never came back again. I had an idea he was-n't going to return.

"I was putting pressure on him to bring him under discipline, and this was the thing that Ali did not get. He was always trying to discipline his superiors, the people who were working with him.

To tell you the truth, the boy needed a good spanking, but I wasn't sure who could give it to him. And the saddest time I had with him was when he left the Salt Mine. I had to keep my propriety up. I'm a great instructor and a great teacher, but I was sad when he left. I loved him like a son and I could see a lot of revenue leaving with him, but I had my dignity. So I had to say, 'Well, go ahead. If you want to go, I don't want to prevent you from doing anything you want to do. If you want to go home, that's your prerogative.' And then after he left there was nothing for me to do but watch his rise and eventually his fall."

Shortly after Clay left, Archie wrote his pupil in Louisville wishing him all the best. Cassius responded a week later with a handwritten letter:

Dear Archie,

I received this letter and it was very nice. They [The Louisville sponsoring group] want me to fight on the Patterson card, and I think it would be nice if I could get a chance like that. My Mother and Father are going to move to California this summer, and I will be there with them, but at this time I will have to stay around here. But all I'm doing is training here in Florida for a few fights, but as soon as I can I will be right back at the Salt Mine. So right now I am going along with my backers for these few fights. Tell your wife and the kids that I said "hello." Tell Dick [Sadler] I said "hello" and that I will be back sooner or later. I am using what you told me and it is doing the trick. We had a good write up in The Ring *this month. Good Luck in the title fight.*

You are the "boss."

Cassius

There would be no return for Clay at the Salt Mine. His backers agreed on Florida-based trainer Angelo Dundee to take over the reins for the young heavyweight prospect. Hank Kaplan, a boxing historian from Miami and longtime friend of Clay's and Dundee's, recalls, "I was Cassius's best friend when he lived in Miami. I asked him how training had gone with Archie Moore, who also was a close friend. Clay responded, 'That old man is crazy. He was making me run up steep hills backwards!' Muhammad always had a great respect for Archie Moore. One of Ali's difficulties in San Diego was the isolation. Archie kept him on a pretty short leash."

Archie passed along his account of the final breakup to friend Mel Durslag of the *L.A. Times*. "I tried to explain to Ali there is no reason squandering energy going 15 [rounds] when you can render an opponent unconscious in two. But he was a talker, not a listener. So I walked away from his account. I figure it cost me $6 million, but I gained in a cultural way not having to hear him."

Despite the loss of his star pupil, life continued on for the old war horse. On January 10, 1960, Archie became one of 11 members inducted into the original San Diego Hall of Champions and Hall of Fame. A few weeks after the induction, old friend George Plimpton paid Moore a visit. In his book, *Shadow Box*, Plimpton wrote: "Archie was a fine host. He loved showing things off. He even showed me some of his ring secrets. One, a can of what he called his 'magic oil,' [was] a sort of milky fluid which he rubbed into his skin—'The stuff penetrates your muscles and keeps them loose'—and which he said with a straight face was emu bird oil from Australia. 'Very hard to get your hands on emu bird oil,' he told me. 'Very hard to get your hands on the bird and very hard to get the oil off him.' He never made it clear to me how this was done—my mind troubled with the thought of fleet-footed men corralling these ostrich-sized birds and moving toward them with suction cups and pliant sponges—and Moore would never elaborate on the process itself, except to say that he had 'powerful connections' who provided the stuff for him."

Archie also took Plimpton on a tour of the 120-acre Salt Mine spread and confessed that the property had been a nudist camp before he took over ownership. Plimpton was amused by the large rocks painted in bright red with the names of some of boxing's all-time greats like Sugar Ray Robinson and Stanley Ketchel. In *Shadow Box* Plimpton noted, "I noticed one crag on which a rude likeness of him had been chiseled out with the legend underneath: ALL-TIME K.O. CHAMP. He took me over to a flat terrace—one of the sunbathing spots—where his name had been painted flat in huge letters, which he told me was to let people flying overhead in the airliners know they were above his camp. 'Do you think someone can read that from 30,000 feet?' he asked. 'I would think so,' I said truthfully."

While negotiating to defend the remnant of his light heavyweight title—the New York, Massachusetts, California and the European boxing commissions still recognized Moore as the world's champion—Moore kept busy. He planned to consider himself champion until he lost the belt in the ring. While Kearns negotiated his next ring venture, Archie refereed local professional and amateur boxing shows and rehearsed for an episode of *The Twilight Zone*. Finally Doc inked a deal for a return engagement against Guilio Rinaldi on June 10, 1960, in New York's Madison Square Garden.

Once again, Archie decided to fight himself into championship condition. Archie won another 10-round decision over Buddy Turman, but this time the bout was in the Philippines. Archie boxed in a series of exhibitions and before leaving for New York stopped Cliff Gray in Nogales, Arizona. A month before the Rinaldi bout, Archie tipped the scales at nearly 200 pounds. It had been nearly two years since Archie had defended the title, and given that and his almost 50 years, it was felt in some quarters that he would be forced to relinquish what remained of his claim to the title.

Upon arrival in New York a few weeks before the bout, Moore set up training camp at Kutsher's in the Catskills. There he was visited by a former foe who questioned Archie's chances against the Italian. "Rocky Marciano...was appalled by his training methods," reported *The New Yorker*. 'I don't believe Rinaldi can lose the fight,' he said. 'The weight making will beat Archie—that's the big thing.'"

Marciano wasn't the only one with doubt. The promoters of the fight, terrified that it wouldn't come off because of Moore's inability to reduce to the class limit, went to Harold Johnson, who'd won NBA recognition as light heavyweight champion by beating Jesse Beaudry, and requested that he make himself available to step in as Archie's replacement if Moore defaulted on the scales. Johnson received a reported $5,000 fee to act as standby. But after a few trips to the scales, Moore finally made the weight on the day of the fight. "I'll never forget the look on Harold Johnson's face," Archie recalled. "His jaw dropped and he said, 'I knew Archie wasn't gonna give me a shot at that money!'"

After that, Moore did something equally astounding. He took an easy 15-round decision over his Italian challenger. The crowd of 9,500, one of the largest turnouts for a fight in years at Madison Square Garden, cheered loudly for boxing's longest reigning world champion as Archie dominated Rinaldi. Moore almost had his rival going a few times, but as he later told *Sports Illustrated,* "We were exactly the same age going into the ninth round, then he got older. Am I right? I was under the impulse to take him out when he hurt his ankle in the fifteenth, but I did not want to take advantage of him. He's a visitor and I wanted him to feel welcome. Why spoil a youngster's record?"

But immediately following the final bell, Archie had more important matters on his mind, as *The New Yorker* reported. "Moore has seldom made an issue of his color, and, unlike baseball's Jackie Robinson, say, has not been known as a supporter of the National Association for the Advancement of Colored People and allied causes. For this reason, many of his admirers were surprised when, seizing the microphone after his Madison Square Garden victory over Rinaldi, he used the prize ring as a platform for endorsing both the NAACP and the Freedom Riders. He announced, with some 19 million people listening, that he was donating a thousand dollars of his purse to the Freedom Riders, another thousand to the United Fund in San Diego, and five hundred dollars to B'nai B'rith, and was also purchasing a $500 lifetime membership in the NAACP. Certain fight fans, particularly in the South, wondered where he got the idea, and whether he had been coached. A man who had known Moore for a long time asked him later on whether the incident had been simply an impulsive act. "I wouldn't be telling the truth if I said it was an impulse," Moore replied. "I'd thought about it. This had been brewing inside me for a long time. I knew what I wanted to do. Of course, I always rough out my speech before a fight, because I always anticipate victory." He smiled. Then he was asked whether the idea had been his own. "Nobody puts words in my mouth," he said sharply. With less heat, he added, "Let me tell you how I feel about this. As a colored champion, I have a responsibility to my race. I have a minor voice. So long as I have popularity, I can make my voice heard, though that isn't always enough. Joe Louis had great popularity, but he wasn't articulate. Some of my white friends were surprised when I spoke out, because they know I am not a militant man—they know I am not militant outside the ring. But they don't know the depth of my feelings.

"I read something not long ago that expresses what I believe. The writer said, 'He who would deny one person freedom does not himself deserve freedom.' I believe that. I knew I would vex certain people, but it didn't matter. In my own way, I will do whatever I can that is right, because right will always stand."

Although Archie was praised for speaking out, he also received some cruel responses. Noted *Sports Illustrated*: "A Nashville attorney wrote: 'You are a slob. You could not fight your way out of a paper bag. Try a freedom ride'....He signed off, gratuitously: 'No member of NAACP.' Another telegram called Archie 'boy,' a Southern euphemism for 'nigger.' The wires riled Moore more than Rinaldi did. 'When do I cease being a boy?' he asked. 'What do I need to do to gain respect? I try to be a good man. This is a fight you can not give up. There is no compromise for freedom. This is something *everyone* wants. I sympathize with all minorities. I'm one myself. The Negro had to have a hand in the making of America. Now it is his duty to try to see the light. Is that wrong? I want my children to be able to sit down in a restaurant, eat and then get up. I want them to ride on the roller coaster as it goes up and down. I want them to be able to go up and down on it.'"

Speaking of roller coasters, boxing fans wondered how much longer the Mongoose could keep boxing at the championship level. The secret, Archie related, was contained in his mystical science of "relaxism." "The main part of exact relaxism is diversion. People with no hobby have no life." Archie had a wide range of interests. He loved listening to his vast collection of jazz albums, playing the piano, shooting pistols at targets at the Salt Mine, and entertaining guests.

Honing in on 79 himself, Doc Kearns had a simpler, probably more accurate explanation for *Newsweek*. "Sure, Archie's getting older," he said. "Don't worry about him. As long as there's a big payday, Archie'll be around to pick up the check."

After a few months of relaxism, swami Moore got ready for an October 1961 date with former world heavyweight title challenger Pete Rademacher, in what would be Moore's twenty-second ring appearance in Baltimore.

Rademacher, a 1956 Olympic gold medalist, had made history when he challenged Floyd Patterson for the heavyweight crown on August 22, 1957. It was Rademacher's very first professional fight. He actually floored Patterson, but Floyd lowered the boom on him in the sixth round. Four years later, he suffered the same fate against Moore. Reported the *Baltimore Sun*: "Ageless Archie Moore floored Pete Rademacher eight times and scored a six-round technical knockout." Recalled Rademacher later, "I did well against Archie Moore in the early going. I had him down, although I believe they ruled it a slip. I was spinning Archie and moving him. I was positioning him; then he hit me with a left hook to the belly that I still feel today. I have so much respect for Archie Moore."

On February 10, 1962, the New York State Athletic Commission and the European Boxing Union withdrew their recognition of Moore as world light heavyweight champion for failure to defend the title within a six-month period. Massachusetts and the British Commonwealth soon followed suit. The New York Commission had warned Archie several times that he needed to sign for a defense against either Harold Johnson or

Doug Jones. Moore refused to knuckle under, citing financial reasons. For years Archie had demanded $100,000 to defend his title. He even placed ads in newspapers seeking a promoter who would guarantee him $100,000 for a title defense against Johnson. There were no takers. The best offer Archie received would have given him 40 percent of the box office receipts. Archie told the *San Diego Union*, "It sounds great, but how much is 40 percent of nothing?"

Before being stripped of his last vestige of the title, Archie had hoped to defend it in San Diego's Balboa Stadium against world middleweight champion Gene Fullmer. Now, as a mere civilian, the potential payday against Fullmer was out. Moore vented to the media: "The commission has taken the title—that it took me 20 years to attain—without reason. And it places me in the earning capacity of a club fighter."

Doc Kearns added his two cents' worth, telling the *San Diego Union*, "We want to lose the title in the ring, not by politics. Archie has held the title for 10 years and defended it nine times. We're disappointed in the commission's action…It seems that all the commissions in the country are becoming matchmakers and promoters."

Now a champion without a portfolio, The Mongoose wasn't about to go quietly into boxing's sunset. There were still big fish to fry, and he no longer needed to swim upstream to make 175 pounds.

CHAPTER 18

Losing to Father Time and Cassius Clay

Boxing's governing bodies may have had it with him, but Archie was still a hero in the real world. Just days after being stripped of his championship, Los Angeles Mayor Samuel Yorty proclaimed February 17, 1962, as "Archie Moore Day," and presented him with the key to the city. Moore was motorcaded to a special ceremony at City Hall, where he combined business with pleasure. "I'm always promoting something," Archie told the press, displaying a milk bottle and plugging the new "Archie Moore Milk Company," based in Los Angeles. The milk was low-fat, for those poor souls concerned with such matters. That no longer included Archie, who was bulking up for his fight one month hence against the third-ranked heavyweight contender at the L.A. Sports Arena.

Legend had it that Alejandro Lavorante had been discovered by Jack Dempsey on a refereeing tour in South America. That may have been laying it on a little thick, but the Argentina fighter had KOed top-ranked Zora Folley since headquartering in Los Angeles and had suffered only one loss. His manager, Pinky George, was no slouch at ballyhoo himself, as evidenced when he bragged about his tiger's special "Keyhole Punch."

"I call it that because it requires pinpoint accuracy," explained George. "It takes speed, timing and power and is particularly effective against an opponent with his guard up, a la Moore."

What Lavorante needed against Moore was a battering ram, and lacking that the Old Master took him apart. After the fight was stopped in the tenth round, with Archie in control the whole way, the South American collapsed and had to be carted out of the ring on a stretcher. About 40 minutes later, ring announcer Jimmy Lennon Sr. announced to worried spectators that Lavorante had been more exhausted than hurt and was chatting with reporters and even planned to hit the post-fight party.

Vastly relieved, Moore heaped encomiums on his vanquished foe. "He has a harder left jab than Sonny Liston," Archie told reporters. "Nobody has ever hit me with a jab like this guy. He knocked my bridgework out in the ninth round. All this kid needs is experience. I could take him to my Salt Mines in San Diego and make a champion of him in two years." (Unfortunately, in two years Lavorante would be dead. Knocked out by Cassius Clay in his next fight, Lavorante then collapsed in a comeback fight against journeyman Johnny Riggins. This time it wasn't exhaustion, but massive brain trauma. Lavorante lived in a semi-vegetative state until he died in 1964.)

Now Moore wanted bigger game. "From here we go to Patterson or Liston," he told the *Los Angeles Examiner*. "Yes, I think I could beat either one of them. I am the superior fighter. I am the elder statesmen." When one reporter barked, "What about that gray in your hair?" The Mongoose replied, "The boys shouldn't be worried about my gray hair; they should be worrying about these gray fists."

To back up the claim, Archie laid out tough Howard King in the first round at the bullring in Tijuana. It was the first time in six fights against King that Moore was able to put him away and also the 135th knockout of his career.

Just three weeks later, Archie and future light heavyweight titlist Willie Pastrano faced off in Los Angeles. The match was arranged by Joe Louis, working for World Enterprise Boxing. The deal was sealed at the U.S. Grant Hotel, Doc Kearns's headquarters. "Whenever Doc wanted to put together one of his big business deals," Joan Moore recalled, "he would get dressed in his best suit and rent out the most expensive suite at the U.S. Grant Hotel. When Joe Louis came to town, Doc did his best to impress."

Pastrano had Angelo Dundee in his corner. Recalls Dundee: "I had known Archie for a long time from when he fought in the hinterlands. He tried to get into Pastrano's mind from the onset. Moore changed a lot of the innovations of boxing. If a guy won a world title, he would send them a postcard. Moore was one of the first guys to use the media as a marketing tool. I picked up a few of his tricks through the years and copied them."

Archie did his best to aggravate Pastrano by referring to him in public as "Pastrami." It worked. "Archie's choice of cold cuts is strictly from hunger," Pastrano replied. "They tell me Archie intends to make a sandwich out of pastrami—someone better tell him pastrami is harder to digest!"

In Peter Heller's book *In This Corner*, Pastrano recalled the weigh in on the day of the fight: "[Moore] weighed about 224 pounds and I weighed about 185. He was about 51 years old—had to be at least. This was a rumor around the boxing grapevine. At the weigh-in, he couldn't even see the eye chart. He was saying, 'A...B...C...D...' and it was, like, P...Q...R. The doctor says, 'For chrissakes, Archie that's not right.' He says, 'Well, Willie ain't gonna be that far [away], anyway.'"

Instructed by Dundee to ignore Archie's blather and to box him from a safe distance, Pastrano promptly forgot all about that as the Mongoose cast an enchanting spell in the ring. "I wasn't thinking about what he could do to me," he told Heller. "He looked so old, you know. I felt sorry for him in a way. But that was taken care of, because in the first round we go out, the guy is boxing me and he starts talking to me: 'Oh, you're looking good, kid, looking good.' All I see is his forehead and eyes. He was behind two big arms like tree trunks; he crossed them in front of him. He would shake one, he called it his 'Rattlesnake.' When he'd throw it, he would throw it from behind, freaky sneak right-hand. 'You're looking good, kid, you're looking good.' He was hitting me with that bullshit, so I start showboating and he gives me that bullshit for a whole round and he eats nothing but left jabs. I'm hitting him all over the forehead, bop, bop, in the first round. I come back to my corner, I told Angie, 'I love this old man. He's beautiful.' Angie says, 'Why?' I said, 'Man, he's telling me such pretty things in there.' And Angie says, 'Don't listen to him. Don't listen.'

"So I went out there and he started again: 'You're looking good, kid. You're the next champ. Dance, dance pretty, Willie.' So I started dancing, putting on a show, 'Oh, you're looking so good, stepping nice. Stand still!' And when he said 'stand still,' automatically, I don't know what it is, some type of mechanism in my mind, I just said to myself, 'What'd he say?' When I did that, that was all he needed. He set me up. He hit me with a right-hand that landed. I remember getting hit, then I remember sitting on the last rope and I saw three Archie Moores coming after me, and I got out of there. He used psychology in there. He was a wise old man."

After that Willie rode his bicycle around the ring, with Moore in pursuit. At the end of 10 not-too-exciting rounds, the decision was a draw. To Dundee, that amounted to a win for his man. Referee Tommy Hart scored it 5-4-1 for Moore and told Pastrano's hometown paper, *The Times-Picayune*, "Archie won the fight. Pastrano was doing all the holding." Angelo Dundee remembered, "They called it a draw, but it was a win for Willie. To score a draw against a living legend like Archie Moore equaled a win for Pastrano."

The living legend himself naturally disagreed, his reaction suggesting that the voting officials would have done worse at the eye exam than he did. The only losers of record were Joe Louis and his promotional group, who dropped at least $20,000 on the fight. Both fighters had been guaranteed $40,000, and the gate had come to just $35,000.

Moore clearly had taken Pastrano lightly. Archie looked fat and actually gained four pounds during training. But he'd bear down harder preparing for his next match, motivated by a strong desire to take an upstart former pupil back to school.

Cassius Clay was coming to Los Angeles to fight Lavorante. If Clay looked impressive in his West Coast debut, Archie was next in line for the heavily hyped Olympic loudmouth.

With Moore watching from a third-row seat, Clay put Lavorante away in the fifth round as he had publicly predicted he would. As Clay exited the ring, reported *Boxing Illustrated*, "by the light of a diamond-studded neck-pin Cassius recognized the wily old Mongoose himself sitting comfortably in the third row. Putting on his fiercest scowl, Clay stuck an accusing finger into Moore's bemused face: 'You're next!' he growled."

Recalls Dundee, "When Cassius KOed Lavorante in the fifth, I grabbed and told him that Moore was near ringside and that Cassius should issue a challenge to him. Clay grabbed the microphone from the puzzled ring announcer and went into his act. 'Archie, I want you next, old man. Moore will fall in four.' I cringed at the rhyme. I used to help Cassius with his poetry, but I want no credit for that line. After that crack, I did my best to get the microphone back in the announcer's hand."

The match was made, and at a press conference Archie donned his scholarly robe and claimed, "That kid's got a lot to learn. And I'm afraid the ol' Professor is gonna have to teach him. I've discovered a few chinks in his armor."

The duel of tongues between boxing's most verbose orators was as entertaining as a fist fight. Archie was one of the few who could match Clay word for word and even come out on top. They appeared together on a program called, appropriately enough, *The Great Debate*, and Moore drew blood after one of Clay's obnoxious sallies with the rejoinder, "Cassius, I don't see how you can even stand yourself."

When Clay promised that, if he lost, he would kiss Archie's feet and leave the country, Moore told him, "Don't humiliate yourself. Our country's depending on its youth." Moore continued,

"Really, I don't see how you can stand yourself. I am a speaker, not a rabble rouser. I'm a conversationalist; you're a shouter."

Cassius tried to keep up, promising to "give him his pension plan" and reciting more doggerel, but it was point, set and match for Professor Moore when Archie told *Sports Illustrated*, "I view this young man with mixed emotions. Sometimes he sounds humorous, but sometimes he sounds like a man that can write beautifully but doesn't know how to punctuate."

Archie told Jack Murphy at the *San Diego Union*, "He's a nice fighter, considering his age [20] and lack of experience, but his boasting is pathetic. Clay's problem is that he lacks maturity both as a fighter and a talker. He's blabbed so much, it ceases to mean anything. I tuned him out long ago. I wonder if that kid has any idea how ridiculous he sounds. Not even Joe Louis after 15 fights was the man this brat thinks he is today."

The difference in the fighters as orators was perfectly delineated by *Los Angeles Herald* sportswriter Mel Durslag: "Archie was such a unique character, which you don't always find with fighters. Ali was fun to be around, too, but he wasn't quite the poet that Archie was. Overall Archie was a more engaging type of personality. He was smarter than Ali. Muhammad was a great coffee shop orator, but Archie was more of a philosopher."

Since there would also be a contest with gloves, Archie worked hard in the gym. Despite being at least 10 years past the mandatory retirement age for boxers in California (waived for him), Moore's body looked solid when he entered the Sports Arena ring. And, thanks to modern chemistry, his hair was black again. Nevertheless, the betting odds were 2-1 in favor of Clay, appearing in only his sixteenth pro fight.

To Doc Kearns, it boiled down to one simple proposition, as he stated in the *San Diego Union*. "Moore knows how to fight; Clay doesn't. Moore can punch; Clay can't."

Angelo Dundee defended the choice of Moore as an opponent for his relatively inexperienced charge. "I don't have any qualms about Clay fighting Moore. The way I look at it, Cassius has everything to gain and nothing to lose. I've never doubted his ability to beat Moore since Willie Pastrano, another of my fighters, earned a draw with Archie." Dundee continued, "I knew Ali was the real thing then, a future great. Archie was getting on in years and he had always had more difficulties with true heavyweights like Ali. Archie's best weight was 175, not 200-plus like he was for Ali."

Jack Murphy was convinced, at least. "Mark it down to wishful thinking, sentiment, loyalty, or friendship—things that have nothing to do with logic—I'm picking The Mongoose and his lip-buttoner to quiet Clay inside nine rounds," he wrote. "If I have to eat these words—well, the worst they can give me is indigestion."

The crowd of 16,230 fans was a California indoor record, but what they saw in the ring wasn't half as much fun as the hype leading up to it. From the opening bell it was obvious that Moore's feet weren't as nimble as his tongue or those of his younger rival. Archie fought out of a crouch with his arms in a crab-like defense. He gamely pressed the attack and managed to land a hook followed by a right to the body near the end of the first round. Clay was in no hurry. Before leaving his dressing room he had scribbled "Moore in Four" on a chalkboard.

In the second round, Archie pushed forward but was rarely given the opportunity to land anything, as Clay always stayed just out of his range. When Moore did launch a blow, Clay would side-step the effort and return fire. Archie managed to land a right near the end of the round, but it didn't affect Cassius, who continued to rain punches on the Mongoose until the bell. Moore's trainer, Dick Sadler, later told *Sports Illustrated*, "Clay missed 100 punches—but he threw 200."

In his corner, Archie stayed on his feet, trying to pump life into his tired legs and as a psychological ploy to make Clay think he was fine. He even threw in a few knee bends. But in the next round the Salt Mine dropout continued to punish his former taskmaster. Archie managed to land a solid right-hand, but that only brought further chastisement. Clay wobbled Moore with an uppercut to the jaw followed by an overhand right. Archie trembled like the last leaf of autumn.

Moore survived and again stood between rounds, but when the bell sounded for the fourth he stumbled toward the middle of the ring. The crowd sensed the end and became mute when Clay crashed a right to Moore's jaw and sent the old man to the canvas. Archie rose at eight, and Clay again jumped all over him and soon sent him down again from another right-hand.

After another eight-count Clay really opened the floodgates, and when Archie sank down for a third time, referee Tommy Hart called off the slaughter as Clay did a victory dance over his foe.

It was the third time in as many fights that Clay predicted the round in which he would stop his opponent. "Who is the world's greatest?" he shouted at the crowd. But in his dressing room, a more restrained Clay told the press he hated beating up on Moore, but had no choice but to use Archie as a stepping stone to his goal of the heavyweight throne.

For his part, Archie was a graceful loser. "Cassius proved that he was everything that I thought he wasn't," he told *Sports Illustrated*. "I had hoped to stay close to him, wear him down, but it didn't work. I couldn't hit him." As for the future, Moore said, "I don't know whether I'll retire. This might just have been a cloud that covered the sun. It was a cloudy night, but every morning brings a new ray of sunshine, new hope. I'm hopeful. And why should I complain? I've been stacking them up like cordwood for many years."

Jack Murphy put a different meteorological spin on things. "The sun finally went down for the patriarch of boxing, obscured by a barrage of red leather thrown by an impudent and talented youngster named Cassius Marcellus Clay. It was the end for Archie Moore and a beginning for the boy who destroyed him. Moore had nothing but courage, courage that enabled him to last until one minute and 35 seconds of the fourth round. The boy had everything, including the satisfaction of calling his own shot."

Later, Moore told Mel Durslag: "[Clay] laid a trap to catch a lion. But all he caught was an old, mangy fox. He stopped me in four, and he laughed and he danced around my ancient carcass."

In *Muhammad Ali, His Life and Times*, Archie said his own peculiar defense had been his downfall. "I was made for him in that I used a wrap-around defense to cover up. I would leave the top of my head exposed, and that's what he wanted. You see he had a style. He would hit a man a lot of times around the top of the head. And if you hit the top of a man's head, you shake up his thought pattern. You disturb his thoughts. A fighter has to think, but if someone is plucking you on top of the head, you cannot think correctly. And this is what he did. He made me dizzy and knocked me out."

"People ask me now if we'd fought when I was young, would the outcome have been different? I don't think so. One never knows for sure, but I told you before, Ali would have beaten Joe Louis four times out of five. And I think I was a pretty good light heavyweight, but I think Joe Louis would have beaten me."

Three weeks after the Clay match, Archie was contacted by Jack Murphy in San Diego, where the Mongoose had returned to tend to the psychological and physical wounds inflicted by Clay. "I have been remorsefully recounting things," Archie said, "It's a good general who can recount his mistakes." When Murphy pressed him about retirement, Moore said, "A lot of people don't like to go to funerals because they hate to admit what they already know. Maybe I'm like that."

Wrote Murphy, "With his 50th birthday coming up on December 13, the Grand Old Party of boxing knows he is kaput. But like an office seeker on election night, he is reluctant to make a formal concession. He is through as an important figure in boxing; yet, like all old troupers, he is still intoxicated by the smell of grease paint."

A few weeks later came the announcement that close friends and fans feared. Archie told a San Diego Lions Club audience that he intended to continue his career and that Kearns was trying to close a deal for a fight in England. But Moore was also making plans for the time when he would no longer answer a ringside bell, if it ever arrived. "When I stop fighting," he said, "I'll step into another arena, the biggest fight anyone could encounter—helping boys with their problems at the Archie Moore Salt Mines boys farm."

The latter fight was as important to Archie as any with gloves. Says his daughter Rena: "Maybe because he never had a father figure, he wanted to make sure every child he came in touch with did. He was always helping kids with some type of program."

CHAPTER 19

Archie the Instructor

A rchie went on location for a guest appearance on the *Perry Mason* TV show. In the episode called "The Case of the Drowsy Mosquito," Mason had to defend his client in a saloon courtroom. Archie portrayed the bartender and the key witness in the murder trial.

When Moore signed to take on "Iron" Mike DiBiase in Phoenix, Arizona on March 15, 1963, Jack Murphy feared it might be another acting assignment instead of a real fight. DiBiase was a professional wrestler. Wrote Murphy in the *San Diego Union*, "It was bad enough when Archie Moore surrendered to a precocious child named Cassius Clay in just four rounds. But now, alas, he is shedding all semblance of dignity by doing a carnival routine for a Phoenix wrestling promoter. All those who have admired Moore during his long, distinguished career as a boxer were dismayed to learn that he again is working for nickels and dimes. Moore has agreed to go on with a wrestler named Mike DiBiase—trading his good name for 27 percent of a $1,000 gate. So now when he is entitled to live leisurely, Moore is scrubbing for small change by working with a wrestler. I said earlier in this piece that he is shedding all semblance of dignity, but that isn't quite true. If Moore feels humiliated, he does a good job of hiding his shame. He's fooling nobody, not even himself, but he keeps up the pretense that his match with the wrestler is a legitimate competition."

Predicted the writer, "DiBiase has boxed a bit, and he will wear gloves—at least at the start of the match. This is a time-worn formula, and it will come as no surprise if the wrestler strips off his gloves and tries to catch Moore in a step-over toehold or something equally frightening."

Responded Moore: "He'd better not try that nonsense, or I'll flatten him fast."

Also dismayed was fellow San Diegan Ted Williams, the Boston Red Sox slugger and also a friend of Moore. "Why doesn't he quit?" wondered the Splinter. "His day is over and he should get out gracefully while he can. Does he need money so much that he can't retire?"

It was a good question. Archie admitted to Murphy that his walking-around money was in limited supply, and that precious little of the $3 million brought in at the box office at his fights made it into his bank account. He was still in litigation trying to collect his $90,000 purse for boxing Guido Rinaldi.

The 10-round main event at Phoenix's Madison Square Garden was promoted by Paavo Ketonen. He hoped for a sellout based on the fact that "DiBiase has made so many enemies since he has been wrestling here, the wrestling fans who'd like to see him get his head knocked off ought to fill the house themselves."

Not hardly. Only 800 fans turned out for the match. Archie entered the ring in an old brown sweater, explaining later that "I wore a peasant's costume because the Loudmouth has stolen my act." The reference was to Cassius Clay, who Moore said was "too commercial" and had "ruined poetry for all time."

A Moore left hook in the first round split DiBiase's eye wide open. The unskilled brawler gave it his best, but, not surprisingly, did more wrestling and holding than fighting. The referee finally stopped the one-sided assault in the third round.

Moore stayed in the ring and signed autographs for fans. Several big-city reporters were in town covering their teams on baseball's Grapefruit League circuit. Some of them had chronicled Moore's historic campaigns against Rocky Marciano in Yankee Stadium and the memorable come-from-behind victory over Durelle. Jack Murphy noted that Archie seemed a bit embarrassed to have them view his match with a professional wrestler in front of 800 people for a gate of less than $2,000.

Archie had hoped the DiBiase match would serve as a tune-up for a lucrative match in England against former British champion and world title challenger Brian London seven weeks later. But during negotiations for the bout, Doc Kearns became severely ill and the deal fell apart. That wasn't the worst of it. After a month in the hospital, Kearns was transferred to his son's home in Miami, where he passed away in his sleep on July 7, 1963. He was 80 years old.

The loss of his manager and close friend was felt keenly by Archie, who told the *San Diego Tribune*, "I'm very saddened by this. The sports world will surely miss him because there will never be another Doc Kearns." Regarding their relationship, Moore added, "There was never a signed contract, just a handshake. Doc's word was his bond. I'm sure anybody who had any dealings with him would vouch for that. The things I learned from Doc were amazing. I learned more from the 10 years I was with Doc than I did in the other 20 years I was with other managers. Doc taught me how to work bargains, how to work the media, and how to market myself."

The death of Kearns finally closed the book on Archie's boxing career, and he turned to other pursuits. Archie acted in *The Carpetbaggers,* starring George Peppard, who played a thinly veiled version of Howard Hughes. Alan Ladd was also in the film.

Archie stayed close to boxing by managing a few fighters in his spare time. One of them, light heavyweight Allen Thomas of Chicago, achieved a world ranking and came close to getting a title bout with Harold Johnson. When Thomas knocked out Sixto Rodriquez in St. Louis, the bout was held at a $100-a-plate Teamsters Union benefit at which Archie was the guest star.

The highlight of the trip home was a reunion with old friend Monroe Harrison, the man who taught Archie the cross-arm defense. Monroe had been coaching local fighters since Moore had left town.

Thomas fell short of the brass ring, but the Mongoose was so sure he had the right stuff as a coach that he was even willing to let bygones be bygones and avail himself to the man who had ruined poetry. "Clay is the most underrated fighter to come along in a long time," he told Jack Murphy. "Cassius is a most devious, a most deceiving young man. He has fooled lots of people because he is hiding his talent behind his big mouth. Cassius has intelligence bordering on brilliancy. Cassius learned from me in three months things it would take the average fighter three years to absorb. It was then that I came to appreciate his unusual ability. I don't say Clay would win if he fought Liston, but I do say it would be a good fight, an interesting fight. Further, if I could have two months to work with Cassius—if I could have him by myself, with nobody peeping over my shoulder—I would be willing to bet on Clay against Liston. The boy has good boxing intelligence; he has imaginative foresight."

Clay stayed with Angelo Dundee and eventually defied the odds by winning the world title on February 25, 1964, when the supposedly indestructible Sonny Liston failed to answer the bell for the seventh round. Although the fighter, who then changed his name to Muhammad Ali, and Archie never again worked together, they remained friends and saw each other many times through the years. "Archie always loved Muhammad," recalled Joan Moore. "How could you not?"

In early '64, Archie opened Archie Moore's Restaurant on 30th and Market St. in San Diego. The bistro featured a lunch and gourmet menu. Naturally, Archie's favorite, fried chicken, was a specialty. Joked Moore, "I don't have to say I'm the greatest; others do it for me, but everyone in town knew my reputation with a skillet."

For the grand opening of the restaurant Archie dressed up in a tuxedo and invited judges, professional football players, reporters, boxers, businessmen and freeloaders. "One thing Doc Kearns taught me, it's important to make a good display," he said. "Doc always told me to put on a good front. He said it's not the money you spend, it's the way you spend it." Casting his eyes over the crowd, Archie continued, "You will note we are well represented here tonight by doctors and lawyers. This is very fitting, because I always seem to need one or the other."

Moore also did speaking engagements, sometimes for extra income and sometimes just for the cause. At prisons in Southern California, Archie showed the film of the first Durelle fight to make the point that, "No matter how bad you're down and out, with the right attitude and perseverance, it's never too late to come out on top."

He enjoyed his prison appearances. "I knew I reached some people," Archie said. "I was always respected at these facilities. I never had any hecklers and no one ever walked out on my speeches."

Archie also accepted an invitation to go to Jamaica and aid government officials, including the police and the army, in imparting lessons in physical education and boxing basics.

Upon returning to San Diego, Archie signed on with the Boy Scouts of America. He toured the country recruiting black youngsters into the Scouts. This eventually led Archie to conceive of his own youth program, which he called "ABC—Any Boy Can." It blended ritual, discipline, old-fashioned morals and a large dose of Archie Moore.

In the late summer of 1965, riots tore up the Watts section of Los Angeles, and racial tensions were peaking elsewhere around the country. A real estate friend in the northern California city of Vallejo recruited Archie to come there and help in the fight against vandalism. Destruction caused by delinquents in tract homes totaled over $7,000 in damage per month. They threw rocks through windows of unoccupied homes, dislocated the plumbing and stole everything they could get their hands on.

The Los Angeles Times reported that the American Savings and Loan Company, which held mortgages on most of the houses in the primarily black housing development, put Archie on a $12,000 salary as a "public relations representative" to combat the vandalism.

He got right to work, setting up a makeshift gym in one of the tract homes. *Parade* magazine reported that "One day a black boy of about eight observed the former champion punching at the bag. 'I can do that,' the lad piped. 'Maybe you can,' Moore said. 'Come back with some more kids tomorrow and we'll see.' The boy returned the next day with 30 other kids.

"Holding out the punching bag as bait, Archie explained that learning to box is as simple as ABC. 'But before the B and C,' Moore said, 'you must first learn the A.' For the next hour, using parable and wry humor, quoting from his favorite philosopher—a black man named Aesop—Moore related to the eager boys the essence of morals and religion. Perhaps only for a fighter, but a very articulate one, would the slum kids have been so attentive."

Within a matter of weeks there was a sharp drop in vandalism in Vallejo, and the houses started selling at a fast pace. Archie had passed on lessons in morality, a sense of pride and respect for property, to the youngsters who stopped by daily to see the former champ pound on the heavy bag. "My goal was to teach faith in God, in country and our fellow man," Archie recalled later. "If a bigot could misguide, then I certainly can guide. I wanted the kids to know that anyone can improve himself that really wants too."

Moore was no starry-eyed dreamer. "You have to get the kids young. After 15 it's almost too late," he told *Parade*. Soon he opened an ABC program in San Diego at his own residence. The age span in ABC was from 8 to 15. The program included boys of all nationalities and races. A Seventh Day Adventist, Moore made religion a part of the script and had his students recite passages from the Bible. Archie had the youngsters he called "students" call him "Instructor Moore," explaining to *Parade*, "It is a subtle way of telling them to be students, not dropouts." ABC kids attended real school, of course, and had to show their homework to Archie for review. Good grades were a prerequisite for ABC membership.

A typical ABC meeting was described in the *Parade* article:

"After a recitation in unison of the Pledge of Allegiance, Moore asks: 'Students, what is the meaning of ABC?'

"The boys respond: 'Any boy can—if he wants to.'

"'If he wants to what?' Moore prompts.

"'If he wants to improve himself,' the boys shout back. 'To become a better student and a better American.'

"'What can a good student become in life?' Moore inquires. The answers roll out—'doctor, dentist, teacher, preacher, politician, mayor, governor, president.'

"Archie continued, 'What does a good student do?' 'Go to church….be a good American…go to school…be a good citizen.' Next Archie demands, 'And what doesn't a good student do?' Again the answers flowed: 'A good student doesn't steal…doesn't drink…smoke…sniff glue…take narcotics.'"

At the conclusion of the roll-call recitation, the boys were free to play ping-pong, softball, or take boxing lessons.

For the first few years, ABC financing came from a number of places: contributions from service clubs, business corporations, private donations and Archie's own pocket. At times it was difficult, but Archie always seemed to find a way. Two young men with whom Moore developed a special relationship were Billy McDaniels and Tommy Brooks. Brooks went on to fame as a boxing trainer, eventually handling Evander Holyfield and Mike Tyson. McDaniels was eventually adopted by Moore.

Brooks started boxing at the Boys Club, but after that program closed he moved on to Moore's ABC program. "Archie Moore meant everything to me," he told *KO* magazine. "He told me from the beginning, 'Kid, I'm giving you a gift.' For 20 years I never understood what he was talking about. But he taught me all about boxing, and it was a way to make a living. But at the time, I didn't know what the hell he was talking about. You know, he was from the old school. He always spoke in riddles and poems. 'When a task is once begun, never leave until it's done.' 'Shoot for the moon, land on the stars.' Stuff like that."

Asked how much of his life had been affected by Archie Moore, Brooks replied, "Everything. If I wasn't a good student or if I didn't pay attention to what he was teaching...for every action there is an equal reaction. It's all about cause and effect. And that's what he taught. You gotta be cagey. You gotta be crafty. You gotta be forceful. You gotta know when to lay back.

"Mr. Moore always looked to the children as the future and often compared them to seeds. He felt that in order to blossom, children needed to be nurtured. 'If you don't water it, it won't grow' is how he looked at it."

Recalls Billy Moore: "My dad was a strict disciplinarian. He could be a tyrant. His toughness was worse than anything I ever encountered on the street. But he knew that I would end up in boxing before I did. He always let me know that just because I was Archie Moore's son didn't mean I would get any breaks. I'll never forget the summers when dad converted an old bread truck into a gymnasium. It would get up to 120 degrees with no ventilation. Dad used to push Tommy Brooks and me like there was no tomorrow.

"Dad's interest in young men was a gift. He recognized where help was needed. 'Any Boy Can' was open to anyone of any ethnic background. It didn't make a difference to Dad. If a boy needed help, Dad wanted to be there for him."

Although Billy had a respectable amateur boxing career, he made a bigger mark on the gridiron. After receiving a scholarship to Cal State-Northridge, Billy ended up playing defensive end for the Philadelphia Bell of the old World Football League until his career ended prematurely due to injury.

Some of the fondest memories Billy has of his father concern the time they spent talking during long rides. "We used to drive in the car and he would relate driving to life. He always presented his own unique outlook on topics. He'd say, 'See that car boxed in traffic by the truck? It is important as a person to continue to grow and avoid being boxed in. You don't want to be boxed in life. You always want to be where you can move to your right or your left.' I think a lot about the times Dad and I used to drive through the San Joaquin Valley. We would be on our way to a speaking engagement and we would stop off in a cotton field and change clothes.

Some people think just because he was Archie Moore he would have to change clothes at the Hilton or something. Dad always prided himself on being a common man.

"Dad wanted to teach youngsters to put their best foot forward without cowardliness but with honor and dignity. That's part of the problem today, because gangs provide protection for those that can't protect themselves. ABC taught young men how to respect and defend themselves. I am hoping to one day revive the program."

During the late '60s, Archie took his youth program national by publishing this letter in newspapers across the country.

The devil is at work in America, and it's up to us to drive him out. Snipers and looters, white or black, deserve no mercy. Those who would profit from their brother's misfortunes deserve no mercy, and those who would set fellow Americans upon each other deserve no mercy.

I'll fight the man who calls me an "Uncle Tom." I have broken bread with heads of state, chatted with presidents and traveled all over the world. I was born in a ghetto, but I refused to stay there. I am a Negro, and proud to be one. I am also an American, and I'm proud of that.

The young people of today think they have a hard lot. They should have been around in the '30s when I was coming up in St. Louis. We had no way to go, but a lot of us made it. I became light heavyweight champion of the world. A neighbor kid down the block, Clark Terry, became one of the most famous jazz musicians in the world. There were doctors, lawyers and chiefs who came out of the ghetto. One of the top policemen in St. Louis came from our neighborhood.

We made it because we had a goal, and we were willing to work for it. Don't talk to me of your "guaranteed national income." Any fool knows that this is insanity. Do we bring those who worked to get ahead down to the level of those who never gave a damn? The world owes NOBODY—black or white—a living. God helps the man who helps himself!

Now then, don't get the idea that I didn't grow up hating the injustices of this world. I am a staunch advocate of the Negro revolution for the good of mankind. I've seen almost unbelievable progress made in the last handful of years. Do we want to become wild beasts bent only on revenge; looting and killing and laying America bare? Hate is bait, bait for simple-minded.

Sure, I despised the whites who cheated me, but I used that feeling to make me push on. If you listen to the professional rabble rousers adhere to this idea of giving up everything you've gained in order to revenge yourself for the wrongs that were done to you in the past—then you'd better watch your neighbor, because he'll be looting your house next. Law and order is the only edge we have. No man is an island.

Granted, the Negro still has a long way to go to gain a fair shake with the white man in this county. But believe this: if we resort to lawlessness, the only thing we can hope for is civil war, untold bloodshed, and the end of our dreams.

We have a meeting of qualified men of both races. Mind you, I said qualified men, not some punk kid, ranting the catch phrases put in his mouth by some paid hate-monger. There are forces in the world today, forces bent upon the destruction of America, your America and mine. And while we're on the subject, do you doubt for a minute that communism, world communism, isn't waiting with bated breath for the black and white Americans to turn on each other full force? Do you want a chance for life, liberty and the pursuit of happiness in the land of your birth, or do you want no chance at all under the Red heel?

Africa's a Great Place to Visit

There are members of the black community who call for a separate nation within America. Well, I do not intend to give up one square inch of America. I'm not going to be told I must live in a restricted area. Isn't that what we've all been fighting to overcome? And then there is the element that calls for a return to Africa.

For my part, Africa is a great place to visit, but I wouldn't want to live there. If the Irishmen want to go back to the Emerald Isle, let them. If the slaves want to return to the Iron Curtain area, OK by me. But I'm not going to go to any part of Africa to live. I'm proud of ances-

try, and of the country that spawned my forefathers, but I'm not giving up my country. I have fought all my life to give my children what I'm able to give them today; a chance for development as citizens in the greatest country in the world.

I do not for a moment think that any truly responsible Negro wants anarchy. I don't think you'll find intelligent—no, let's rephrase that—mature Negroes running wild in the streets or sniping at total strangers. God made the white man as well as the black. True, we haven't acted as brothers in the past, but we are brothers. If we're to be so many Cains and Abels, that's our choice. We can't blame God for it.

Teach That "Any Boy Can"

Something must be done to reach the Negroes and the whites in the ghettos of this country, and I propose to do something.

As a matter of plain fact, I have been doing something for the past several years. I have been running a program which I call the ABC— Any Boy Can. By teaching our youth—black, white, yellow and red— what dignity is, what self-respect is, what honor is, I have been able to obliterate juvenile delinquency in several areas.

I would now expand my program, change scope. If any boy can, surely any man can. I want to take teams of qualified people, top men in their fields, to the troubled areas of our cities. I know that the people who participated in the recent riots, who are participating and who will participate, are misguided rather than mad.

If some bigot can misguide, then I can guide. I've spent too much of my life building what I've got to put to torch just to satisfy some ancient hatred of a man who beat my grandfather. Those men are long dead. Do we have to choke what could be a beautiful garden with weeds of hate? I say NO! And I stand ready to start "Operation Gardener." I invite the respected Negro leaders of our country to join me.

One who did was Moore's brother-in-law, Sidney Poitier. "It's a funny thing," Archie told the *San Diego Tribune*, "We were both struggling artists—he in the theater, me in the boxing ring. We both came up from poverty. Sidney's father, you know, was a tomato picker in Nassau. And we both had to make our way into the fields of great competition. Poitier had won an Academy Award for his role in *Lilies of the Field.*

"Sidney feels that what we can do best along the same lines is to reach the kids, and the public generally, through the kind of movies he makes, for instance, *To Sir, With Love.*'"

The film stars Poitier as a teacher in a London ghetto who is overwhelmed by a disorderly class. The students show little respect for themselves or their teacher—until his fortitude and tolerance win them over and help prepare them for the world beyond school.

Continued Archie: "I'll tell you what Sidney is concerned about. It's the father image. In some Negro families, the father, no matter how talented or educated he is, can't find a job. So the mother has to work. When she comes home, she has to take care of the house. The boy sees that, and all his sympathy goes to her. The kid loses respect for the father. He thinks maybe he's lazy. So, first there's disrespect for the father. That turns to dislike, then to hatred. Either he or the father has to leave. Usually it's the boy. He goes out in the cruel world. And after a while he finds how tough it is for him to get work, especially if he has no education. I've done a lot of research on this, and what worries Sidney and me is that in a home like that, the boy has no one to be a model for him. There's no father image."

Joan Moore recalled those days well. "Archie constantly had kids over to the house. He was trying to project a father image to all children, especially the ones without a male role model. He would even take some of them to church with him on Sunday. Some kids would just come over to play. I enjoyed the kids and would help out if one skinned their knee or needed a button sewn on. Some looked at me as a mother figure, I suppose, because Archie was a father figure for them."

Children weren't the only ones Moore boosted whenever he could. At the invitation of the State Department, Archie entertained the troops during the war in Vietnam. His responsibility in his overseas tours was to referee amateur bouts for the Ninth Marines at Hill 55. The ring consisted of two strands of rope wrapped around four trees. The boxers and Archie were forced to maneuver around tree stumps within the roped-off section. It was a risky venture, but not as much as what happened when Lt. Col. Felix Salvador, an old San Diego friend of the Mongoose, offered to let Archie shoot his M-16 rifle. Moore demonstrated his expert marksmanship by blasting a couple tin cans. Compliments were not the only reaction forthcoming. Alerted by the gunfire, a Viet Cong sniper returned fire. As Moore ducked, Salvador ordered 25 rounds of artillery in the direction of the sniper. Moore recalled to Jack Murphy, "Unless that sniper went underground, he was a goner. But the Viet Cong are ingenious at building tunnels. They have hundreds of miles of tunnels in Vietnam."

During his 30-day trip to Vietnam, Moore visited 57 units, making speeches, refereeing and showing highlight videos from his career. The soldiers questioned Archie about world heavyweight champion Muhammad Ali, who had declared himself a conscientious objector and refused to be inducted into the armed forces. Is he a good fighter? Is he coming to the army? "He has a responsibility to serve his country just as you men do," Archie told the troops. "I think he belongs in the army. Clay would perhaps be a great entertainer; he is virtuoso, a man of many parts."

Moore was no flaming hawk himself. "I feel rice is the prize [in Vietnam]," he said, "and the price of rice never should come so high. Boys become men in a hurry in Vietnam; they grow up overnight. They've discovered this isn't a novel; people get shot and killed, and the other side doesn't surrender just because you tell him to. It's not a polite war. When an American is taken prisoner, he knows he'll soon be dead. With his throat slit."

1966 was also an active year on the screen for the former champion. Archie played "Mr. Jackson" in the comedy *The Fortune Cookie*, starring Jack Lemmon and Walter Matthau. For his role Moore had his hair dyed white (and confessed that he stopped sporting a beard because that white hair was real). Moore also made guest appearances on the television shows *Family Affair* and *Batman*. In the latter, Archie played alongside guest villain Art Carney, who was "The Archer." But after *The Fortune Cookie*,

Archie put his acting career in low gear, calling Tinseltown "too fancy, too unreal."

Archie's commitment to troubled kids was anything but artificial, and the gratification he got from it meant more than an Academy Award. A group of fourth graders at San Diego's Foster Elementary spent a year putting together a scrapbook of "Good Americans," and of all the nation's celebrities, only Moore and "Godfather of Soul" James Brown were included. Archie was recognized for his work with "Any Boy Can," and Brown for his efforts to restore peace in the aftermath of the assassination of Dr. Martin Luther King Jr.

In 1968, Archie became the seventeenth recipient of the "Mr. San Diego" award presented by the Grant Club, an organization of prominent business leaders. Mayor Curran handed Archie a super-sized key to the city and praised the Any Boy Can program as "the key to a brighter future for boys in San Diego." Telegrams poured in from all over, including messages from Jack Dempsey and a "hats off" from Gene Tunney. From Harry Markson, administrator of Madison Square Garden, came a wire asking, "Are you sure ABC does not mean 'Archie Begins Comeback?'" Jack Murphy called Archie a "philosopher, fighter, humorist, a friend of just about everybody in every walk of life."

After 90 minutes of plaudits, Archie took the podium. He talked about his feelings about the problems of lawlessness and race riots and spoke of qualities like spiritual faith, courage, and liberty, "the things that have made America great." Race riots, he stated, "served a purpose—to bring to the forefront that something must be done now. There is a great gap, and we need ABC to close that gap. ABC is a sure way to get youth to communicate with authority."

Quoting from the Bible, Archie said, "A little child shall lead them." But, he asked, "How should that little child lead you? With a miniskirt, with a Beatle haircut? That little child needs someone to teach him to lead.

"We don't have much time to think," he concluded. "Let's do something!"

A week after the award dinner, Archie and eight of his ABC boys were invited to Washington D.C. by Sen. George Murphy of California. Archie spoke of his organization at a luncheon in the Senate dining room.

Archie's renown as a humanitarian was overtaking his fame as a great boxer. His letter about juvenile delinquency was now being circulated abroad through the U.S. Intelligence Agency. The ABC program was finally getting the recognition it deserved. It seemed that Instructor Moore would live out his life combating delinquency. But in 1968, an impromptu encounter with another Olympic gold medal boxer would once again put Archie back in the boxing spotlight.

CHAPTER 20

Assisting George Foreman to the Heavyweight Title

Shortly after winning his heavyweight title at the 1968 Olympics in Mexico City, George Foreman dropped by unannounced at the Moore residence. Recalled Archie: "I was in Pennsylvania at the time when Foreman stopped by the house. Joan answered the door, and George told her that he was going to turn pro and that he wanted my assistance. It wasn't until after his pro career got under way that I could help train Foreman. I would have loved to have trained Foreman from the beginning of his pro career, but at that time I had commitments scheduled with my 'Any Boy Can' program."

Foreman had been saved from delinquency himself by the federal Job Corps program, with which Archie was familiar. He had visited Job Corps sites across the nation, including a women's Job Corps location in Albuquerque, New Mexico, in whose honor he changed his program to "Any Girl Can" for the occasion.

As in his prison appearances, one of the methods Moore used to give hope to the youngsters was to show a tape of the first Durelle bout. "These kids were all walking up a glass hill in life. I wanted them to realize with hard work and respect for your fellow man that anything was possible. I felt that the Durelle fight showed them no matter how close defeat seems, it's never too late to pull yourself up from the bootstraps and finish a winner."

Besides, Archie added, "I never did get tired of watching that tape."

For all its successes, the ABC program constantly battled for funding, and in June 1971, Archie was stunned and disappointed when the ABC's volunteer board threw in the towel. The program then included 300 San Diego inner-city kids. "I venture to say we have dramatically changed 70 percent of the boys who came here," Moore sadly remarked.

But he wasn't giving up. Archie then funded the venture out of his own pocket. Recalls daughter Rena, "Daddy kept the program going as long as he could, but without any outside financial aid it eventually came down to food on the Moores' table or the ABC organization. He still worked with children through the Boy Scouts, and if anyone ever stopped by the house, he was always willing to provide boxing instruction or advice."

Months after the program officially disbanded, Archie received this letter from a former ABC student, Overton Clabourne of Vallejo, California.

Dear Instructor Moore,

I have learned a great deal and have acquired that self-motivation that I used to hear you speak about. Your basic morals of life have sunk deep within my heart and have become a habit of every day. I know nothing in this world comes easy and that anything worth something is worth working for.

As I look back to when we used to recite the concept, I never really gave much thought to what the words meant, but now the words are like a message from God himself.

I want you to know that this was made possible in part by you because of the right road I was placed on. Over the years, I've gotten a lot of people concerned about me wanting to be something in life. These people I won't let down.

"I don't know what I did for him, but I do know what he did for me," Archie said. "It doesn't take much to teach a boy how to fight. To teach him what to fight for is even more important. This letter went straight to my heart."

George Foreman was 37-0 as a professional and had signed to fight heavyweight champion Joe Frazier for the title. As he had at the start of his career, he sought out the master for help.

Recalls former welterweight contender Charlie Shipes, a member of Team Foreman: "I was in camp with Sonny Liston back in the early '60s. I sparred with Liston quite a bit. I was pretty young at the time. I remember when Archie came by for a workout. I couldn't hit him. I had sparred with Bobo Olson and Liston and could tag them on occasion, but not Archie. I only had a few fights at the time, but Archie treated me like a world champion. I paid close attention to Moore and how he conducted himself. He was a fantastic motivator of people. When Foreman and Dick Saddler had a falling-out, I mentioned to George about bringing Archie on board."

In his 1996 autobiography, *By George*, Foreman recalled that Archie actually rejected his first proffered salary, but accepted a second proposed sum plus "a hefty bonus if I won," with one caveat: 'I can be with you six days a week, but not on Saturday,' Archie said. "I'm a Seventh Day Adventist and have to go to church."

The fight with Frazier was set for January 22, 1973, in Kingston, Jamaica. In preparing Foreman for Frazier, Archie recalled, "I worked on George's jab and the accuracy of his awesome punching power. Most importantly, I built up his self-belief. Foreman was the best fighter in the world going into the Frazier fight, and I made sure he knew that. I knew that Frazier could hurt Foreman if he hit him. So my plan was to stop Smokin Joe's barrage at arm's length—to catch Frazier with a stiff jab coming in. Before the fight Foreman was dropping his hand after delivering a straight left. I educated him on delivering it like a piston—*pop-pop-pop*."

There was also play, with a purpose. Archie recalled in George Plimpton's book, *Shadow Box*, "We would play ping-pong and the loser would have to squeeze a toy mouse that shrieked when handled. Nobody ever wanted to squeak the mouse because then everyone else knew who was the loser. I was pretty good at ping-pong, but near the end of training camp Foreman won every time. I used to say, 'What's it gonna be George, man or mouse?' It was a mental exercise meant to develop confidence. The goal was to get Foreman to believe he could do anything."

The fireworks between the fighters began at the weigh-in. Frazier threw an elbow in Foreman's direction because he felt that the challenger had moved inside his comfort zone. George then jumped on the scale, giving Frazier a long icy stare that didn't waver. Several inches taller than Frazier to begin with, Foreman really towered over the champ standing on the scale. "All this time," George wrote in his autobiography, "Archie stood behind me, rubbing my neck. Frazier got right up in my face, or as close as his four-inch height disadvantage allowed. 'I should kill you right now,' he said. Frazier had stepped on a land mine packed with hate. I exploded instantly, 'Shut up,' I yelled. 'Don't you say another word.' If Joe had taunted me again, or stared in silence, or even turned around and walked back to his seat, I'd have thought he was playing the same game. But he said, 'You can't tell me to shut up.' He shouldn't have done something that polite. Chink in his armor."

But the challenger's psychological advantage was short-lived. After weigh in, Foreman picked up a newspaper with an article predicting that he would be destroyed by Frazier. Again, master psychologist Archie reached into his bag of tricks to bolster his man's confidence.

In the ring, Foreman admitted, "My quivering knees barely carried me to center ring to hear the referee's instructions. I stomped the floor a few times to try to still them. Joe and I faced off. I found his eyes and held them in mine. Archie had taught me that if you could get your man to turn away first in the staring contest, then you'd won the fight. Here, if Joe broke first and looked down, he'd see my knees shaking. I kept telling myself not to be scared, but the knees didn't listen."

The night before, Archie had rehearsed fight strategy with Foreman. "I knew George could handle Frazier without difficulty. I knew Joe would come out 'smokin' right at him. Then Frazier would bend down in a crouch and expose the top of his head. I told Foreman that once he saw the top of that head to use his right hand and throw some thunder behind it. If you ever see a film of the fight, that is exactly what happened. George connected with a mighty right to the top of Joe's head, and Frazier went up in the air like he was doing a jackknife."

At first Moore's strategy was disputed by Dick Sadler, who was in camp despite his differences with Foreman. "Sadler was afraid Foreman was gonna break a hand hitting Frazier on top of the head," Archie said. "But I knew that catching Frazier on top of his exposed head while he rushed in was the key to victory for George. I convinced Sadler that there is nothing on top of a man's head except skin, bone, and a little fluid. The plan worked; Frazier hit the deck six times in two rounds. Frazier even tried to run out of the ring on one occasion, but where could he have gone, the Bahamas?"

After Foreman's stunning second-round KO, Archie told *Sports Illustrated*, "After the first round I said to him, 'You can't do it any better. Apply the pressure.' Well, he responded…with a shot that resounded around the world. Quite something. The fight surely should motivate any young violently prone person in Jamaica to try on the gloves. Watch them in the streets tomorrow. You'll see hundreds of re-creations, people staggering around who will be Frazier, but most of all will be the kids who want to be Foreman. Yes sir. We showed George how to put Frazier on Queer Street."

Other fighters sought Moore's counsel and expertise. Hard-punching heavyweight Earnie Shavers, managed by Don King, was set to fight former WBA heavyweight champion Jimmy Ellis on June 18, 1973. King brought The Mongoose in to help. "Archie and I hit it off right away," recalls Shavers, "him being a great puncher himself. As soon as Archie arrived, he announced that we needed a training camp. King arranged with Muhammad Ali for us to use his training facilities in Deer Lake, Pennsylvania. It was a beautiful and well organized camp. Ali gave us full use of the camp. Archie had me chopping trees to tone my body and increase my power. Archie's assistance boosted my confidence going into the Ellis fight."

Ten days before the fight, Moore and Shavers relocated to New York to wind up training and throw some psychological grenades at Shavers's opponent. "Archie was a master of psychology and he had a plan to con Ellis," Earnie said. "Archie went down to watch Ellis train one day. Upon exiting the workout, Archie announced to Ellis, 'James, you can't punch.' A few days later the press noted that it seemed unusual for a caliber of fighter like Ellis to be beating up sparring partners this close to the fight. Archie had gotten inside his head with his comment."

After the fighters weighed in, the Moore-Shavers head games continued. Remembers Shavers, "When Angelo and Jimmy were leaving the weigh-in, I told the security guard to go and protect Dundee and the 'oversized middleweight.' That remark angered Ellis. Ellis bumped into Archie in the hallway and voiced his frustration. 'Mr. Moore, I'm going to hurt Earnie tonight. I'm telling you because I don't want any blood on my hands.' Archie responded, 'James, if you don't want blood on your hands tonight, don't wipe your face during the fight.'"

The fight ended in the very first round when Ellis tried to prove he could punch and ended up on his back for the 10-count. A devastating right uppercut put him there. The next morning Archie was up to his old tricks. Said Shavers, "Archie and I went down to breakfast at our hotel across from the Garden. Some reporters came into the restaurant and Archie saw them. He then took a small brown bottle of cough syrup out of his coat pocket, took the top off and said, 'Take a swallow and let out a loud roar, then stand up and roar again.' The reporters wrote that Archie had given me some secret potion from Australia, but it was only cough syrup without a label. Archie was a sly fox."

They made a good team, The Mongoose and the man Ali would nickname "Acorn." "I believe Archie and I got along so well because I didn't mind hard work," Shavers said. "Archie would kill time by telling stories on how the top fighters ducked him for years. But he remained in shape in case the opportunity arose. Archie taught me all about the human body and where to hit your opponent to cause the greatest harm. He also taught me how to eat right and how to properly cook food. On the days that I fought after meeting Archie, I would eat two steaks but not swallow the meat. I would only swallow the juices because that gave me strength without forcing my body to digest the meat. Archie made sure I did my roadwork by 5 a.m. because the air was fresh. The trees put out fresh oxygen in the morning. Archie made sure I didn't run near traffic where automobiles pollute the air with carbon monoxide. Archie was the best I knew at putting together a fight plan that worked."

Shavers was training to fight Jerry Quarry at the Garden when his jaw was broken by sparring partner Jeff Merritt. The bout was postponed, and Archie got the hook. Explained Shavers: "I had my mouth open and I got hit with one of Merritt's left hooks, and it fractured my jaw. The Quarry fight was postponed. Matchmaker Teddy Brenner of Madison Square Garden had spent several thousand dollars promoting the fight, and he was livid. Someone had to be blamed, and they fired Archie and made him the scapegoat. Brenner reasoned that Archie should not have let me spar with a big hitter like Merritt. Don King replaced Archie with his friend Tiger Brown. I had a lot of confidence in Archie that I was unable to get with Brown."

In *Only in America, The Life and Crimes of Don King*, Shavers blamed King for axing Archie and said losing Moore "killed [his] concentration and confidence" to the point that, when the Quarry fight was held, he got knocked out in the first round.

Truth be told, Jeff Merritt was also one of King's fighters, and it was King who put him in the ring with Shavers. When Archie suggested Merritt was too tall for Earnie, King told him, "Who asked you? I pay you to train fighters, not give me advice." But after Shavers got hurt, it was Archie who left, not King.

But Moore was still a fixture in the corner of the heavyweight champion of the world. He worked with George Foreman when Big George defended his title against Joe Roman in Tokyo and Ken Norton in Caracas, Venezuela.

Norton was a native of Illinois who ended up in San Diego. "I was always aware of Archie Moore," he said. "I had began my professional career in San Diego, and Archie was an icon in the area. There were times when I would see him at the fights and we would converse. I always addressed him as Mr. Moore. I had the utmost respect for him. In 1973 I beat Muhammad Ali in San Diego and I attracted a decent following in the area, but it never reached Archie's popularity. San Diego was his town. As the years passed we eventually became close friends. They will never make another one like him."

En route to Venezuela for the Foreman-Norton fight, Archie made a detour to the Argentine Embassy in Washington D.C. By order of Moore's old friend Juan Peron, Ambassador Alejandro Orfila rolled out the red carpet for Archie, Joan, sister-in-law Juanita Poitier and Archie's "godson," famed Los Angeles criminal attorney Charles E. Lloyd. Although in exile for 18 years, Peron kept in touch with Moore frequently. Recalled Lloyd, "It was the most elegant black-tie event I had ever seen. My godfather has been toasted all over the world, but nothing could top the bash that Peron threw for him at the Embassy. Archie could have gone around the world without a wallet. He had such a commanding presence."

In the summer of '74, Archie headed to Johannesburg, South Africa, to work with South African champion Norman "Pangaman" Sekgapane, in his bout against Jorgen Hansen of Denmark. At a press conference, Archie addressed more than mere boxing matters. "You blacks in South Africa gotta realize that you are now in the biggest room for improvement," he said. "You can be anything. I was born in a ghetto but refused to stay there. I am black and proud of that. I am also an American and proud of that.

"Jeez, how I'd really love to talk to your youngsters down here," Archie continued. "Youth problems, I believe, are the same all over the world. The only difference is the punishment. How I'd love to start the ABC program here. Do you want me to teach your kids how to fight? No! I can teach them what to fight for."

Archie had both black and white reporters eating out of his hand.

A few days later, Sekgapane knocked out Hansen, and Moore returned to the States to spend time with his family before jetting back to the African continent for what would be one of the biggest events in boxing history.

Don King had raised $10 million to put Foreman and ex-champ Muhammad Ali in a ring in Kinshasa, Zaire. Formerly the Belgian Congo, Zaire was ruled by President Mobutu Sese Seko, who thought that hosting a heavyweight title fight would put his struggling country on the map. Of course it wasn't just any heavyweight title fight, but one pitting a young, undefeated titlist—Foreman—against a man considered by many—and himself—as the greatest of all time. "Rumble in the Jungle," indeed.

For all that, Ali was considered to be on the down side of his career, and few in the media gave him a chance against Foreman. Neither did Archie. "I feared for Ali's safety and prayed beforehand that Foreman would not seriously injure him," he said. "Foreman was a murderous puncher, and Ali had lost some leg speed. Ali and I originally parted company because he didn't think he needed to learn in-fighting back in those days. Ali had hot feet under him and he thought he had learned it all. He started down that high-way to fame, confident he could go on indefinitely with that great natural speed of his. But the footsteps of time are in his ears now, and he's meeting himself coming back."

In Zaire, Archie was always seen carrying a picnic basket he guarded with his life. When asked about it, he said, "I abstain from duffel bags." The rumor started that the basket contained lion meat that Moore fed to Foreman to fuel his anger. That appealed to Archie, and he happily did everything he could to keep the rumor alive.

Moore didn't just school the champion in ring technique and diet. Another interest Archie passed on to Foreman was his love of jazz. Foreman was accustomed to loud music and often blared his stereo. Archie asked him to turn down the volume and really listen to the music. He turned George onto jazz singer Billie Holliday, and in Zaire they often passed time listening to jazz.

Ali was up to his old tricks, calling Foreman "The Mummy" and predicting "the whole world is gonna bow down to me, because the stage is set. Everbody's talking about how great George Foreman is, how hard he hits, but I'll be king again. I'm fighting another Sonny Liston."

During the opening round, Ali boxed from long range. But then, at the beginning of the second round, Ali retreated to the ropes and stood there flat-footed. It was the last strategy anyone would have advised against the power-punching Foreman. Even Ali's corner yelled at him to move and box. But Ali had other notions, and eventually his "rope-a-dope" scheme to stand and absorb punishment wore out Foreman. George punched himself out and was stopped in the eighth round.

In *Muhammad Ali, His Life and Times*, Archie recalled, "George was the most dangerous puncher of his time. And what I remember most about that fight was Ali rushed out at the opening bell, showing no fear, and struck George on top of the head. Plans upset; do you know what I mean? Right at the start, George knew he had something different to contend with. But George only knew one way to fight, so he swung and he swung, and he pinned Ali up against the ropes, determined to wear him down. At first that seemed like a fine strategy. Everything we'd planned was to get Ali on the ropes, where George could hit him. But George got him there, and when Ali stayed there, George didn't know what to do."

The fight started in the pre-dawn hours to accommodate closed-circuit telecast buyers and viewers in the States. Later that Zaire afternoon, at 4 a.m. San Diego time, Moore phoned Jack Murphy to give his take on the fight. "Ali has to be the greatest ever, the greatest fighter I have ever seen. Like Floyd Patterson, he came back and won the title a second time, and he did it against a much more dangerous opponent. Ali psyched George out of his system of fighting. It shows what inexperience will do to a young fighter. George didn't seem to realize he couldn't maintain the same speed for 15 rounds. He should have gone to his jab.

"Give Ali's people some credit. They came into the ring and loosened the ropes. The ropes had been taut. They loosened them, and that's why Ali was able to lean back so far. It's an old, time-worn trick and they got away with it. Give some credit to Drew Brown, the one they call 'Bundini.' He had Ali leaning on Foreman, pushing him down. It tired George; it was as though he had fought 14 rounds instead of seven."

To George Plimpton, Archie put an automotive spin on the events in Zaire: "Ali swayed so far back on the ropes that it was like he was sitting in an old convertible Cadillac. The '54 model. Now, George tried to enter from the side doors. But they were shut. So George began to bang at them, hitting at Ali's arms that had the elbows protecting his hips, on up to the gloves protecting the lower mandible. On occasion, George struck Ali some tremendous blows on the upper cranium, causing Ali no little discomfiture. But Ali weathered that, and he cunningly convinced George that he could not punch, and other nonsensical things, until George began to behave like he actually believed it, until this tremendous [boxer] lost his power from punching at that Cadillac's doors and he turned from an atomic force into a firecracker. In short, as they say in the idiom of Brooklyn, he blew his cool."

After Foreman's defeat to Ali, he fought on until suffering a decision defeat to Jimmy Young on March 17, 1977. He then took a 10-year hiatus from boxing before again reuniting with Moore for the amazing comeback that put Big George back on the heavyweight throne.

A few months after "The Rumble in the Jungle," Archie was back in Africa, this time in Lagos, Nigeria. He was working for the country's Director of Sports, assisting the nation's top amateur boxers. It was supposed to be a short-term assignment, but the Nigerian government was so pleased with his work that Archie was persuaded to stay on. He wrote Joan explaining the situation:

December 21, 1975

My darling wife,

The Director of Sports, as I told you via phone, like the work I've done in the area of youth. This is part of his overall plan to help in education. Well, dear, get yourself together and get all the personals you will have to have, as it looks possible you and the family will be leaving soon. It would be a gas if you could all come over on a ship. This would be an unforgettable experience for all. How are my darling children? Has Hardy found any hobbies besides chasing girls? What is Billy doing besides waxing the car? My best to Joanie and Rena. Warn them about priorities, education, school first. Then profession, or position in life.

Bye my sweet little girl (big girl).

All my love,
Daddy

Eventually the family did join Archie in Africa. Recalls daughter Rena: "We were well taken care of in Nigeria. We were put up in a country club area with other foreign guests of the government. I was just finishing high school, and Nigeria was much different than what I was used to in the States. We attended a nice private school, but I missed my friends back home. It was the disco age in California, but not Nigeria. As African Americans returning back to Africa, my sister and I faced a different kind of prejudice. Black Africans held a certain prejudice against blacks from the States. It was different for my dad because he was a celebrity of sorts. I even got spit on once. Things were going real well for Daddy; he was put in charge as the head boxing coach for the Nigerian Olympic team headed to the 1976 Olympics in Montreal."

J'Marie recalled, "I was rather young to appreciate the experience. I did feel that going to the 'Motherland' was going to be exciting. Dad convinced us that the house was only a small step down from our San Diego home."

The trip there was certainly different from any they'd taken before. "We flew from London to Lagos on Nigerian Air," says J'Marie. "I couldn't believe it; people brought chickens and goats right on the plane. When we landed in Lagos the first night, it was pitch black and the heat almost turned me into a Hershey chocolate bar. We were instructed by the Nigerian Embassy to take a cab to the hotel. There was a note for us to meet Dad at the hotel buffet once we arrived. The buffet was very elegant with a standard European table setting, including fresh flowers, although it had an odd aroma. I don't eat seafood, especially when the eyes are staring at me. At the end of the buffet was a huge pig with an apple in its mouth. It didn't look too appetizing. Finally I settled on some stew because I thought that couldn't be messed up too bad. I was wrong; when I got back to the table I took a bite and bit into something hard. It was a baby goat hoof!"

The Moores stayed in a two-bedroom house without air conditioning. Rena recalls, "Wall geckos climbed the screen, and goats and roosters were running wild near the yard. It was hot and humid. We each took several baths a day just to cool down. Two fans provided the only relief from the hot weather. But it was too hot for them to have any real effect. To clean our clothes Dad would fill the tub, add some soap, and stomp away. It was quite different in Nigeria."

The distaff Moores begged Archie to call the U.S. Embassy for some Western fare. Archie's favorite food there was a variation of the grilled chicken he loved so much back home. Archie would build a brick circle and fill it with rocks and wood. Then he'd take an iron grate, slant it, and wait for the rocks to get hot. Moore tilted the grill to let the grease drip off.

As hard as they tried to fit in, the other Moores had trouble adapting to the local ways and culture. "Nigerian women didn't wear pants, so they thought my sister and I were crazy," says J'Marie. "I purchased some African garb and got my hair braided to fit in, but we never really did. The Nigerians referred to us as 'Oibo,' meaning that we were of mixed ancestry. After being in Nigeria on and off for four years, it was good to get back home."

It was in Nigeria where Archie adopted the trademark beanie-type cap that made him instantly recognizable for the rest of his life. The distinctive caps were crocheted by Joan. "Archie's sensitive about his hair because he's going bald," she told a reporter. "Plus, I'm taller than he is. With the hat on, he's up there with me."

Whenever Archie took on a new fighter, Joan got an order for a beanie. "Every time I looked around, someone said, 'I like his hat, can I get one?'" Joan estimated that she crocheted over 100 lids. "Archie was always telling me that somebody wants a hat. I used to laugh and joke with him after his hundredth request. I'd say, 'I'll have to think about that or, better yet, I'll teach you how to do it.' He just smiled and never bothered to learn how to crochet."

Although most of Moore's training was done with Nigeria's top amateurs, he also managed to teach some of the less privileged. Recalls J'Marie, "My Dad had his own driver in Nigeria, and whenever he saw a large group of young kids he would ask the driver to pull over. Dad would then take out his stick and trace out a 20-by-20 foot area for his ring. Dad would first run through the basics and then sparring would commence. Sometimes I had to demonstrate jabbing, uppercuts, pivots, and combinations. The kids all loved it. As Dad drove off the kids would chase after the vehicle yelling 'Of couch! Of couch!'"

One time, The Mongoose himself got back into action. Archie was out sightseeing one afternoon and he noticed construction workers heaving sand from the banks of the Ikorodu River into a boat. Archie pulled over and snapped a photo. The foreman of the work crew, a young, well-muscled man, didn't like having their picture taken and confronted Moore. "You people come up here to take our pictures and then take it back and ridicule us poor people," he yelled. Archie apologized and offered to turn over the film, but it was the entire camera that the angry foreman demanded. When the construction worker punctuated his demand by tossing a punch at Moore, Archie retaliated with a left hook, a right to the belly and a final left-hand that dropped the foreman—no Foreman—like a sack of grain. It was like old times with one exception; Archie was bitten in the hand during the fight and it became infected. "If a man can bite my fist before I can get it out of his mouth," he said later, "I'd better stop fighting in the streets."

Much more serious were the consequences when Archie became involved in an auto accident several months later. It was originally erroneously reported back to the States that Archie had severed his spinal cord in the incident. Fortunately, his back injuries weren't that severe, and after an overnight stay in the hospital, he and Joan, who suffered a broken wrist and internal injuries, were released.

Archie stayed in Nigeria for four years. When he finished there, he agreed to spend a year in New Brunswick, Canada, lecturing youngsters on drug abuse and vandalism and teaching boxing fundamentals. That put him just a couple hundred miles from Yvon Durelle's home. Durelle had recently been acquitted of a second-degree murder charge stemming from a fight at a tavern he owned. It was a messy, headline-making incident that left the old fisherman in financial difficulty from big legal fees.

The two former adversaries were given a reunion dinner in honor of the twentieth anniversary of their historic championship battle. A thrilled Durelle told the audience, "I never made a dime from boxing, but I was fortunate to become good friends with people like Archie Moore."

That last sentiment was shared by people all over the world.

CHAPTER 21

The Battle Against the Beehive

After returning home from Canada, Archie reached an agreement in late August, 1979, to train unbeaten heavy-weight prospect James "Quick" Tillis. A Tulsa native, Tillis began his professional career in Chicago and ran his record to 9-0 when his manager, Dean Kaulentis, hired Moore to oversee the former rodeo cowboy's training.

Increasingly frugal in his later years, Archie moved into Tillis's small studio apartment in downtown Chicago to save on rent. Being so close to the old Mongoose was a double-edged sword, Tillis recalled in his autobiography, *Thinking Big*. "I got to know Archie better than anyone wanted to know Archie," he wrote. "He'd talk in his sleep, first sayin, 'mumbo, mumbo, mummmbo, jumbo, jummmbo'— at least it sounded that way—then he'd start jabberin some African language, 'haku miko bamsu.'"

Tillis's first fight under Moore was on September 7, 1979, in Chicago against Jimmy Cross. After easily disposing of his opponent in two rounds, Tillis stood at ring center unsure of what to do next. Shouted Moore, "Bow! Bow!" Tillis did as instructed, and Moore signaled in approval.

Of course the old master imparted more than the proper ring etiquette to his charge. "Archie was teaching me moves I ain't even seen," Tillis later recalled. One of them was called "The Pool Table," whereby the fighter threw a left hook out of the corner followed by a pivot and a left jab. The mysteries of "Escapology," "Breathology" and other Archieisms were also revealed, but, Tillis said, "I can't talk about them. They're trade secrets."

"Excellent, excellent," Moore told *Chicago Sun-Times* columnist John Schulian when apprised of Tillis's refusal to break the magician's code. "If he continues to listen and to believe, I can have him fighting for the championship in 18 months."

Tillis eventually did fight for the World Boxing Association heavyweight title, but by then he and Archie were no longer professionally related. In fact, after just two additional bouts under Moore's supervision, they went their separate ways.

Back home in San Diego, Archie continued to pass on his knowledge to economically challenged youngsters. "It made me proud when someone would mention that they would sit by the radio and listen to my fights or when someone became excited just to shake my hand," he said. "I believe it meant a great deal to my community for a black man to receive so much recognition. It was important to me to pass on this hope to others. My goal was to reach these kids early, teach them things that their parents should have taught them. Boxing was one way to reach these youngsters so they could go on to a decent life. It can keep them busy enough so there is no time for drugs, the street, or whoremongering."

Another opportunity to widen his influence came in 1980, when Archie was appointed to a post in the U.S. Department of Housing and Urban Development by President Ronald Reagan. He single-handedly ran "Project Build," centered in a 490-unit HUD-funded housing project in the Watts section of Los Angeles. Archie stayed in an apartment there, and sometimes with his brother Samuel in Compton. He drove a Toyota truck equipped with its own boxing gym in the trailer. "My goal was to teach self-defense so that kids wouldn't be bullied into buying drugs," he said. "I was happy to be helping kids again, but I worked in some scary areas."

While working on the HUD project, Moore befriended Dr. Marilyn Douroux, an inner-city high school teacher. Dr. Douroux recalled, "Archie came to my office in 1983 and wanted to know how he could get involved with working with children. I received permission from my school district for Archie to work with my students in Los Angeles. Archie would pull in people off the street and show them how to box. He would also preach morals and his 'Any Boy Can' creed. At first, some of the younger kids took him for granted because they didn't know who he was. Then one day I rented a limousine for some of the meanest inner-city kids from a variety of ethnic backgrounds to ride with Archie to a boxing match at the Great Western Forum. Each boy was provided a shirt with 'Team Mongoose' printed on the back. The troubled teens were not convinced until the limousine pulled up to the arena. As soon as Archie got out he was flooded by fans and reporters. The unconvinced kids soon changed their tune. After that night they worshipped Archie. If Archie didn't come to town, the kids would be disappointed. He was one of the most brilliant men that I ever met."

And, sometimes, one of the most frustrating, too. "My husband and I spoiled Archie," Dr. Douroux said. "He had his own room at our house and we gave him the run of the place. He'd stop by the house with a big grin and ask, 'What's for lunch?' Archie and I worked together with some kids from some really tough gangs. Sometimes we had a difference of opinion. Archie wasn't one for details. He never wore a watch. We used to fuss back and forth a lot. He once told my husband, 'I know she means well, but if she was a trainer her men would hate her.' Archie's HUD office was on Wilshire Blvd. He did a lot of positive work for underprivileged youth in the projects. It was an honor to my husband and I to become so close to him."

Archie was astonishing in many ways, Dr. Douroux said. "Even in his '70s, he amazed kids by walking on his hands. He also had a penchant for buying things he'd never use. His taste could be awful. He once gave me an armadillo lamp that he was so proud of. He was a very sensitive guy who cared a great deal about others."

On September 24, 1980, Jack Murphy died of cancer in San Diego. In the 29 years that he had been sports editor at the *San Diego Union*, the city grew into a truly major league sports venue. Murphy's vision and initiative helped bring the football Chargers to town in 1961. His daily editorials and behind-the-scenes work played a contributory role in getting the city council's approval for the construction of a new stadium in 1965, which brought the baseball Padres to town in 1968. Five months after Murphy's passing, the sports stadium was named in his honor.

His old comrade's death was a heavy blow to Moore. "From the day he became a sports journalist we bonded," Archie said. "Jack and I always kept in close touch well after my career had ended. Jack used to joke that in 29 years he hadn't made much progress because he still held the same job! But in reality, he was a journalistic giant who was instrumental into turning San Diego into a professional sports town."

*   *   *

In a freak accident, Moore's own life was almost taken on June 2, 1985. Archie was on his way to a press conference in Chula Vista to talk about his 7'2" heavyweight prospect, Tom Payne. But before leaving his house Archie was attacked by a swarm of bees and ended up being taken to Physicians and Surgeons Hospital instead.

"Those bees almost killed me," Archie told *The Ring*. "They covered me like a robe. I kept them in a wooded box in the back yard. I liked them for their honey. I attempted to move the hive to put up a punching bag in the hive's current location. When I moved the hive, one of the drawers came out and there were bees all over me.

"In a split second, I was covered in a black buzzing cloud. In a flash, I felt them up my shirt and pants. I was getting stung all over my body. I covered my face with my hands. It felt like I was on fire.

"I ran into the house followed by a swarm. Aunt Willie Pearl was yelling from the window. I knew if the bees got to her, she'd be a goner. I ran into the house, peeled my clothes off and jumped into the shower. I hoped it was all a nightmare, but the pain was real. I began to swell from all the stings. I was rushed to the hospital; I don't even remember it. I was out cold for two days and in intensive care for three. In all of my career, I had never been defeated like that."

Archie continued to work hard in the HUD program, and he played hard, too. He spent his off days at University Pool Hall in L.A., perfecting his game of eight-ball bank and looking out for the other habitués of the place. Pool hall manager Lefty Barton told the *Los Angeles Times*, "You know what Archie does once in a while? He'll come in with a whole box of pastrami—not Pastrano—sandwiches for everybody. He's a real man, Archie is."

In October of 1985, San Diego paid tribute to its favorite fistic son with a testimonial dinner recognizing Moore as the city's greatest fighter. Former ring opponents Muhammad Ali and Joey Maxim were on hand, although the latter took an indignant powder before his scheduled remarks after a tape was shown of Archie beating him up in 1952. Ali more than filled the void, "roasting" Archie for 15 minutes. He made the crowd laugh by saying he "hated" The Mongoose for being so humble, and recalling when Archie told him not to "brag so much," because "you may have to back it up."

When International Boxing Federation heavyweight champion Larry Holmes put his title on the line against Michael Spinks on September 22, 1985, Holmes brought Archie to camp as a special adviser. Holmes's regular trainer, Eddie Futch, was also Spinks's trainer and had decided to sit the fight out because of his conflicting loyalties.

Spinks was the undisputed light heavyweight champion of the world. As Archie knew well, no 175-pound champion had never successfully challenged for boxing's greatest title. The match had added significance for Holmes because a win over Spinks would raise him to 49-0 as a professional, tying the mark of Rocky

Marciano, the only heavyweight titlist to go through his career with an unblemished record.

A 5-1 underdog, Spinks used his awkward style to confuse Holmes and capture the heavyweight crown via a close and controversial decision that outraged the deposed champion. The now 48-1 Holmes lashed out not only at the judges but also at the memory of Marciano. "Rocky couldn't carry my jockstrap," Holmes said. While he was at it, Holmes also fired his special adviser, Archie. When Moore wondered, via letter, what he had done wrong, Holmes wrote back:

Dear Archie:

I received your letter and felt I would answer with some of my thoughts.

I have always considered you one of the greatest fighters of all time.

Archie, I noticed when we were in Las Vegas everything seemed to be a secret with you. In spite of what people did in my camp, they at least tried to help by working as a team with the coaching, training, etc.

You did not act as a team player by including the rest of my corner people. Everything had to be private with you.

I thank you for being there and being my friend.

Yours Truly,
Larry Holmes

Of course, Holmes wasn't the first boxer to chafe under Archie's rule, and he wouldn't be the last. Former Canadian judo champion Pierre Marchand trained under Archie when he broke into boxing in San Diego. Marchard told San Diego's *Tuned In*, "Archie Moore is very intense, always giving 100 percent. It's like a flashback of his fighting days when you're with him. He has old methods. It's like a military camp with him. You have to say 'Yes sir.' He's tough, but he has good intentions."

Added Marchand's manager, Dan Hamel: "We had a tough time working with him as a trainer because he demands so much respect. He's a great person, was a great champion, and I do respect the man, but he's not very subtle in his approach to anything. He force-feeds knowledge rather than working with a fighter's personality. But like him? You bet. He's got that twinkle in his eye, and you can't help but like the guy."

It took someone as eccentric as Archie to really appreciate his methods, and when former champion George Foreman decided after being out of boxing for 11 years to go after his old title again, one of his first calls was to the Moore house. "I answered the phone when George called," recalls Rena Moore. "At first I wasn't even sure if it was really him. The family hadn't heard from him for so long. But then Daddy got on the phone with him and later confirmed that Foreman wanted his help for his comeback.

"When it was announced that Daddy was going to be helping Foreman, it seemed like the whole world thought they were both off their rockers. Daddy always believed from the beginning that George had what it took to regain the title."

Foreman was 37 years old and scaled around 315 pounds. "Dad understood George's situation," says Billy Moore. "He realized that Foreman already knew how to fight and that conditioning was key. Dad didn't train him like he would a 21-year-old professional fighter. Dad rarely had Foreman spar. He figured there was no need for a man George's age to take a beating in the gym."

"It was George's idea to bring in Archie," recalled Charlie Shipes, Foreman's chief trainer. "Archie was a great motivator. Archie worked on Foreman's defense, instilling the cross-arm defense into George's arsenal. He also worked on the preciseness of George's delivery of punches."

With an eye to the ex-champion's girth, Moore also counseled Foreman on his dietary habits, extolling the virtues of the fabled Aborigine diet. The cheeseburger-loving Foreman gave it the old college try. "I would try some of the things, chew the meat and not swallow it, things of that nature," he said. "But when Archie was not looking, I'd eat it anyway."

Unlike the younger, slimmer Foreman of a decade or so earlier, whose perpetual glower and sullenness qualified him for the "Sonny Liston Congeniality Award," this Foreman was easy-going, funny and forthcoming about his reason for donning the gloves again. "After 10 years of me preaching and not working out," he said, "we were so poor you could drop the second 'o' and the 'r' and call us 'po.' My wife told me to get out and make some money."

The first bout of Foreman's comeback took place on March 3, 1987, in Sacramento, California. Trained down to a portly 267 pounds, Big George stopped journeyman Steve Zouski in four. Four months later and 20 pounds lighter still, Foreman faced no-hoper Charlie Hostetter.

"Hostetter entered the ring looking like a guy who knows the sentence before he faces the judge," said the *San Diego Tribune*. "Few ever have reflected a sense of terror as well as did the Texan, and his agony was compounded when the start was delayed 10 minutes while the promoters searched for a boxing glove. One of the originals had split a seam; ringsiders meanwhile noted that Foreman's trunks were threatening to do likewise at any moment."

But George's trunks held up better than poor Hostetter, who folded in round three. Foreman then called for a fight with heavyweight champion Mike Tyson. Boxing purists cringed, but the media had fun with the Foreman circus, and Archie was having his kicks, too. He would report to camp three weeks before each fight, enthusiastic and ready for business. Recalls Rena Moore: "Daddy was really happy when he started working with Foreman on his comeback. He loved being around the big-time boxing again and the opportunity to reunite with former associates."

It was a mutually beneficial partnership. "Archie Moore is the greatest teacher of boxing who ever lived," Foreman told the *San Diego Tribune*. "I want to win not just for George Foreman, but for Archie Moore. I'm a better fighter today than I was 10 years ago. Mr. Archie Moore has taught me some things nobody has since fighters fought in pits and holes."

The Foreman Express rolled along. In September, Bobby Crabtree fell in six in Springfield, Missouri. Two months later, Tim Anderson lasted four rounds in Orlando. These weren't first-rate heavyweights, but capable opponents with winning records. Truth is, it didn't matter that much to the crowds that instantly bonded with the new, improved (at least personality-wise) Foreman. Wrote the boxer in his autobiography, *By George*: "The people came and stood for me, their applause filling the hall and my heart. I drank it in like a thirsty man. This was what I missed the first time out. No one ever appreciated it more than I did. What's more, I think they saw I appreciated it and saw how much I loved them back. That was a new experience for both of us."

Evidence of Foreman's growing popularity was the additional seating needed to accommodate the crowd for George's bout against Rocky Sekorski at Bally's in Las Vegas, even though it was televised nationally on ESPN.

Sekorski exited in the third round after absorbing tremendous shots. Between rounds, Foreman stood and leaned over the top rope to consult with Moore, dressed in his trademark beanie cap. The live crowd and television audience were taken with the unique partnership. That went for younger journalists as well, who laughed at Foreman's cheeseburger jokes and at Archie's pronouncements about the secrets of longevity he had imparted to George.

Not so copacetic was Moore's relationship with the administration of President George H. Bush, who took over from Ronald Reagan in 1988. Bush installed Jack Kemp as HUD's secretary, and under his stewardship, Archie's youth-counseling job was phased out. Unhappy about the move and hoping to spur a reversal of the action, Moore sent Secretary Kemp a photo that had been taken of Archie when he was a light heavyweight champion, standing with the crew-cut quarterback of the San Diego Chargers—Kemp himself. It didn't work. "I never heard from him," Moore said, laughing. "I think I'll send him another one."

In 1988, George the boxer registered nine victories, including a stoppage over former light heavyweight champion Dwight

Muhammad Qawi. Archie told the press, "I have no doubt he can come back and win the heavyweight championship of the world. This is the most powerful puncher I have ever seen, and I have seen them all, back to Joe Louis. We're going to shake up some people. Thirty-nine years old? I think this is where I began."

After steamrolling five more opponents of modest credentials, Big George—19-0 on his comeback—signed for his biggest test against former contender George Cooney. Cooney was embarking on a comeback of his own after three years outside the ropes. In his first ring incarnation, Cooney's brutal left hook had taken him all the way to a title fight against Larry Holmes, which "Gentleman Gerry" lost by technical knockout.

The fight was informally labeled "Two Geezers at Caesars" and derided by some as akin to professional wrestling. But Foreman was taking it very seriously. He said of Cooney, "He's a great fighter. No doubt he deserves all the attention the people have given him in the past. During the time he was fighting his greatest fight with Holmes, I was preaching on the streets. I was out there doing something else, so I didn't pay much attention to his career. I see him as a fighter now, and I've heard him as a speaker. He seems to be confident, which he is supposed to be. I'm optimistic about the whole situation, too."

With The Mongoose in his corner, Big George was the last dinosaur standing. Cooney caught and shook him with a hook in the first round, but Foreman nailed him with a huge barrage in the second. Cooney fell hard, and when he got up he was retired again.

The old guy could still belt, and under Professor Moore's tutelage, Foreman seemed to be putting his punches together better than he did as a young lion. Archie explained to the *Houston Chronicle* his formula for success: "It's like putting together a watch or an automobile. A mechanic knows what makes a car tick, or what makes it outsprint another. With George, I make him aware of the things that are at his disposal. Everyone who knows George knows that his forte is punching power.

"But there are so many other things that will accelerate that punching power, or guide that power in a way that can bring it into fruition without harming himself or tiring himself. And I know these things. I can't tell you what they are, because if I tell you one, it leads into the other. It's just a system that is highly developed. It can be copied, so I won't talk about it."

What it all boiled down to, Moore said, was chemistry. "Really, I just love George," he said. "It's like a brotherly love, you know. Like father to son."

The feeling was mutual. "That man [Moore] has done more for me than anyone else I've met in boxing," Foreman said. "He can get me to do that little extra bit in a workout. He can get me to run that extra mile when I really don't want to. Maybe we relate so much because we are so close in age. You know, he's a youthful 76, I'm a youthful 41. We're just two young kids hanging out on the block having a whole lot of fun."

After three years on the comeback trail, Foreman signed to face Brazilian Adilson Rodrigues on June 16, 1990. The 36-3 South American was ranked eleventh by both the World Boxing Council and the World Boxing Association. He was the first ranked contender George faced since March 17, 1977 when he lost a decision to Jimmy Young.

On the other half of the doubleheader in Las Vegas was Mike Tyson, who'd been shockingly dethroned by 42-1 underdog Buster Douglas the previous winter. Tyson was starting out on his own comeback trail against Henry Tillman. Big George took the opportunity to draw an important distinction between himself and the sneering Tyson. "I'm not like Tyson, who is a rude dude. I'm nice to people. I talk to them, spend time with them. If a guy will pay $400 to see me fight, I'll jump out of the ring and dance with him."

Prior to the Rodrigues fight, Archie talked boxing and cardiology with his friend Mel Durslag of the *Los Angeles Times*. "George is not too old to render into unconsciousness any opponent. And you better believe there is no opponent right now the quality of Rocky Marciano. Yet at roughly George's age, I came close to rendering Rocky into unconsciousness with one punch.

"People who fought Marciano developed heart palpitations. At one point, I think my heart stopped for three minutes. But there are no Marcianos around now. Anything around I think George can render into unconsciousness."

That's just what Foreman did to Rodriques, putting him out in the second round.

That was a special month for The Mongoose. Not only was Foreman victorious in his biggest comeback fight, but Archie received one of his highest honors when he was inducted as one of the 53 charter members in the International Boxing Hall of Fame in Canastota, N.Y. The initial class also included Joe Louis, Rocky Marciano, Muhammad Ali and Sugar Ray Robinson.

Foreman was in negotiations to fight the winner of the upcoming title clash between James "Buster" Douglas and top contender Evander Holyfield. In the meantime, he and Archie flew to London, where George had a bout scheduled against Terry Anderson. Anderson was, pugilistically speaking, a creme puff. Foreman devoured him in less than a round. The British press, meanwhile, devoured with relish the performance of the other elder statesman, Archie Moore. Speaking of Foreman, Moore disclosed with a straight face that "He has the belief in himself, and it's because of a man he met in Africa years ago who gave him some secret powder and told him to rub it on his elbow and shoulder to become more powerful. George didn't believe it, but I told him to go ahead and use it, and I have seen him developing ever since.

"There is no more potion left now; it's all in the mind. But I am afraid he's going to hurt somebody."

Archie was having the time of his life. Recalls daughter Rena: "Daddy was enjoying all the hoopla surrounding Foreman's comeback. He was making more money than he had during his fighting days and he enjoyed being back in the eye of the boxing public. If a reporter needed a quote, Daddy was always happy to oblige."

Evander Holyfield ended the Cinderella reign of Buster Douglas, knocking out the blubbery champion in three rounds. Then, it was announced that on April 19, 1991, Holyfield would risk the title against Foreman, with the latter pulling down $12 million as his end of the purse.

What should have been one of the greatest and most satisfying times of Archie's life instead turned sour. Archie joined the Foreman camp on the Caribbean Island of St. Lucia, but things did not go well there for him. "His health was not the best," recalls Dr. Marilyn Douroux, "and a few days before the fight, Angelo Dundee was brought in to help in the corner. Archie was hurt. I don't think Archie was dutifully rewarded for the help and dedication he gave to Foreman. Archie would never talk about it."

Says Rena Moore: "I know that when Dundee was brought in, Daddy was upset. He called from camp and said that he wanted to come home. I urged him to go through with the fight. I didn't want him to have any regrets. It was going to be the best payday of his life, and he had earned it working with Foreman for so many years.

"With Dad, George Foreman and Angelo Dundee, you're dealing with three huge egos. There just didn't seem to be room for all three. I think Daddy felt pushed aside once Angelo Dundee was brought in."

In a surprisingly competitive fight broadcast over pay-per-view TV, Big George dropped a close but unanimous 12-round decision to Holyfield, who later told *The Ring*, "He made me do things I didn't want to do, punch when I didn't want to punch. He cut off the ring. At 42, George is not dead."

But his partnership with Archie Moore was. Moore helped in the Holyfield fight, but he never worked with Foreman again.

An article in the *Houston Chronicle* quoted Foreman's brother Roy's reasons for the breakup. "Moore's temperament, more than any other factor, has worked against him. Archie is getting older. It's not that you can't use his mind; he just gets testy with people.

"Archie's about 80 years old. He gets upset if you touch him, he gets upset at some of the things people say to him, he doesn't like to sign autographs any more. We just don't want a blow-up in public. It's best that Archie contribute from afar now."

Foreman tried to heal the breach in a letter to Archie dated November 4, 1991. In the letter, which thanked Archie for his help, Foreman reassured Archie that his decision was "nothing personal" and that he planned to ask for his help in the future, if he was still available.

Although their partnership remained dissolved, the letter smoothed Archie's ruffled feathers. "Dad and George separated on good terms. I was a little angry about it because Foreman promised he would keep Dad throughout his career," said Billy Moore.

But Moore was not done counseling professional boxers. There was none of that father-son stuff with his next client, either. It was strictly—and literally—father-daughter.

CHAPTER 22

There Goes a Man

On May 22, 1993, the City of San Diego celebrated "Archie Moore Day." It wasn't just in recognition of past ring glory, but also in gratitude for Archie's continuing work with youngsters. All proceeds from a $100-a-plate luncheon went to the Bates Street Boxing club. It was in one of the city's toughest neighborhoods, and Archie periodically stopped in and worked with the young boxers, advising them not only on ring technique but also techniques for getting the most out of life. "I'm friends to all youngsters," he said. "'Anything I can do to help'— that's my motto."

Archie often cruised to the gym, wearing a yachting cap, in his red Thunderbird. Asked why he wore the yachting cap, Moore replied, "It lends the impression that you own a yacht."

A month after his special day, Archie was invited to help honor Muhammad Ali in a televised tribute from Washington D.C., billed as "The Great Ones." Rena escorted her father on the trip, which turned into a nail-biter for her thanks to Archie's dogged independence. Recalls Rena: "Once we arrived in

Washington, D.C. Daddy was a little fussy. Perhaps he was jet-lagged. As soon as we reached our hotel, Daddy was complaining about having to get dressed up and speak onstage. Dad was given a script at the rehearsal to read about Ali on television, about how Ali's career had meant so much to him. Daddy would rather have talked about his own career. That is just the way he was. I convinced him that going through with the planned speech would make him look good on national television. If I played to Daddy's ego, I could usually win him over.

"After the rehearsal we attended a special reception to meet the president and Mrs. Clinton at the White House. At first I was excited about meeting the president, but soon I became extremely concerned. I remembered that Daddy never shook hands. It was a cleanliness thing. He always bumped fists with people instead. I was afraid he was going to give the Clintons the fist! Daddy was not in a good mood, and I sensed a drama alert. He just didn't want to be there.

"To my relief, Daddy extended his hand to the president. I couldn't help but give a slight laugh of relief. Hillary looked at me like I had lost my mind."

Rena's relief was short-lived. "After we left the White House, we arrived at the awards," she relates. "Since the entire program was being taped, there were several lulls allowing for commercials and re-takes. Daddy pulled out his eyeglasses with the duct tape and started practicing his lines. As each speaker took turns going up to the podium, I could hear Daddy practicing his lines. But each time he repeated his lines, he improvised a little bit more, adding and deleting sentences. In a short time the speech he was reading to me in no way resembled the original.

"Dad was called to the stage, where he began reading his speech. I felt a big sense of relief when I realized he was not adding any lines. I began to smile. But right then, Dad peers over his glasses, looks out at the audience and says, 'You know, I didn't write any of this.' As I sink down in my seat, trying to disappear, I catch myself and realize that in some bizarre way I'm actually proud of him. How many of us actually say exactly how we feel or what is on our mind? Dad was never shy about speaking up on any subject."

In this case, however, it was for naught. Says Rena: "When the special aired, Dad's original lines were cut down to, 'Muhammad Ali, I salute you.' Of course, Dad had a fit and stormed off to type a few letters of protest. I tried to explain that's what happens when you try to get cute and ad-lib.

"Over the years, I learned that Dad was a law unto himself—sweet and unpredictable, at his funniest when he wasn't trying to be, proud, stubborn and quick-tempered, overly generous with time and money when it came to helping others. He was both creative and impatient. Like the rest of us, he was human. But unlike the most of us, he refused to be silenced. You had to love him for that."

That same year, the much-in-demand Archie was invited to Uruguay to celebrate the fortieth anniversary of his match against Dogomar Martinez. "At first I wasn't too keen on the idea of Dad going to a third-world country," says Rena. "I didn't know anything about Uruguay. But the officials there promised they would have an ambulance follow his every move. Not that I anticipated any trouble, but I was concerned for his safety."

This time Archie was accompanied by daughter Elizabeth's husband, John Stump. An attorney, John knew nothing about boxing when he married Elizabeth, and when they began dating he'd never even heard of her famous dad. "But after my marriage, Archie and I became good friends," John says. "Getting to know him was quite a bonus."

John picked up the airplane tickets for Uruguay from the travel agent. The first-class fare, paid by Martinez's people, ran $8,000 for what Archie's son-in-law laughingly remembers as "a wild ride."

"We flew from San Diego to Los Angeles, and then boarded a plane to Peru. Archie woke up once we landed in Peru and said, 'Where are we? Where are we going?' I told him we were going to Montevideo, Uruguay. He gave me a confused look and replied, 'For what? I don't know anyone in Montevideo.' I didn't know what to think then. I was starting to get concerned. I didn't have any contacts in South America, and I wondered if maybe he was showing some signs of Alzheimer's. I was becoming quite concerned."

From Peru it was on to Sao Paulo, Brazil, with Archie singing a song from the film *Huckleberry Finn* most of the way. At one point he looked at Stump and said. 'You look nervous.' Then Moore fell asleep. In Montevideo, Stump says, they landed at "a small, rundown airport. Nobody greeted us as we got off the plane, and Archie didn't seem to remember a thing. My only comfort was knowing that I had my American Express card and I could charge two tickets to get us safely on the next flight home.

"At customs two large Samoan-looking men approached us. They grabbed our bags and walked us through two large glass doors. Once we walked through the doors there were cameras flashing and lots of reporters and a TV crew waiting. I was worried because Archie earlier said he had no idea why we were going to Uruguay. Then it happened. Archie broke out in perfect Spanish for the news people. He had been putting me on the whole time!"

They were in Montevideo five days, "and had a wonderful trip," Stump says. "Archie knew everyone in Montevideo. He was a hit everywhere he went. Everyone wanted to be photographed with him. Archie was a true professional in every way. He realized that in order to be ready for the celebration he needed to be rested. He knew what he was doing. He never wasted physical or mental energy. Archie was 'on' for the entire five days. He had learned how to manage himself a long time ago."

In 1983, 15-year-old amateur boxer John Scully came across Moore's home address in *The Ring* magazine. He wrote to Archie, and a long-distance friendship developed as they exchanged letters from opposite ends of the continent. Eventually Archie's pen pal became John "Iceman" Scully and challenged for the 175-pound title his hero had once owned.

Scully's first person-to-person meeting with his idol was at a boxing dinner in Massachusetts where Archie was a speaker. The local press turned out to cover Scully's long-awaited meeting with the legend with whom he had corresponded for six years.

Says Scully: "The first time that I saw Mr. Moore in person was in the reception area backstage at the dinner. Mr. Moore told me that he wanted to meet me 'in secret.' We went into the small bathroom area and Mr. Moore shut the door behind us. He held up his right hand and said, 'Let's see the jab.' We were both wearing tuxedos and dinner was about to start. It was also a very warm evening. But I could not say no to Archie Moore. So I jabbed into his palm. I remember he was not happy with it, so he had me do it again. He had me do it again and again. He was very intense and it felt like I was in the gym training for a fight. He shouted instructions—'Faster! Harder!'

"Then former world heavyweight champion Floyd Patterson entered the small bathroom area. There was no room for the three of us, so I assumed my training session was over. But then Mr. Moore took me into the shower area and resumed his lesson. We were only inches away from Patterson at the urinal, and he and Mr. Moore were engaged in a conversation. I was in awe sharing the bathroom with two boxing immortals."

The bathroom boxing lesson wasn't the only memorable part of the evening for Scully. At the conclusion of his after-dinner talk, Archie called Scully up to the podium. "Let me show you a beautiful person," he told the audience, referring to Scully.

Former world welterweight champion Carlos Palomino grew up hearing his dad talk about the great Archie Moore. After Palomino's retirement from boxing, he made appearances with Moore before youth groups. "Archie always tended to kids' needs," Palomino says. "He did his best to give back to the community because he understood where he came from."

In the spring of '94, Archie was admitted to the intensive care unit of Sharp Memorial Hospital for triple coronary bypass surgery. The night before the operation, Archie joked to son Billy about opting for the old family remedy instead: wheat grass. The surgery was successful, and The Mongoose made a full recovery.

On November 5 of that year George Foreman regained the heavyweight championship by knocking out Michael Moorer in Las Vegas. Archie was thrilled for his fellow Methuselah, telling the

San Diego Union-Tribune, "I think it's wonderful. I thought he would put up a good fight, because George is a fighter from the heart and George is afraid of nobody, being a Texas street fighter. But I wouldn't have bet he would have won against this young man. George can punch. When you talk about punchers, these men can knock your head off, can give you a concussion with one punch. Moorer got nailed and, man, he was out."

While Billy Moore followed in his dad's footsteps by working with several of San Diego's finest professional and amateur fighters throughout the years, the only one of Archie's children to put the gloves on for pay was, of all people, daughter J'Marie.

After 10 years as a flight attendant, J'Marie decided to give boxing a try as women's boxing was gaining a foothold. "Dad didn't push anyone in the family to box," she says. "My brother Billy had competed as an amateur, but I wanted to become a professional. Ever since I was four years old I've been around it, mostly sparring with my brothers. In school I was always athletic, especially in track. But I had never been in a fight.

"One morning, shortly after the death of my brother Hardy, I said, 'Dad, I wanna box!' He said, 'Let's shake, rattle n' roll.' From that day forward we began training. I became a professional because there was no time to be an amateur. I saw Dad's health going down, especially after Hardy died."

Billed as—what else?—"Lady Mongoose," the tall and attractive J'Marie became the first in a fast-growing line of daughters of ex-champions putting on the gloves. Joining her later would be the daughters of Muhammad Ali, Joe Frazier, George Foreman and Ingemar Johansson.

Archie's advice to J'Marie was simple: "Always remember what you were taught, and that you will always do things with pride and integrity, and for a higher purpose."

Training camp was set up behind the glove-shaped swimming pool at the Moore residence. Sister Rena acted as manager.

The conditioning regimen consisted of morning roadwork and wood chopping. J'Marie also used newer wrinkles like the Stair Master and treadmill, which Archie viewed with some skepticism. J'Marie told the *San Diego Union-Tribune*, "People say things have progressed, but the old ways are good, too. My father taught me that. I asked him a lot of things. He's so good because he takes everything in stride. He reminds me of a specialist, a fine tuner. He's done that with me."

Still, the distaff Mongoose's professional debut didn't come off without a hitch. Two weeks before her June 27, 1997 fight with Greta Daniels, and a week after Archie had a cardiac pacemaker installed, her mom underwent double-bypass surgery. Then, in the ring at the Tropicana Hotel in Atlantic City, the shorter Daniels actually raised her leg to kick Moore. But J'Marie won the four-round decision.

When he wasn't training his daughter, Archie spent time at the pool hall. Recalls J'Marie: "The crowd at Dad's favorite pool hall had changed drastically in recent years. There was a younger crowd, including some gang members. I felt uncomfortable dropping off my father there. But he insisted. One time I came in and Dad had finished a game of pool and was leaving the hall. A young tattooed gang member said respectfully, 'See you later, Archie.' Dad stopped abruptly and spun around. 'That's Mr. Moore,' he told him. I just froze, worried about the reaction of the gang member. But he said, 'Yes, Mr. Moore.' I let out a sigh of relief. Dad always had a way of commanding respect."

In the gym, Archie passed on some of his boxing secrets to his daughter. "Dad knew he wouldn't be around physically in my corner," J'Marie says, "so he showed me some of the greatest moves I've ever seen in boxing. Then he taught me how to execute them, how to pull and push power. He wanted to make sure that I knew the tactics it usually takes many years and fights to learn."

But it would be almost three years until J'Marie again fought professionally. There were plenty of offers in the meantime, but a much more important matter demanded her time and attention. "Dad's health was wavering," she says. "Eventually a series of seizures started, so I stayed in San Diego and just trained."

Even the staunchest of fighting hearts must one day give out, and at 2:30 in the afternoon on Wednesday, December 9, 1998, Archie Moore passed away at a San Diego hospice.

On December 17—exactly 46 years after Archie won the world light heavyweight title from Joey Maxim—a "Celebration of Life" was held at the Cypress View Mausoleum.

A film clip of that heart-stopping first round of the Moore-Durelle fight was shown to the large crowd. When it was over, Durelle himself, who'd made the long journey from Baie St. Anne, spoke. "I broke down crying when I heard he died," said the Canadian. "I feel privileged that I knew him. I'm glad we became friends."

Former heavyweight champion Ken Norton had the honor of holding the bell from the long-gone San Diego Coliseum as boxing official Danny Milsap rapped it 10 times in a final tribute to The Mongoose. "This is very emotional," Norton said. "Archie, to me, was what you wanted everyone to be like. He was a very good role model, a very good person, a very good Christian. A perfect person, just about."

In a message to the Moore family, Mayor Susan Golding said, "The boxing career of Archie Moore is legendary; he was known throughout the world. But as San Diegans we had the blessing of knowing him just a little more than the rest of the world did. He had a selfless spirit. He was a man who brought out the best in others."

The one and a half-hour, mostly lighthearted service also included video clips from Archie's television and film career. About 10 large-screen televisions lined the mausoleum walls, allowing the 1,000-plus celebrants to view varied scenes from a remarkable life.

The final video clip was from the movie *Huckleberry Finn*, with Archie as the slave Jim, poignantly saying "Bye everybody, God bless you."

George Foreman did not attend Moore's funeral, but provided this eulogy for *Time* magazine:

When I think of Archie Moore, an old proverb comes to mind. Suppose you want to build a tower. First you sit down and figure the cost. Then you see if you have enough money to finish it. Otherwise, if you lay a foundation and can't complete the building, everyone will make fun of you. In all the years we talked while Archie was teaching me, he never complained about the years of being the number one contender and of being mistreated as champion. All I ever heard were these pieces of the foundation of a great American—the traveling on boxcars and sleeping where he could. On the night he won the light heavyweight championship but no money, there was that gleam in his eyes. When he uttered the word "champion," that made me, too, want to be a champion. Working for me and other boxers, he made it clear: I love God, my family, and I will love you if you work hard. So Archie laid the foundation, and today he stands as a tower for all athletes, saying, "If you want it, leave your excuses behind and come get it."

Will he be missed? No—he lives! Every time a boxer or any athlete is told, "You are too old or too little," we will see Archie Moore smiling as big as life, saying, "No, I did it." Rest in peace, champ. You fought a great fight.

Over the years, various sources have listed Archie's total number of knockouts anywhere between 129 and 141. He always claimed that the record keepers misplaced a few along the way. It's unlikely that the real total will ever be known, but stranger things have happened. Not long after Archie's death, *The Ring* reported the discovery by boxing historian John Buchanan of the name Archie L. Wright in a Missouri census from January, 1920. It listed his age then as three and a half, which would confirm 1916 as the year of Archie's birth.

But that is all really quite immaterial. Archie himself once told his friend Jack Murphy, "When I'm finished, I want people to say only one thing of me. I want them to say, 'There goes a man.'"

That is simply not debatable.

AFTERWORD

by Pete Ehrmann,
Boxing Historian and Journalist

The Fraternal Order of Eagles is a 104-year-old organization of over a million members throughout the United States of America and Canada. Many of history's most prominent boxers have belonged, including John L. Sullivan, Jim Corbett, James J. Jeffries, Jack Dempsey, Joe Louis and Rocky Marciano. Many of them spoke at one time or another at the sports banquet that was for almost 50 years a staple of the Eagles' annual convention. But going into the last decade of the 20th century, the preponderance of speakers came from the ranks of football and baseball. As one banquet organizer put it, "Is there anybody in boxing any more you would want to invite into your home?" And thus, by extension, to your sports banquet?

The answer, in 1991, came in a letter from San Diego. "I am an experienced speaker and one who can charm, disarm and entertain and cause people to feel refreshed," wrote the former light heavyweight champion of the world.

There, in a nutshell, was the secret to the enduring appeal of Archie Moore. Invited to that year's Eagles convention in Cincinnati, Ohio, Archie held an audience of several thousand men enthralled as he picked 10 of them to join him on stage and proceeded to teach them the fundamentals of jabbing and footwork.

The audience was used to off-color locker-room stories from their speakers. But as "Instructor Moore," as Archie insisted his 10 pupils address him, put his students through their paces, the audience watched in hushed awe. Many had been wearing diapers when Moore was boxing, but true greatness has no shelf life. The Eagles loved him.

They weren't alone. That afternoon, Archie had walked from his downtown Cincinnati hotel in search of a bookstore to buy a copy of *The Guinness Book of World Records*. He wanted to show someone where he was credited in the book with the most KOs in boxing. Purely by chance, Moore was spotted by the president of the City Council, who rushed back to City Hall and demanded a "Key to the City" to present to Archie at the sports banquet that evening.

W.C. Heinz, who started writing sports in the Joe Louis era and is still cranking out books today, calls Moore "the most scientific fighter of my time, and, outside the ropes, the most inventive." His inventiveness was rooted in Archie's ardent belief that it would be awful indeed to "go through a day—even one day— without a little music and laughter."

Archie never did. That day in Cincinnati, Archie was decked out in a finely tailored gray suit, blue tie and matching blue handkerchief. Topping off the impeccable ensemble was a white beanie, on the front of which were three small pins. Two of them were likenesses of Moore's heroes, baseball great and civil rights pioneer Jackie Robinson and Dr. Martin Luther King, Jr.

"And this," he told a fan, pointing to the pin in the middle, "is me."

In fact it was Bugs Bunny, a cartoon character equally renowned but never truly as wily as the character under the hat, whose career and life charmed, disarmed and entertained and caused people to feel refreshed.

ARCHIE MOORE BOXING RECORD

Date	Opponent	Site	Result/Rounds	Title
1935				
Unknown	Piano Mover Jones[1]	Hot Springs, AR	KO/2	
9/3/35	Bill Simms[2]	Poplar Bluff, MO	KO/3	
1936				
1/31/36	Pocohontas Kid[3]	Hot Springs, AR	KO/3	
7/14/36	Murray Allen[4]	Quincy, IL	KO/5	
8/36	Sammy Christian	Quincy, IL	D/6	
9/30/36	Murray Allen	Keokuk, IA	KO/3	
10/9/36	Sammy Jackson	St. Louis, MO	W/5	
12/8/36	Sammy Jackson	St. Louis, MO	D/5	
1937				
1/5/37	Dynamite Payne	St. Louis, MO	KO/1	
1/18/37	Johnny Davis	Quincy, IL	KO/3	
2/2/37	Joe Huff	St. Louis, MO	KO/3	
3/23/37	Ham Pounder	Ponca City, OK	KO/2	
4/9/37	Charley Dawson	Indianapolis, IN	KO/5	
4/23/37	Karl Martin	Indianapolis, IN	KO/1	
5/1/37	Frank Hatfield[5]	Cincinnati, OH	KO/1	
6/1/37	Al Dubinsky		KO/1	
8/19/37	Deacon Logan	St. Louis, MO	KO/3	
9/1/37	Billy Adams	Cincinnati, OH	L/8	
9/9/37	Sammy Slaughter	Indianapolis, IN	W/10	
9/17/37	Charley Dawson	St. Louis, MO	KO/5	
11/16/37	Sammy Christian	St. Louis, MO	W/5	
12/1/37	Sammy Jackson	Jackson, MO	KO/8	
1938				
1/7/38	Carl Lautenschlager	St. Louis, MO	KO/2	
5/20/38	Jimmy Brent	San Diego, CA	KO/1	
5/27/38	Ray Vargas	San Diego, CA	KO/3	
6/24/38	Johnny Romero	San Diego, CA	L/10	
7/22/38	Johnny Sikes	San Diego, CA	KO/1	
8/5/38	Lorenzo Pedro	San Diego, CA	W/10	
9/2/38	Johnny Romero	San Diego, CA	KO/8	
9/16/38	Frank Rowsey	San Diego, CA	KO/3	
9/27/38	Tom Henry	Los Angeles, CA	KO/4	
10/1/38	Bobby Yannes	San Diego, CA	KO/2	
11/22/38	Ray Lyle	St. Louis, MO	KO/2	
12/7/38	Bob Turner	St. Louis, MO	KO/2	

Date	Opponent	Site	Result/Rounds	Title
1939				
1/20/39	Jack Moran	St. Louis, MO	KO/1	
3/2/39	Domenic Ceccarelli	St. Louis, MO	KO/1	
3/16/39	Marty Simmons	St. Louis, MO	W/10	
4/20/39	Teddy Yarosz	St. Louis, MO	L/10	
7/21/39	Jack Coggins	San Diego, CA	NC/8	
9/1/39	Jack Coggins	San Diego, CA	W/10	
9/22/39	Bobby Seaman	San Diego, CA	KO/7	
11/13/39	Freddy Dixon	Phoenix, AZ	TD/8	
11/27/39	Billy Day	Phoenix, AZ	KO/8	
12/7/39	Honeyboy Jones	St. Louis, MO	W/10	
12/29/39	Shorty Hogue	San Diego, CA	L/6	
1940				
3/30/40	Jack McNamee	Melbourne, AUS	KO/4	
4/18/40	Ron Richards	Sydney, AUS	KO/10	
5/9/40	Atilio Sabatino	Sydney, AUS	KO/5	
5/12/40	Joe Delaney	Adelaide, AUS	KO/7	
6/2/40	Frank Lindsay	Hobart, TAS	KO/4	
6/27/40	Fred Henneberry	Sydney, AUS	KO/7	
7/11/40	Ron Richards	Sydney, AUS	W/12	
10/18/40	Pancho Ramirez	San Diego, CA	KO/5	
12/5/40	Shorty Hogue	San Diego, CA	L/6	
1941				
1/17/41	Clay Rowan	San Diego, CA	KO/1	
1/31/41	Shorty Hogue	San Diego, CA	L/10	
2/26/41	Eddie Booker	San Diego, CA	D/10	
1942				
1/28/42	Bobby Britton	Phoenix, AZ	KO/3	
2/27/42	Guero Martinez	San Diego, CA	KO/2	
3/17/42	Jimmy Casino	San Francisco, CA	KO/5	
10/30/42	Shorty Hogue	San Diego, CA	KO/2	
11/6/42	Tabby Romero	San Diego, CA	KO/2	
11/27/42	Jack Chase	San Diego, CA	W/10	
12/11/42	Eddie Booker	San Diego, CA	D/12	For California Middleweight Title
1943				
5/8/43	Jack Chase	San Diego, CA	W/15	Won California Middleweight Title
7/22/43	Willard Hogue	San Diego, CA	TKO/5	
7/28/43	Eddie Cerda	San Diego, CA	KO/3	

Date	Opponent	Site	Result/Rounds	Title
8/2/43	Jack Chase	San Francisco, CA	L/15	Retained California Middleweight Title
8/16/43	Aaron Wade	San Francisco, CA	L/10	
11/5/43	Kid Hermosillo	San Diego, CA	KO/5	
11/26/43	Jack Chase	Hollywood, CA	W/10	
1944				
1/7/44	Amado Rodriguez	San Diego, CA	KO/1	
1/27/44	Eddie Booker	Hollywood, CA	KO'd/8	
3/24/44	Roman Starr	Hollywood, CA	TKO/2	
4/21/44	Charley Burley	Hollywood, CA	L/10	
5/19/44	Kenny La Salle	San Diego, CA	W/10	
8/11/44	Louis Mays	San Diego, CA	KO/3	
8/18/44	Jimmy Hayden	San Diego, CA	KO/5	
9/1/44	Battling Monroe	San Diego, CA	KO/6	
12/18/44	Nate Bolden	New York, NY	W/10	
1945				
1/11/45	Joey Jones	Boston, MA	KO/1	
1/29/45	Bob Jacobs	New York, NY	KO/9	
2/12/45	Nap Mitchell	Boston, MA	KO/6	
4/2/45	Nate Bolden	Baltimore, MD	W/10	
4/23/45	Teddy Randolph	Baltimore, MD	KO/9	
5/21/45	Lloyd Marshall	Cleveland, OH	W/10	
6/18/45	George Kochan	Baltimore, MD	KO/6	
6/26/45	Lloyd Marshall	Cleveland, OH	TKO/10	
8/22/45	Jimmy Bivins	Cleveland, OH	TKO'd/6	
9/17/45	Cocoa Kid	Baltimore, MD	KO/8	
10/22/45	Holman Williams	Baltimore, MD	L/10	
11/12/45	Odell Riley	Detroit, MI	KO/6	
11/26/45	Holman Williams	Baltimore, MD	TKO/11	
12/13/45	Colion Chaney	St. Louis, MO	KO/5	
1946				
1/28/46	Curtis Sheppard	Baltimore, MD	W/12	
2/5/46	Geogie Parks	Washington, DC	TKO/1	
5/2/46	Verne Escoe	Orange, NJ	TKO/7	
5/20/46	Ezzard Charles	Pittsburgh, PA	L/10	
8/19/46	Buddy Walker	Baltimore, MD	KO/4	
9/9/46	Shamus O'Brien	Baltimore, MD	KO/2	
10/23/46	Billy Smith	Oakland, CA	D/12	For California Light Heavyweight Title
11/6/46	Jack Chase	Oakland, CA	D/10	

Date	Opponent	Site	Result/Rounds	Title
1947				
3/18/47	Jack Chase	Los Angeles, CA	K/O9	Won California Light Heavyweight Title
4/11/47	Rusty Payne	San Diego, CA	W/10	
5/5/47	Ezzard Charles	Cincinnati, OH	L10	
6/16/47	Curtis Sheppard	Washington, DC	W/10	
7/14/47	Bert Lytell	Baltimore, MD	W/10	
7/30/47	Bobby Zander	Oakland, CA	W/12	Retained California Light Heavyweight Title
9/8/47	Jimmy Bivins	Baltimore, MD	K/O9	
11/10/47	George Fitch	Baltimore, MD	KO/6	
1948				
1/13/48	Ezzard Charles	Cleveland, OH	KO'd/8	
4/12/48	Dusty Wilkerson	Baltimore, MD	KO/7	
4/19/48	Doc Williams	Newark, NJ	KO/7	
5/5/48	Billy Smith	Cincinnati, OH	W/10	
6/2/48	Leonard Morrow	Oakland, CA	KO'd/1	Lost California Light Heavyweight Title
6/28/48	Jimmy Bivins	Baltimore, MD	W/10	
8/2/48	Ted Lowry	Baltimore, MD	W/10	
9/20/48	Billy Smith	Baltimore, MD	KO/4	
10/15/48	Henry Hall	New Orleans, LA	L/10	
11/1/48	Lloyd Gibson	Washington, DC	LD/4	
11/15/48	Henry Hall	Baltimore, MD	W/10	
12/6/48	Bob Amos	Washington, DC	W/10	
12/27/48	Doc Williams	Baltimore, MD	KO/7	
1949				
1/10/49	Alabama Kid	Toledo, OH	KO/4	
1/31/49	Bob Satterfield	Toledo, OH	KO/3	
3/4/49	Alabama Kid	Columbus, OH	KO/3	
3/23/49	Dusty Wilkerson	Philadelphia, PA	KO/6	
4/11/49	Jimmy Bivins	Toledo, OH	KO/8	
4/26/49	Harold Johnson	Philadelphia, PA	W/10	
6/13/49	Clinton Bacon	Indianapolis, IN	LD/6	
6/27/49	Bob Sikes	Indianapolis, IN	KO/3	
7/29/49	Esco Greenwood	North Adams, MA	KO/2	
10/4/49	Bob Amos	Toledo, OH	W/10	

Date	Opponent	Site	Result/Rounds	Title
10/24/49	Phil Muscato	Toledo, OH	TKO/6	
12/6/49	Doc Williams	Hartfard, CT	KO/8	
12/13/49	Leonard Morrow	Toledo, OH	KO/10	
1950				
1/31/50	Bart Lytell	Toledo, OH	W/10	
7/31/50	Vernon Williams	Chicago, IL	KO/2	
1951				
1/2/51	Billy Smith	Portland, OR	TKO/8	
1/28/51	John Thomas	Panama City, PAN	KO/1	
2/21/51	Jimmy Bivins	New York, NY	TKO/9	
3/13/51	Abel Cestac	Toledo, OH	W/10	
4/26/51	Herman Harris	Flint, MI	TKO/4	
5/14/51	Art Henri	Baltimore, MD	TKO/4	
6/9/51	Abel Cestac	Buenos Aires, ARG	TKO/10	
6/23/51	Karel Sys	Buenos Aires, ARG	D/10	
7/8/51	Alberto Lovell	Buenos Aires, ARG	KO/1	
7/15/51	Vincente Quiroz	Montivideo, URU	KO/6	
7/26/51	Vincente Carabajal	Cordoba, ARG	TKO/3	
7/28/51	Americo Capitanelli	Tucuman, ARG	TKO/3	
8/5/51	Rafael Miranda	Tucuman, ARG	TKO/4	
8/17/51	Alfredo Lagay	Bahia Blanca, ARG	KO/3	
9/5/51	Embrell Davison	Detroit, MI	KO/1	
9/24/51	Harold Johnson	Philadelphia, PA	W/10	
10/29/51	Chubby Wright	St. Louis, MO	TKO/7	
12/10/51	Harold Johnson	Milwaukee, WI	L/10	
1952				
1/29/52	Harold Johnson	Toledo, OH	W/10	
2/27/52	Jimmy Slade	St. Louis, MO	W/10	
5/19/52	Bob Dunlap	San Francisco, CA	KO/6	
6/26/52	Clarence Henry	Baltimore, MD	W/10	
7/25/52	Clinton Bacon	Denver, CO	TKO/4	
12/17/52	Joey Maxim	St. Louis, MO	W/15	Won World Light Heavyweight Title
1953				
1/27/53	Toxie Hall	Toledo, OH	KO/4	
2/16/53	Leonard Dugan	San Francisco, CA	TKO/8	
3/3/53	Sonny Andrews	Sacramento, CA	KO/5	
3/11/53	Nino Valdes	St. Louis, MO	W/10	
3/17/53	Al Spaulding	Spokane, WA	KO/3	
3/30/53	Frank Buford	San Diego, CA	TKO/9	
6/24/53	Joey Maxim	Ogden, UT	W/15	Retained World Light Heavyweight Title

Date	Opponent	Site	Result/Rounds	Title
8/22/53	Reinaldo Ansaloni	Buenos Aires, ARG	TKO/4	
9/12/53	Dogomar Martinez	Buenos Aires, ARG	W/10	
1954				
1/27/54	Joey Maxim	Miami, FL	W/15	Retained World Light Heavyweight Title
3/9/54	Bob Baker	Miami, FL	TKO/9	
6/7/54	Bert Withehurst	New York, NY	KO/6	
8/11/54	Harold Johnson	New York, NY	TKO/14	Retained World Light Heavyweight Title
1955				
5/2/55	Nino Valdes	Las Vegas, NV	W/15	
6/22/55	Carl ("Bobo") Olson	New York, NY	KO/3	Retained World Light Heavyweight Title
9/21/55	Rocky Marciano	New York, NY	KO'd/9	For World Heavyweight Title
1956				
2/20/56	Howard King	San Francisco, CA	W/10	
2/27/56	Bob Dunlap	San Diego, CA	KO/1	
3/17/56	Frankie Daniels	Sacramento, CA	W/10	
3/27/56	Howard King	Sacramento, CA	W/10	
4/10/56	Willie Bean	Richmond, CA	TKO/5	
4/16/56	George Parmentier	Seattle, WA	TKO/3	
4/26/56	Sonny Andrews	Edmonton, Canada	KO/4	
4/30/56	Gene Thompson	Tucson, AZ	TKO/3	
6/5/56	Yolande Pompey	London, England	TKO/10	Retained World Light Heavyweight Title
6/25/56	James Parker	Toronto, Canada	TKO/9	
9/8/56	Roy Shire	Ogden, UT	TKO/3	
11/30/56	Floyd Patterson	Chicago, IL	KO'd/5	For Vacant World Heavyweight Title
1957				
5/1/57	Hans Kalbfell	Essen, GER	W/10	
6/2/57	Alain Cherville	Stuttgart, GER	TKO/6	

Date	Opponent	Site	Result/Rounds	Title
9/20/57	Tony Anthony	Los Angeles, CA	TKO/7	Retained World Light Heavyweight Title
10/31/57	Bob Mitchell	Vancouver, BC	TKO/5	
11/5/57	Eddie Cotton	Seattle, WA	W/10	
11/29/04	Roger Rischer	Portland, OR	KO/4	
1958				
1/18/58	Luis Ignacio	Sao Paulo, BRA	W/10	
2/1/58	Julio Neves	Rio de Janeiro, BRA	KO/3	
3/4/58	Bert Whitehurst	San Bernardino, CA	TKO/10	
3/10/58	Bob Albright	Vancouver, BC	TKO/7	
5/2/58	Willie Besmanoff	Louisville, KY	W/10	
5/17/58	Howard King	San Diego, CA	W/10	
5/26/58	Charlie Norkus	San Francisco, CA	W/10	
6/9/58	Howard King	Sacramento, CA	W/10	
8/4/58	Howard King	Reno, NV	D/10	
12/10/58	Yvon Durelle	Montreal, Canada	KO/11	Retained World Light Heavyweight Title
1959				
3/9/59	Sterling Davis	Odessa, TX	TKO/3	
8/12/59	Yvon Durelle	Montreal, Canada	KO/3	Retained World Light Heavyweight Title
1960				
5/25/60	Willie Besmanoff	Indianapolis, IN	TKO/10	
9/13/60	George Abinet	Dallas, TX	TKO/3	
10/29/60	Guilio Rinaldi	Rome. ITA	L/10	
11/28/60	Buddy Turman	Dallas, TX	W/10	
1961				
3/25/61	Buddy Turman	Manila, Philippines	W/10	
5/12/61	Clifford Gray	Nogales, AZ	KO/4	
6/10/61	Guilio Rinaldi	New York, NY	W/15	Retained World Light Heavyweight Title
10/23/61	Pete Rademacher	Baltimore, MD	TKO/6	
1962				
3/30/62	Alejandro Lavorante	Los Angeles, CA	TKO/10	
5/7/62	Howard King	Tijuana, MEX	KO/1	

Date	Opponent	Site	Result/Rounds	Title
5/28/62	Willie Pastrano	Los Angeles, CA	D/10	
11/15/62	Cassius Clay	Los Angeles, CA	TKO'd/4	

1963

Date	Opponent	Site	Result/Rounds	Title
3/15/63	Mike DiBiase	Phoenix, AZ	TKO/3	

Final Record:

Won—186

Lost—24

Draws—10 (includes one Technical Draw)

KO's—134

No Contest—1

[1] Some record books list Moore's first opponent as "Piano Man" Jones. Archie Moore insisted that it was Piano Mover Jones. This fight could never be verified but occurred while Moore was in the Civilian Conservation Corps.

[2] This bout is not listed in all record books. It was the second bout in the same night for professional boxer Bill Simms, according to *The Daily American Republic* of Poplar Bluff, AK, 9/4/35.

[3] This bout is verified in the Hot Springs, AK newspaper *New Era*, 2/1/36.

[4] Moore knocked out Murray Allen in the fifth round, not the sixth round as many records indicate.

[5] Moore's bout against Frank Hatfield occurred in Cincinnati, OH according to the *Cincinnati Post*, 9/1/1937.

BIBLIOGRAPHY

"Archie 'Kayo' Moore Visits Mother Here." (September 30, 1937). *St. Louis Argus*

"Archie Moore Flattens Romero in Second Heat." (November 7, 1942). *San Diego Tribune*

"Archie Moore Gets Divorce." (May 22, 1954). *New York Times*

"Archie Moore Honored by Ring Hall of Fame." (December 14, 1970). *San Diego Union*

"Archie Moore Out for No. 6 on Card." (January 29, 1937). *St. Louis Argus*

"Archie Moore Scores 'K.O.' in Pro Debut." (July 17, 1936). *St. Louis Argus*

"Archie Moore Sued." (November 29, 1956). *New York Times*

"Archie Moore Wins Fifth Pro Battle." (November 18, 1937). *St. Louis Argus*

"Archie Turns on the Charm." (May 11, 1956). *Boxing News*

"Babe Davis is out to Slug Baer." (September 9, 1936). *Keokuk Daily Globe*

"Boxing Bout Tonight, Henneberry v Moore." (June 27, 1940). *Sydney Morning Herald*

"Boxing Stir, Decision for Moore." (June 28, 1940). *Sydney Morning Herald*

"Clash in Return Bout at Armory." (April 23-24, 1937). *Indianapolis Staff*

"Crowd Boos Max Baer in Boxing Show." (October 1, 1936). *Keokuk Daily Gate*

"Dixon-Archie Moore Match Tops Legion Arena Ring Card Tonight." (November 13, 1939).
     Arizona Republic

"Early Coliseum Sellout Looms." (December 11, 1942). *San Diego Union*

"Elder Statesman." (June 12, 1961). *Newsweek*

"Five Knockouts on Legion Bill." (February 1, 1936). *Hot Springs Sentinel-Record*

"George Reeves, TV Superman, Commits Suicide at Coast Home." (June 17, 1959).
     New York Times

"Gibson Wins On Foul, Moore Disqualified." (November 2, 1948). *Washington Post*

"Golden Gloves Ticket Sales Set Single Day's Record." (February 14, 1936).
     St. Louis Daily Globe-Democrat

"Grand Fight. Moore's Success." (July 12, 1940). *Sydney Morning Herald*

"Great Boxing Expected. Tonights Bout Richards and Moore." (April 18, 1940).
     Sydney Morning Herald

"Hall Gains Duke in Negro Brawl." (October 20, 1948). *Times-Picayune*

"Harrison Memorial Tournament Huge Success." (August 23, 1979). *St. Louis Argus*

"It Must Be Moore." (June 1, 1956). *Boxing News*

"King Arch Kayoed By Wrestler." (August 19, 1960). *San Diego Union*

"Matthews Puts Away Deathpain in 5th." (September 4, 1935).
     Poplar Bluff Daily American Republic

"Middleweight Boxers, Moore and Richards Tonights Contest." (July 11, 1940).
     Sydney Morning Herald

"Middleweight Boxers, Moore and Sabatino, Tonight's Stadium Match." (May 9, 1940).
     Sydney Morning Herald

"Moore a Formidable Opponent." (June 5, 1956). *London Times*

"Moore and Lorenzo Pedro Tangel In 10 Round Main." (August 5, 1938). *San Diego Union*

"Moore Axes Lumberjack Parker in Ninth Round." (July 26, 1956). *Toronto Evening News*

"Moore Battles Bobby Seamon." (December 12, 1942). *San Diego Union*

"Moore Betters Rival In New Fight 'Scare'." (April 1, 1962). *Miami Herald*

"Moore Blasts NBA for Lifting Title." (October 27, 1960). *San Diego Union*

"Moore Calls Shot; Wins by KO in 3rd." (March 5, 1949). *Columbus Dispatch*

"Moore Cries 'Foul' at NBA Action, says He's Ready to Fight." (October 29, 1960).
     Newark Star Ledger

"Moore Dethroning Won't Apply Here." (October 27, 1960). *Herald Wire Services*

"Moore Faces Morrow at Arena." (December 13, 1949). *Toledo Blade*

"Moore Flattens Durelle, Challenger Decked Four Times in 3rd by Ancient Champ."
     (August 13, 1959). *San Diego Union*

"Moore Guns for Two Titles After Blasting of Morrow." (December 13, 1949). *Toledo Blade*
"Moore Hit By $750,000 Suit." (November 29, 1956). *Chicago Tribune*
"Moore Impresses Railbirds in Preps for Lane Field Go." (May 19, 1938). *San Diego Union*
"Moore Knocks Out Sikes In Third." (June 28, 1949). *Indianapolis Star*
"Moore Outpoints Bolden." (December 19, 1944). *New York Times*
"Moore Slight Favorite Over Bivens Tonight." (April 11, 1949). *Toledo Blade*
"Moore Stops Muscato; Maxim Bout in the Making." (October 25, 1949). *Toledo Blade*
"Moore Stops Neves." (February 1, 1958). *San Diego Union*
"Moore Technical Winner Over Big Boy." (July 22, 1943). *San Diego Union*
"Moore to Box Hall Tonight." (November 15, 1948). *Baltimore Sun*
"Moore to Meet Lyle in Fight Here Tonight." (November 22, 1938). *St. Louis Post Dispatch*
"Moore Triumphs in Ignacio Fight." (November 19, 1957). *New York Times*
"Moore Victor When Bivens Fails to Answer Bell for Tenth Round." (February 22, 1951).
        New York Times
"Moore Wins, Contest Stopped." (May 10, 1940). *Sydney Morning Herald*
"Moore Wins, Fight Ends in Ten Rounds." (April 19, 1940). *Sydney Morning Herald*
"Moore, Hall Meet Tonight in Negro Ring Attraction." (October 19, 1948). *Times-Picayune*
"Moore-Billy Day set for 10-Round Feature." (November 27, 1939). *Arizona Republic*
"Munsell Kayoes Vincent Parrille, Moore Stops Pounder." (March 24, 1937). *Ponca City News*
"'Ol' Archie Staggered, Bows to Rinaldi in 10." (October 10, 1960). *Miami Herald*
"Old Arch Helps a Good Cause." (August 17, 1979). *St. Louis Globe-Democrat*
"Referee Gives Bacon Verdict on Low Blow." (June 14, 1949). *Indianapolis Star*
"Richards is Confident, 'Can Beat Moore'." (June 6, 1940). *Sydney Morning Herald*
"'Richard's Problem; Solving Moore's Tricks." (July 11, 1940). *Sydney Morning Herald*
"Seeks 3rd Win as Pro, this Friday, at Coliseum." (October 9, 1936). *St. Louis Argus*
"St. Louis Negroes Beat Kansas City Boxers 5 to 3." (April 19, 1936). *St. Louis Post Dispatch*
"'Sugar Ray' Does It Again, Now He's After Archie Moore." (May 25, 1956). *Boxing News*
"The Amazing Moore." (September 27, 1957). *Boxing News*
"Three Champions Crowned at Golden Gloves." (February 8, 1936).
        Poplar Bluff Daily American Republic
"Time Runs Out for Archie." (November 7, 1960). *Sports Illustrated*
"Two Supporting Bouts Arranged for Baer Show." (September 28, 1936). *Keokuk Daily Gate*
"We Were Fortunate to Have Him." (September 17, 1998). *CNNSI.COM*
Adams, Wilbur. "Archie Moore has Easy Time Taking 10 Rounder from King."
        (March 26, 1956). *Sacramento Bee*
Adams, Wilbur. "Moore Decks King 3 Times, Wins Easily." (June 10, 1958). *Sacramento Bee*
Allen, Johnny. "Starr Mixes with Moore in Legion Feature Tonight." (March 24, 1944).
        Los Angeles Daily News
Allison, Bob. "Archie's Not Emeritus, And He Retains Dignity." (March 14, 1963).
        Phoenix Gazette
Allison, Bob. "Rassler DiBiase Tries Ole Arch." (March 15, 1963). *Phoenix Gazette*
Anderson, Dave. *In the Corner: Boxing's Greatest Trainers Talk about Their Art.*
        New York: William Morrow & Company, 1991.
Aoki. "Archie Moore Says 'Foreman Can Beat Tyson." (March 1989). *Boxing Scene*
Author Unknown. "Five Knockouts on Legion Bill." (February 1, 1936).
        Hot Springs Sentinel-Record
Baltar, Sam. "Moore Too Good For Game, Outclassed Tony." (September 21, 1957).
        Los Angeles Herald Express
Batcha, Becky. "A Boxer Beanie Worth Fighting For." (April 29, 1991). *Philadelphia Daily News*
Beyette, Beverly. "Archie Is Hailed As New 'Champ'." (September 26, 1967). *San Diego Union*
Bojens, Ken. "Moore Flattens Montana 'Boxer'; Program Brief." (July 23, 1938).
        San Diego Union
Bojens, Ken. "Moore Flattens Ray Vargas in Third; Rival No Match." (May 28, 1938).
        San Diego Union
Bojens, Ken. "Moore Steals the Show." (May 21, 1938). *San Diego Union*
Boni, Bill. "The Champ Draws Customers." (March 17, 1953). *Spokane Review*

Borden, Eddie. "Australia the Land of Sportsmen." (February 1939). *The Ring*

Bosson, Roy. "34 Rounds of Boxing to be Held Tonight." (January 31, 1936).
      Hot Spring Sentinel-Record

Bosson, Roy. "Five Knockouts on Legion Bill." (February 1, 1936). *Hot Spring Sentinel-Record*

Brean, Herbert. "A Fighting Man Who is a Writing Man Too." (July 18, 1955). *Life*

Brean, Herbert. "Archie, The High-Style Champ." (July 18, 1955). *Life*

Brietz, Eddie. "Good Supporting Card is Arranged for Boxing Show." (March 23, 1937).
      The Ponca City News

Briordy, William. "Moore Favored to Defeat Johnson in Title Defense." (August 11, 1954).
      New York Times

Briordy, William. "Moore Title Bout in Spring Likely." (November 6, 1960).
      The New York Times

Brooks, Tommy. "You Can't Be A Friend And A Trainer." (1998). *KO*

Brown, Brian. "Moore Abuzz over Latest Charge." (June 6, 1985). *The San Diego Tribune*

Buck, Al. "Moore's Title is Eyed by Many." (October 1956). *The Ring*

Burnes, Robert L. "Old Arch Helps a Good Cause." (August 17, 1979).
      St. Louis Globe-Democrat

Cadou Jr. Jep. "Calls 'Em'." (May 26, 1960). *The Indianapolis Star*

Canepa, Nick. "Foreman Boxes Critics' Ears." (March 2, 1988). *San Diego Tribune*

Canepa, Nick. "Old Mongoose get a Lift from New/Old Champ Foreman."
      (November 17, 1994). *The San Diego Union-Tribune*

Canepa, Nick. "The Old Mongoose Remains Young." (October 5, 1985). *The San Diego Tribune*

Cannon, Jimmy. "Archie Plays the Garden." (August 10, 1997). *New York Post*

Cannon, Jimmy. "What Archie Knows, They Don't Teach." (November 14, 1962).
      New York Journal-American

Carey, Ed. "Fifteen Race Boxers Bid for A.A.U. Championships." (April 4, 1934). *St. Louis Argus*

Casey, Jack. "Portland Punches." (April 1951). *The Ring*

Cassidy, Robert. "The Battle of the Ages." *The Ring*

Center, Bill. "His Comeback on Verge of Title Bout, it's Fat City for Foreman."
      (June 15, 1990). *San Diego Union*

Center, Bill. "'Long Count' Recalls when Moore Decked Champion Marciano."
      (February 12, 1990). *The San Diego Union*

Center, Bill. "Moore Just Kept Fighting in Another Era, Ambassador Made San Diego a Winner."
      (October 10, 1985). *San Diego Union*

Clarke, Jack. "Archie Dud in Gladiator Role." (December 1, 1956). *Chicago Daily Sun Times*

Cohane, Tim and Moore, Archie. "My Rocky Road to Rocky." (September 6, 1955). *Look*

Collins, Bob. "Besmanoff On Canvas Twice." (May 26, 1960). *The Indianapolis Star*

Collins, Bob. "Moore, Besmanoff Meet Tonight." (May 25, 1960). *The Indianapolis Star*

Condon, Bob and Archie Moore. *The Archie Moore Story.* McGraw-Hill, 1961.

Conklin, William R. "New York Strips Moore of Crown and Calls for Johnson."
      (February 10, 1962). *New York Times*

Cottrell, John. *Muhammad Ali, Who Once Was Cassius Clay.* England, Funk & Wagnalls, 1967.

Cox, Jimmy. "Moore Cuts DiBiase Eye, Gets TKO." (March 16, 1963). *Phoenix Gazette*

Crittenden, John. "Old Days Gone. Archie Happy with Small Purse." (January 27, 1965).
      Miami News Midweeker

Cronin, Ned. "Booker TKO's Moore in Eighth." (January 22, 1944). *Los Angeles Daily News*

Cuddy, Jack. "Moore Defends Title Tonight." (December 10, 1958). *San Diego Union*

Cushman, Tom. "Fat George Gets Some Belly Laughs." (June 14, 1990). *San Diego Tribune*

Cushman, Tom. "Foreman Spars with his Past." (July 10, 1987). *San Diego Tribune*

Cushman, Tom. "Friends Pack 'Celebration' for Archie." (December 18, 1998).
      The San Diego Union-Tribune

Cushman, Tom. "It's Boxing's Old Man and the 'C'. Foreman-Cooney may be Fight for the
      Ages." (January 13, 1990). *San Diego Tribune*

Cushman, Tom. "Mongoose's Daughter Dons G Loves." (April 24, 1997).
      San Diego Union-Tribune

Daley, Arthur. "He Talks Big." (September 29, 1955). *The New York Times*

Daley, Arthur. "Man Without a Punch." (December 19, 1952). *New York Times*
Daley, Arthur. "Moore 2-1 Choice Over Olson in Fight Tonight." (June 25, 1955).
   The New York Times
Daley, Arthur. "Shall we Dance." (January 29, 1954). *New York Times*
Dalton, John. "Moore's Class Instructs Men, Boys." (May 17, 1972).
   Colorado Springs Gazette Telegraph
Daniel, Dan M. "What Recent Investigations Mean to Public." (April 1956). *The Ring*
Daniel, Dan. "Moore-Anthony Mess In 175 Pound Class is Tradition." (July 1957). *The Ring*
Daniel, Daniel M. "Why is Moore Poison?" (November 1952). *The Ring*
Davis, George T. "Lavo's Secret Punch - 'The-Keyhole!'," (March 30, 1962).
   Los Angeles Herald-Examiner
Deisenroth, Dennis. "Archie Polishes Diamond." (February 27, 1974). *Pleasanton Paper*
Digles, Joe. "Moore Defeats Valdes in Bout Seen by 10,800." (May 3, 1955). *Las Vegas Sun*
Doherty, James. "Fears and Hope of a Heavyweight Contender." (November 1962).
   Boxing Illustrated
Douroux, Marilyn G. *Archie The Ole Mongoose Moore*. Boston,
   Branden Publishing Company, Inc. 1991
Doyle, James E. "Archie Makes 7 Trips to Canvas." (August 23, 1945). *Cleveland Plain Dealer*
Doyle, James E. "Bivens Rules 12-5 Choice to Defeat Moore Tonight." (August 22, 1945).
   Cleveland Plain Dealer
Doyle, James E. "Charles Shakes Off Moore's Rally, Wins by Knockout in Eighth."
   (January 14, 1948). *Cleveland Plain Dealer*
Doyle, James E. "Charles Swings at Moore's Chin Tonight With Eyes on 2 Titles."
   (January 13, 1948). *Cleveland Plain Dealer*
Doyle, James E. "Marshall Will Have Weight Edge Over Moore in Tonight's Fight."
   (June 26, 1945). *Cleveland Plain Dealer*
Doyle, James E. "Moore Drops Marshall 3 Times in Tenth. Wins on Technical Kayo."
   (June 27, 1945). *Cleveland Plain Dealer*
Dundee, Angelo, and Mike Winters. *I Only talk Winning*. Chicago: Contemporary Books, 1985.
Durslag, Melvin. "Archie Moore, Advisor: Give Foreman a Chance VS. Tyson."
   (September 2, 1988). *Los Angeles Herald Examiner*
Durslag, Melvin. "For Client's Happiness, Moore is Better." (May 16, 1990). *Los Angeles Times*
Effrat, Louis. "Moore Halts Johnson in 14th at Garden." (August 12, 1954). *New York Times*
Ehrmann, Pete. "Remembering King Archie Moore." (April 1999). *The Ring*
Eskin, Lew. "Move Far Moore." (October 1957). *The Ring*
Eskin, Lew. "Yvon Durelle, Fisherman, Fighter." (October 1958). *The Ring*
Faherty, Justin L. "Springfield Golden Gloves Champions Due to Arrive Here Today."
   (February 15, 1936). *St. Louis Argus*
Feour, Royce. "Moore Won Only Las Vegas Bout." (December 10, 1998).
   Las Vegas Review Journal
Finnigan, Joe. "Poitier Rates Arch a Natural Actor." (November 13, 1959). *The San Diego Union*
Fisher, Nelson. "Moore Flattens Shorty by T.K.O. in 2nd Frame." (October 31, 1942).
   San Diego Union
Fisher, Red. "Moore Comes Off Canvas to KO Durelle in Thriller." (December 11, 1958).
   Montreal Star
Fiske, Jack. "Archie Delivers Severe Beating." (March 5, 1958). *San Francisco Chronicle*
Fiske, Jack. "Moore Favored to Stymie Norkus Comeback Tonight." (March 26, 1958).
   San Francisco Chronicle
Fitch, Jerry. "Where Are They Now." (December 26, 1998). *Boxing Bulletin Board*
Fleischer, Nat. "Archie Moore the Master Technician." (September 1945). *The Ring*
Fleischer, Nat. "Johnson First in Live." (April 1954). *The Ring*
Fleischer, Nat. "Moore Tops Among World Heavyweights." (August 1956). *The Ring*
Fleischer, Nat. "Moore VS. Patterson, But When and Where?." (October 1956). *The Ring*
Folster, David. "Moore and Durelle: Nearly Neighbors Now." (December 11, 1978). *MacCleans*
Forbes, Dick. "Charles Takes Decision in Close Encounter." (May 6, 1947). *Cincinnati Enquirer*
Frazier, Raymond Joseph with Yvon Durelle, *The Fighting Fisherman*, Doubleday 1981

Freeman, Donald. "The ABC's of Archie Moore." (September 8, 1968). *Parade*

Fried, Ronald K. *Corner Men: Great Boxing Trainers*. New York: Four Walls Eight Windows, 1991.

Furillo, Bud. "Moore's Memory is Testimony to His Ability to Dodge Punches."

Galloway, Clark. "Argentines Like Peron." (June 22, 1951). *U.S. News & World Report*

Gammon, Spec. "Moore-Davis Fight Tonight Features Pro Boxing Show." (March 9, 1959).
    The Odessa-American

Gammon, Spec. "Pudgy Grappler 'Punching Bag' for Champion." (March 10, 1959).
    The Odessa-American

Goldman, Herb. "Solid Gold Man." (April 1986). *The Ring*

Goldstein, Alan. "Moore in Four." (February 1963). *Boxing Illustrated*

Goldstein, Alan. "Moore Fought 22 Mains in Baltimore." (December 10, 1998). *Baltimore Sun*

Granger, Betty. "Archie Moore Weds." (August 25, 1956). *New York Amsterdam News*

Greene, Lee. "The Guy's a Gypsy." (1956).

Gregg, Christy. "Payne Drops Nod To Archie Moore." (April 11, 1947). *San Diego Union*

Grillfin, Jack R. "Even I Must Bow to a Thing Called Youth Says Moore." (December 1, 1956).
    Chicago Daily Sun Times

Gustkey, Earl. "A Gander at the Mongoose…Archie Moore." (September 18, 1986).
    Los Angeles Times

Gutteridge, Reg. *The Big Producers*, Random House, 1983

Hauser, Thomas. *Muhammad Ali: His Life & Times*. New York: Simon & Schuster, 1991.

Hawn, Jack. "Arch, Daniels Vie at Legion." (March 17, 1956). *Hollywood Citizen-News*

Heinz, W.C. "They Mystery of Archie Moore." (September 9, 1955). *Saturday Evening Post*

Heller, Peter. *In This Corner!* New York: Simon & Schuster, 1973.

Hennesey, Hal. "The Miracle of Archie Moore." (March 1959). *Boxing Illustrated*

Herrick, George. "Tony's in Perfect Shape." (September 19, 1957). *San Diego Tribune*

Hinch, Charles. "Fourth Graders Honoring Moore." (May 5, 1968). *San Diego Union*

Hochman, Stan. "Moore Boxes Whitehurst." (March 4, 1958). *San Bernardino Evening Telegram*

Hyvonen, Gary. "The Stars Come Out to Honor Archie Moore." (October 5-11, 1985). *Tuned-In*

Jackson, Richard A. "Henley Loses; Moore Wins." (November 19, 1937). *St. Louis Argus*

Jackson, Richard. "Bostick and Moore Win Bouts." (January 14, 1938). *St. Louis Argus*

Jones, Eddi. "Moore Slight Favorite To Beat Johnson." (January 30, 1952). *Toledo Blade*

Jones, Eddie T. "Amos Ducks Moore KO Punch." (October 5, 1949). *Toledo Blade*

Jones, Eddie T. "Archie Favored Over Alabama Kid Tonight." (January 10, 1949). *Toledo Blade*

Jones, Eddie T. "Archie Moore Stops Satterfield." (February 1, 1949). *Toledo Blade*

Jones, Eddie T. "Archie Moore Trounces Big Abel Cestac." (March 14, 1951). *Toledo Blade*

Jones, Eddie T. "Moore Favored to Beat Cestac Tonight." (March 13, 1951). *Toledo Blade*

Jones, Eddie T. "Moore Knocks Out Alabama Kid." (January 11, 1949). *Toledo Blade*

Jones, Eddie. "Only 2,200 Watch Hall Bow at Arena." (January 28-28, 1953). *Toledo Blade*

Kane, Martin. "Old Archie Wolfs His Lamb." (August 24, 1959). *Sports Illustrated*

Keane, Cliff. "Gus Mell Captures Unanimous Decision." (February 13, 1945).
    Boston Daily Globe

Kearns, Jack, and Oscar Fraley. *The Million Dollar Gate*. New York: Macmillan, 1966.

Kessler, Gene. "Patterson Champ KO's Moore." (December 1, 1956). *Chicago Daily Sun Times*

Kessler, Gene. "Patterson, Archie Meet Tonight," (November 30, 1956).
    Chicago Daily Sun Times

Kirk, Arthur. "Archie Defeats Joey With Ease Before 12, 210." (December 19, 1952).
    St. Louis Argus

Kirk, Arthur. "Archie Moore with Eyes on Title." (December 17, 1952). *St. Louis Argus*

Klewer, Lou. "Moore Flattens Bivens in Eighth Round." (April 11, 1949). *Toledo Blade*

Knack, Joe. "Moore Beats Harold Johnson; Now Seeks Title Bout." (January 30, 1952).
    Toledo Blade

LaConte, Arturo H. "Boxing In Panama." (April 1951). *The Ring*

Lardner, John. "And he Can't Play a Comb." (August 23, 1954). *Newsweek*

Lardner, John. "King of the Share-Croppers." (August 8, 1955). *Newsweek*

Lardner, John. "The Old Man's Price." (July 1, 1957). *Newsweek*

Larnder, John. "A Sudden Dost of Age." (October 13, 1958). *Newsweek*

Linthicum, Jesse A. "Archie Moore Decisions Sheppard." (January 28, 1946). *Baltimore Sun*

Linthicum, Jesse A. "Archie Moore Defeats Hall by Decision." (November 16, 1948).
    Baltimore Sun

Linthicum, Jesse A. "Archie Moore Here Tonight." (November 26, 1945). *Baltimore Sun*

Linthicum, Jesse A. "Archie Moore Wins Decision." (June 29, 1948). *Baltimore Sun*

Linthicum, Jesse A. "Moore Beats Nate Bolden." (April 3, 1945). *Baltimore Sun*

Linthicum, Jesse A. "Moore Halts Cocoa in 8th." (September 18, 1945). *Baltimore Sun*

Linthicum, Jesse A. "Moore Loses to William." (October 23, 1945). *Baltimore Sun*

Linthicum, Jesse A. "Moore Scores T.K.O. Over Bivens." (September 9, 1947). *Baltimore Sun*

Linthicum, Jesse A. "Moore Stops Rival in 11th." (November 27, 1945). *Baltimore Sun*

Loubet, Nat. "What is the NBA?." (1957). *The Ring*

Lownes, Tom. "Cora Lee Sees Archie, and It Really is Great!." (October 15, 1959). *Miami Herald*

Lynch, R.G. "Johnson Wins Over Moore, Low Punch Deciding Factor." (December 11, 1951).
    Milwaukee Journal

Magee, Jerry. "Moore Gains Honor For Life He Has Lived." (August 15, 1989). *San Diego Union*

Marenghi, Anthony. "From Pillar to Post." (January 8, 1961). *Newark Star*

Mareughi, Anthony. "The MBA is Archie's Personal Puppet." (October 30, 1960). *Newark Star*

Matheny, Sean. "Joey Maxim Interview." (August 28, 1999). *International Boxing Digest*

Matthews, Neal. "A Few Rounds with the Mongoose." (September 19, 1985).
    San Diego's Weekly Reader

Matthews, Neal. "A Heavyweight's Speed is in his Hands, and Foreman Still Has That."
    (March 22, 1990). *San Diego Reader*

McConnell, Monroe, "San Diego Middleweight Gets Unanimous Nod in Lane Field Go."
    (May 8, 1943). *San Diego Union*

McConnell, Monroe. "Archie Moore Belts Out Cerda In Third Round." (July 20, 1943).
    San Diego Union

McConnell, Monroe. "Archie Moore Whips Chase." (November 27, 1942). *San Diego Tribune*

McConnell, Monroe. "Booker, Moore Battle to Draw." (December 11, 1942). *San Diego Union*

McConnell, Monroe. "Moore Stows Monroe Away in 6th Round of Coliseum Main Event."
    (September 3, 1944). *San Diego Union*

McConnell, Monroe. "Moore Wins State Title." (May 9, 1943). *San Diego Union*

McDonald, Johnny. "Archie 6-5 Choice Over Pastrano." (May 28, 1962). *San Diego Union*

McDonald, Johnny. "Archie Beats Foe, Faces Ban by NBA." (May 2, 1957). *San Diego Union*

McDonald, Johnny. "Archie Moore Training Site." (October 15, 1978). *Ramona Home Journal*

McDonald, Johnny. "Archie Wins Seven Straight in Australia."
    (September 12, 1955). *San Diego Union*

McDonald, Johnny. "Champ 182, Spots Rival 18 Pounds." (October 10, 1985).
    San Diego Union

McDonald, Johnny. "Moore Back, Claims He Overtrained." (December 11, 1956).
    San Diego Union

McDonald, Johnny. "Moore Crushed in Four." (November 16, 1962). *San Diego Union*

McDonald, Johnny. "Moore Scores KO over King in First Round." (April 18, 1984).
    San Diego Tribune

McDonald, Johnny. "Moore Tests King Tonight." (May 17, 1958). *San Diego Union*

McDonald, Johnny. "N.Y. Strips Archie of Title." (February 10, 1962). *San Diego Union*

McDonald, Johnny. "Ulcers Knock Out Archie, Nearly End Boxing Career."
    (September 13, 1955). *San Diego Union*

McGoogan, W. J. "Archie Moore Barred for Year." (December 8, 1939). *St. Louis Post-Dispatch*

McGoogan, W.J. "Moore Gets His Big Chance in Title Bout." (December 18, 1952).
    St. Louis Post-Dispatch

McGoogan, W.J. "Moore Kayoes Ohio Boxer in Second Round." (November 23, 1938).
    St. Louis Post Dispatch

McGoogan, W.J. "St. Louis Boxers Eliminated." (April 17, 1936). *St. Louis Post-Dispatch*

McGoogan, W.J. "Yarosz - Moore Bout Victor In." (April 20, 1939). *St. Louis Post Dispatch*

McGoogan, W.J. "Yarosz Too Experiences, Wins." (April 21, 1939). *St. Louis Dispatch*

McKinney, Jack. "Archie Moore's Son Hears the Bell." (June 7, 1974). *Philadelphia Daily News*

Meade, James. "Crumbling Career Saved by 'Cookie'." (February 3, 1966). *The San Diego Union*

Meyer, Bob. "Verdict Irks Ancient Arch." (May 29, 1962). *Times-Picaynne*

Miles, Gary. "Daughter Has Archie Moore in her Corner." (June 29, 1997).
   The San Diego Union-Tribune

Miller, Bill. "For Moore Now? Johnson!" (November 1957). *The Ring*

Miller, Bill. "Moore Kayo's Lavorante in 10th Round." (June 1962). *The Ring*

Millstein, Gilbert. "In This Corner, At Long Last, Archie Moore!" (September 11, 1955).
   The New York Times

Miner, Jimmy. "Ezz Charles Wins Split Decision Over Moore." (May 6, 1947). *Cincinnati Post*

Miner, Jimmy. "Heavies Box in Feature at Parkway." (September 1, 1937). *The Cincinnati Post*

Mitchell, Ray. "Boxing is Booming in Australia." (August 1951). *The Ring*

Mladinich, Robert. "The Journeyman Who Made Life Hard for 'The Rock'." *The Ring*

Mooney, John. "Moore Decisions Maxim." (June 25, 1953). *Salt Lake Tribune*

Mooney, John. "Odds Favor Moore at 8 to 5 Over Maxim." (June 24, 1953).
   Salt Lake City Tribune

Moore, Archie and Leonard Pearl. *Any Boy Can*. Englewood Cliffs, NJ: Prentice-Hall, 1971.

Moore, Archie. "Guide or Misguide." (August 8, 1967). *San Diego Union*

Moore, Archie. "I'll Make Him Fight My Way." (September 20, 1955). *Look*

Moore, Archie. "Law and Order Is The Only Edge We Have." (April 15, 1968).
   Republican-Congressional Committee Newsletter

Moore, Archie. "My Secret Diet." (July 4, 1960). *Sports Illustrated*

Moore, Archie. "On Fight Managers." (October 1964). *Boxing Illustrated*

Moore, Archie. "The Greatest Man I Ever Fought." (September 9, 1964). *Boxing Illustrated*

Moore, Archie. "Why I Played Jim, The Slave." (September 1960). *Ebony*

Moore, Archie. *Any Boy Can: The Archie Moore Story*. Englewood Cliffs, NJ: Prentice-Hall, 1971.

Moore, George. "Dixon-Moore Contest is Draw as Low Blow Stops Phoenix Boxer."
   (November 14, 1939). *Arizona Republic*

Muller, Eddie. "Moore Decks Kind 3 Times." (February 21, 1956). *San Francisco Examiner*

Murphy, Jack. "Now Archie Will Do His Acting Before the Hollywood Cameras."
   (September 9, 1959). *The San Diego Union*

Murphy, Jack. "Professor Moore Ready to Spank Upstart Pupil." (November 14, 1962).
   San Diego Union

Murphy, Jack. "28 Years Ago They Didn't Even Know Mr. San Diego Had Landed."
   (September 26, 1967). *San Diego Union*

Murphy, Jack. "Age and Young Challenger Fail to Slow Champ Archie." (August 13, 1959).
   San Diego Union

Murphy, Jack. "Another Obstacle for Moore: He'll Have to Whip Louis Jink."
   (November 30, 1956). *San Diego Union*

Murphy, Jack. "Archie Fought for $3 Million But There's Little to Show for It."
   (March 15, 1963). *San Diego Union*

Murphy, Jack. "Archie Old, Tired But Clay May Have Bitten Off Too Much."
   (November 15, 1962). *San Diego Union*

Murphy, Jack. "Archie Sees Himself Clearly, and Doesn't Like What He Sees."
   (December 12, 1962). *San Diego Union*

Murphy, Jack. "Armstrong Tells Moore's Age and Offers Some Predictions."
   (March 4, 1958). *San Diego Union*

Murphy, Jack. "Candidate Moore Injects Something New in Politics." (1960).
   The San Diego Union

Murphy, Jack. "Chicken With a Personality On Menu at Archie's Eatery." (April 29, 1964).
   San Diego Union

Murphy, Jack. "Childe Arch Reveals a Secret: He was Three at Time of Birth."
   (December 10, 1958). *San Diego Union*

Murphy, Jack. "Even the Critics Now Agree Archie's Not Just a Con Man." (December 12, 1958).
   The San Diego Union

Murphy, Jack. "Heartbreak Accompanies Scribes Covering Mongoose's Exhibition."
   (March 17, 1963). *San Diego Union*

Murphy, Jack. "Here's One More Vote For Ring's Foremost Antique." (September 9, 1957).
San Diego Union

Murphy, Jack. "Mongoose Cheerfully Accepts Decision of the Electorate." (September 20, 1963).
San Diego Union

Murphy, Jack. "Mongoose Learns About Real Danger in Tour of Vietnam." (June 23, 1966).
San Diego Union

Murphy, Jack. "Moore Camp Jittery As Champ Struggles With Weight Issue."
(October 31, 1957). San Diego Union

Murphy, Jack. "Moore Ignores Deadlines, Goes On With Plan to Fight Fullmer."
(February 2, 1962). San Diego Union

Murphy, Jack. "Moore Rated Even Bet." (November 30, 1956). San Diego Union

Murphy, Jack. "Moore Ready to Counsel Clay on How to Win Liston's Title."
(October 18, 1963). San Diego Union

Murphy, Jack. "Moore Stops Anthony In 2:29 of Seventh Round, Keeps Title."
(September 21, 1957). San Diego Union

Murphy, Jack. "Moore's Demand Unreasonable?" (May 2, 1957). San Diego Union

Murphy, Jack. "Patterson Knocks Out Moore in 5th." (December 1, 1956). San Diego Union

Murphy, Jack. "Red Leather Points Blue Ending as Sun Sets For Arch." (December 13, 1962).
San Diego Union

Murphy, Jack. "Sad Ending to a Fighting Era: Pursuit Ends in Frustration." (December 2, 1956).
San Diego Union

Murphy, Jack. "Spar Mates, Handlers Confident Moore Can Dispose of Anthony."
(September 19, 1957). San Diego Union

Murphy, Jack. "The Mongoose Speaks Out On Grudges, Bums, and Joe Louis." (May 17, 1958).
San Diego Union

Murphy, Jack. "The Mongoose." (November 11, 1961). New Yorker

Murphy, Jack. "The Story of a Kindly Angler Who Befriended a Sick Fighter." (April 18, 1973).
San Diego Union

Murphy, Jack. "The Trickery of Ali Earns Archie's Praise." (October 31, 1974). San Diego Union

Murphy, Jack. "Willie Runs From Old Man But Somehow Gets A Stalemate." (May 30, 1962).
San Diego Union

Murray, Jim. "Boxing Given Him Fat Chance." (April 19, 1991). Los Angeles Times

Murray, Jim. "Can George Win? Never Say Never." (April 18, 1991). Los Angeles Times

Newfield, Jack. Only In America. William Morrow & Company. New York (1995).

Neri, Tony. "Moore, Parks Bout Tonight At Turner's." (February 5, 1946). Washington Post

Nichols, Joseph C. "Marciano Will Risk Title Sixth Time." (September 19, 1955).
The New York Times

Nichols, Joseph C. "Marciano, Moore End Heavy Work." (September 19, 1955).
The New York Times

O'Connor, Charles. "Archie Moore of New York Proves Tough Foe for Ezz Charles."
(May 6, 1947). Cincinnati Times-Star

Oliver, Ron. "Have We Seen The Last of Archie Moore as Champion?" (May 31, 1957).
Boxing News

Ontavio, Aldo. "Archie Upset By Rinaldi." (January 1961). The Ring

Other Contributing Periodicals: St. Louis Argus (1936, 1937), Keokuk Daily Gate (1937), Hot
Springs New Era (1936), Poplar Bluff American Republic (1935).

Patterson, Floyd, and Milton Gross. Victory Over Myself. (Pelham Books, 1962).

Plimpton, George "An Eye for an Eye and a Tooth for a …" Sports Illustrated

Plimpton, George. Shadow Box. G.P. Putnam's & Sons, New York (1977).

Plimpton, George. "The Youthful Plimpton VS. The Wily Moore." (October 24, 1977).
Sports Illustrated

Porzio, Alfredo. "From Buenos Aires." (September 1951). The Ring

Price, Engleman J. Thinking Big. ECW Press, Toronto Canada. (2000).

Prime, Jim. "Archie-Moore-Yvon Durelle I." (July 1997). The Ring

Raddue, Gordon. "Moore to Lure Big Crowd." (April 10, 1956). Richmond Independent

Ringwise. "Slapsie Maxie, M'AVOY Mix in Lane Field Main Tonight." (May 20, 1938).
San Diego Union
Rogin, Gilbert. "Archie: More or Less." (February 23, 1961). *Sports Illustrated*
Rogin, Gilbert. "Archie: More or Less." (June 19, 1961). *Sports Illustrated*
Rogin, Gilbert. "For an Ancient Warrior." (November 26, 1962). *Sports Illustrated*
Rosenbaum, Art. "Frugal Archie Bars Sparmates." (May 25, 1965). *San Francisco Chronicle*
Ryan, Jeff. "Archie Moore at 76." (May 1990). *The Ring*
Sabre, Bob. "Archie's Boy." (August 1963). *Boxing Illustrated*
Salak, Johnny. "Sand Bitter, But Wise." (April 27, 1957). *The Ring*
Scheinman, John. "George 2000: A Fighter for The Millennium." (September 1997). *The Ring*
Scheuer, Steven. "Archie Moore in Role." (October 17, 1963). *San Diego Union*
Schmuhl, Bob. "Moore Proves He's Still the Master." (August 28, 1965).
Michigan City News-Dispatch
Schnitzer, Sam. "Moore to Drill for Public This Afternoon." (September 15, 1957).
Los Angeles Examiner
Schroeder, Jack. "Moore Takes Decision to Keep Crown." (June 25, 1953). *Salt Lake City Tribune*
Schulian, John. "Archie Moore is One of a Kind." (October 31, 1979). *Chicago Sun-Times*
Schulman, Arlene. "The Lady Mongoose." (October 1997). *The Ring*
Shhehan, Joseph M. "Moore, Philosophizing in Dressing Room." (June 23, 1955).
The New York Times
Siegel, Morris. "Archie Moore Favored to Win." (June 15, 1947). *Washington Post*
Siegel, Morris. "Moore Mauls Sheppard in Easy Victory." (June 16, 1947). *Washington Post*
Slocum, Bob. "In Archie's Shadow, Billy Moore Strives to be 'Champ at Life'." (April 18, 1984).
Smith, Gary. "After the Fall." (October 8, 1984). *Sports Illustrated*
Smith, Raymond V. "Archie Moore Swaps Blows With Chaney Here Tonight."
(December 13, 1945). *St. Louis Globe-Democrat*
Smith, Raymond V. "Auditorium Fights Tonight." (November 16, 1947).
St. Louis Daily Globe-Democrat
Smith, Raymond V. "Moore Kayoes Ceccarelli in First." (March 3, 1939).
St. Louis Daily Globe-Democrat
Smith, Raymond V. "Yarosz Gives Moore Boxing Lesson." (April, 21, 1939).
St. Louis Daily Globe-Democrat
Smith, Raymond. "'Uncrowded Champ' Faces Wright." (October 29-31, 1951).
St. Louis Globe Daily Democrat
Smith, Red. "View of Sports." (January 7, 1961). *New York Herald Tribune*
Smith, Wendell. "The Life and Times of Archie Moore." (May 1988). *Boxing Scene*
Springer, Steve. "Archie Moore Dies at 84." (December 10, 1998). *Los Angeles Times*
Steinman, Ted. "Moore Easily Beats Pedro." (August 6, 1938). *San Diego Union*
Steinman, Ted. "Moore Stops Foe With Technical Kayo in Third." (September 17,1938).
San Diego Union
Steinmann, Ted. "Archie Moore Ends Romero Threat With K.O. Victory." (September 3, 1938).
San Diego Union
Steinmann, Ted. "Johnny Romero Wins Close Battle Over Archie Moore." (June 23, 1938).
San Diego Union
Stickney Jr. W.H. "Foreman Trying to Roll back Years with Late-in-Life Comeback Touring."
(August 2, 1987). *Houston Chronicle*
Stickney Jr. W.H. "Foreman, Trainer Moore have Mutual Admiration." (June 13, 1960).
Houston Chronicle
Stickney Jr. W.H. "Less of Moore in Foreman's Camp." (April 26, 1992). *Houston Chronicle*
Stone, Joe. "Mr. San Diego To Be Honored." (1968). *San Diego Tribune*
Streshinsky, Shirley. "Up Against the Ghetto and the Freeway." (February 20, 1972).
Lost Angeles Times West Magazine
Sullivan, George. *The Cassius Clay Story*. Fleet Publishing Company, (1964).
Swesey, Ben and Jenkins, Jim. "Foreman Fights to Recapture Form Tonight." (March 9, 1987).
Sacramento Bee
Tinkham, Harley. "Archie Wants Patterson or Liston Next." (March 31, 1962).
Los Angeles Herald-Examiner

Tosches, Nick. "I Think Sonny Liston Died the Day He was Born." (February 1998). *Vanity Fair*

Underwood, John. "NBA Lifts Title from Old Archie; Kearns 'to fight'." (October 26, 1960). *Miami Herald*

Vara, Robert. "Stormin' George Foreman." (July 7, 1991). *Houston Chronicle*

Waina, Jack. "Fistic Headlines in Michigan." (December 1951). *The Ring*

Ward, Alan. "Morrow Wins Title in First." (June 3, 1948). *Oakland Tribune*

Webster, John. "Moore Hands Johnson First Defeat in Ring." (April 27, 1949). *Philadelphia Inquirer*

Webster, John. "Moore TKO's Wilkerson." (March 24, 1951). *Philadelphia Inquirer*

Welsh, Jack. "Vegas Scene." (December 20, 1998). *Boxing Update/Flash*

Whorton, Cal. "Moore Flattens Anthony in 7th." (September 22, 1957). *Los Angeles Times*

Whorton, Cal. "Moore Flattens Chase in Ninth." (March 19, 1947). *Los Angeles Times*

Whorton, Cal. "Moore, Chase Continue Boxing Feud Tonight." (March 18, 1947). *Los Angeles Times*

Will, Bottmley. "Davis-Moore Bout Feature of Ring Show." (January 15, 1937). *Quincy Herald-Whig*

Winters, Mike. "Former Champ in Ring for Youngsters." (April 18, 1869). *Toledo Blade*

Ziff, Sid. "Moore Blasts Fleischer for 'Deliberate Insult'." (December 29, 1958). *Los Angeles Mirror News*

Zimmerman, Paul. "Big Money Bouts Have Eluded Moore." (September 16, 1957). *Los Angeles Times*

Interviews:

Bivins, Jimmy. June 7, 1999.

Breitbard, Bob. March 8, 1998.

Brooks, Tommy. September 17, 2000.

Douroux, Dr. October, 1999

Dundee, Angelo. March 22, 1999.

Durelle, Yvon. December 16, 2000.

Durslag, Mel. November 14, 1999.

Duva, Lou. September 17, 2000.

Frazier, Eddie. March 14, 1998.

Furillo, Bud. October 12, 1999.

Futch, Eddie. March 8, 1998.

Kaplan, Hank. September 8, 1999.

Lloyd, Charles E. November 13, 1999

Lowry, Ted. September 16, 1999.

Maxim, Joey. March 22, 1998.

Moore, Archie and immediate family. September 8-15, 1997.

    Rena Moore

    Joan Moore

    Billy Moore

    J'Marie Moore

Norton, Ken. June 7, 2000.

Palomino, Carlos. April 19, 1999.

Rademacher, Pete. October 8, 2000.

Scully, John. July 11, 2000.

Shavers, Earnie. June 8, 2000.

Smith, Lyle. March 23, 1998.

Smith, Walter. February 23, 1998.

Snipes, Charlie, November 15, 1999

Stump, John. November 15, 1999.

Wright, Arnold. January 14, 2000.

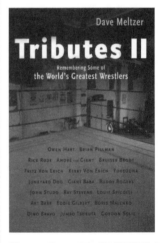